Volume 1

D1388688

ASSESSMENT IN SPEECH AND LANGUAGE THERAPY

REMOVED
FROM
STOCK

City Hospital

WB00022070

ASSESSMENT IN SPEECH AND LANGUAGE THERAPY

Edited by
JOHN R. BEECH AND LEONORA HARDING
WITH DIANA HILTON-JONES

Routledge
Taylor & Francis Group

LONDON AND NEW YORK

First published in 1993 by Routledge

This edition first published in 2019
by Routledge
2 Park Square, Milton Park, Abingdon, Oxon OX14 4RN

and by Routledge
52 Vanderbilt Avenue, New York, NY 10017

Routledge is an imprint of the Taylor & Francis Group, an informa business

© 1993 Selection and editorial matter, John R. Beech and Leonora Harding with Diana Hilton-Jones; individual chapters, the contributors.

All rights reserved. No part of this book may be reprinted or reproduced or utilised in any form or by any electronic, mechanical, or other means, now known or hereafter invented, including photocopying and recording, or in any information storage or retrieval system, without permission in writing from the publishers.

Trademark notice: Product or corporate names may be trademarks or registered trademarks, and are used only for identification and explanation without intent to infringe.

British Library Cataloguing in Publication Data
A catalogue record for this book is available from the British Library

ISBN: 978-1-138-34553-9 (Set)
ISBN: 978-0-429-39880-3 (Set) (ebk)
ISBN: 978-1-138-35292-6 (Volume 1) (hbk)
ISBN: 978-1-138-35299-5 (Volume 1) (pbk)
ISBN: 978-0-429-43448-8 (Volume 1) (ebk)

Publisher's Note
The publisher has gone to great lengths to ensure the quality of this reprint but points out that some imperfections in the original copies may be apparent.

Disclaimer
The publisher has made every effort to trace copyright holders and would welcome correspondence from those they have been unable to trace.

NB00022070
£21.74
WB570

ASSESSMENT IN SPEECH AND LANGUAGE THERAPY

While basic speech and language therapy texts exist, they do not adequately cover the methods available to assess clients in daily practice. *Assessment in Speech and Language Therapy* does this clearly and comprehensively for both specialists and students. The first part consists of reviews on specialist areas of assessment and the second makes an appraisal of tests frequently used within the profession.

Written by specialists in the field, the chapters in the first part cover such areas as receptive language, expressive language, articulation and phonology. This is followed by chapters on specific areas of speech and language problems, such as stammering, acquired language difficulty, children with special needs and assessment within psychiatry.

The test reviews in the second part are organized under convenient headings that give straightforward information on the purpose of each test, its population and how it is administered, scored and interpreted. This is followed by brief technical details such as how the test was standardized, its reliability and validity. Finally there is an overall evaluation of the test.

Assessment in Speech and Language Therapy will be useful not only for specialists, but also for all speech and language therapists and clinical psychologists working with the communicatively impaired, as well as students in this area.

ASSESSMENT IN SPEECH AND LANGUAGE THERAPY

Edited by John R. Beech and Leonora Harding with Diana Hilton-Jones

London and New York

First published in 1993
by Routledge
11 New Fetter Lane, London EC4P 4EE

Simultaneously published in the USA and Canada
by Routledge
29 West 35th Street, New York, NY 10001

© 1993 Selection and editorial matter, John R. Beech and Leonora Harding with
Diana Hilton-Jones; individual chapters, the contributors.

Typeset in Times by
Leaper & Gard Ltd, Bristol
Printed and bound in Great Britain by
T.J. Press (Padstow) Ltd, Padstow, Cornwall

All rights reserved. No part of this book may be reprinted or
reproduced or utilized in any form or by any electronic,
mechanical, or other means, now known or hereafter
invented, including photocopying and recording, or in any
information storage or retrieval system, without permission in
writing from the publishers.

British Cataloguing in Publication Data
A catalogue record for this book is available from the British Library

Library of Congress Cataloging in Publication Data
Assessment in speech and language therapy / edited by John R. Beech
and Leonora Harding with Diana Hilton-Jones.
p. cm. – (Routledge–NFER assessment library)
Includes bibliographical references and index.
1. Speech disorders–Diagnosis.   I. Beech, John R.   II. Harding,
Leonora, 1944–   .   III. Hilton-Jones, Diana.   IV. Series.
RC423.A84   1993
616.85′5075–dc20   92-39593
CIP

ISBN 0-415-07881-4 (hbk)
ISBN 0-415-07882-2 (pbk)

CONTENTS

ILLUSTRATIONS

BOXES

FIGURES

CONTRIBUTORS

Linda Armstrong Lecturer, Department of Speech Pathology and Therapy, Queen Margaret College, Edinburgh.

Julie Dockrell Lecturer, Department of Social Psychology, London School of Economics and Political Science.

Jenny France Speech and Language Therapist, Broadmoor Hospital, Crowthorne, Berks., and Specialist Clinical Adviser for Psychiatry, Eastern Region.

Pam Grunwell Professor of Clinical Linguistics, Head of the Department of Human Communication, De Montfort University, Leicester.

Clare Henry Lecturer in Speech and Language Therapy, School of Speech Therapy, University of Central England.

Jean Kerr Chief Speech and Language Therapist, Kings College Hospital, Kings Healthcare, London.

Armin Kuhr Professor at the Department of Clinical Psychology, Hanover Medical School, Germany.

Janet A. Lees Honorary Consultant Speech and Language Therapist, Wolfson Child Development Centre, The Hospital for Sick Children, Great Ormond Street, London.

Elspeth McCartney Head of the Division of Speech and Language Therapy, University of Strathclyde, Glasgow.

H. Fiona Robinson Chief Speech and Language Therapist, Queen's Medical Centre, Nottingham and Specialist Clinical Adviser for Voice, College of Speech and Language Therapists.

Lena Rustin Director of Speech and Language Therapy Services, Camden and Islington Community Health Services, London.

Sheila L. Wirz Senior Lecturer, National Hospitals' College of Speech Sciences, London.

Jannet A. Wright Lecturer, National Hospitals' College of Speech Sciences, London, and Institute of Education, London University.

SERIES EDITORS' PREFACE

The word 'assessment' conjures an adverse emotional reaction in many people. We have all at some stage undergone an assessment in some form – for instance when sitting an examination – and many of us have found it a distinctly unpleasant experience. Why should we make assessments of people, and even more to the point, why launch a series of volumes on the subject?

Assessment is usually to do with making a judgement about an individual in relation to a large group of people, based on the acquisition of a body of knowledge concerning that individual. In carrying out an assessment the professional believes that it is necessary to make such an assessment as a basis for deciding a particular course of action. This activity is considered to be predominantly in the best interests of the person being assessed, but at times, will also protect the interests of society, or an organization, such as a company. Whether or not one agrees with the concept of making an assessment, the practice continues in our society, even if it waxes and wanes in some professional sectors. Our own view is that assessment is here to stay and in many cases is beneficial to the individual.

It is important that the best available means of assessment are used by professional workers to provide an accurate body of knowledge on which to base decisions. Errors of diagnosis can sometimes have serious consequences. The national press seems to report almost every day on situations in which diagnosis has been problematic, such as releasing a violent prisoner prematurely, or making erroneous accusations of child abuse, and so on. Less dramatic situations would be ones in which a child is inaccurately assessed and is then put on a training programme which is not appropriate for his or her needs, or where an elderly person is inaccurately considered as unable to live in his or her own home and transferred to another environment. Given that many of these assessments are essential, improving their accuracy is a worthwhile goal. If this series of volumes is instrumental in improving accuracy to some degree, we shall be well pleased.

As well as inaccurate use of tests, breakdown of communication between professions can lead to wrong decisions and inappropriate therapy or placement plans. Any one client may be treated, assessed or discussed by a number of professionals with different training, areas of expertise, approaches to assessment and vocabulary. (The term 'client' itself suggests one particular approach to care.) This series is explicitly directed to the sharing of knowledge and to the breaking-down of barriers between professionals. We believe multidisciplinary co-operation and information exchange can only benefit the subjects of assessment. It should be borne in mind, however, that certain tests which have been reviewed in these volumes can only be applied by professionals with the appropriate qualifications. We hope that there will be a certain amount of liberalization of these strictures in the future in order to facilitate co-operation between professionals.

When planning the series we decided early on that we were not going to produce exhaustive manuals, giving thorough reviews of all possible assessment techniques. There are many books of this nature already available. We thought that it would be a much better idea to produce fairly short books targeted at a particular category of person requiring assessment, such as the elderly, or those with speech and language difficulties. Our readership would be the professional workers involved with such groups, either directly as assessors or indirectly as those who use test results in their decision-making. Students training for these professions, or professionals undergoing in-service training will also find these useful. Therefore, we have set our writers a very difficult task. Each contribution has to be easy to read, but at the same time, provide information which the current professional worker will find useful when deciding on an assessment strategy. The writer might point to a new test which has been developed, or highlight the inadequacies of one currently used. The chapters do describe the application of tests within a particular area, but they also provide a range of other useful information, for instance, check-lists, case studies, points to bear in mind with certain types of patient, and so on.

Most of the volumes contain a final section of reviews on the main tests currently applied in that area. Making choices about what to include has been difficult; but the final choice is based on extensive consultation with practising professionals and researchers. The end result should contain the tests used most frequently within an area. The problem is that there is usually a large variety of more minor tests, each of which is probably used by only a few workers. From this group we have chosen those tests which seem to contain a feature or application of outstanding interest, or those tests which we felt deserved wider use.

All of the test reviews were written within a pre-arranged structure. Information is given about the purpose of the test, how to use it and an evaluation is also made. Some technical information is provided, such as the number of people who were tested in order to develop the test. Where available, the reliability and validity are supplied. The reliability shows the extent to which applying the same test again will give the same result. A low reliability indicates that assessment could be inaccurate as the outcome changes on successive occasions. The validity of the test shows how well the test is associated with similar tests measuring the same properties. The reader does not necessarily need any prior knowledge in order to understand these test reviews. However, the interested reader is referred to our book in the series entitled *Testing People: A Practical Guide to Psychometrics* which goes into the statistical basis of testing in more depth. This is a corner-stone volume in the series which is intended for professional people who wish to update their statistical knowledge in order to understand the basis of the tests. It does not assume any previous statistical knowledge.

Turning briefly to the contents of the current book, this volume covers a variety of problem areas involved with assessment in speech and language therapy. We begin with an introduction that examines the epidemiology of the communicatively impaired, and the history of interest in communication disorder, followed by current practice. The second chapter examines the assessment of receptive language in children, from preschool up to the teenager. The third looks at expressive language in the child. This is followed by the assessment of articulation, voice and stammering problems. The seventh chapter covers acquired language problems and includes work from cognitive neuropsychology. The rest of the chapters concentrate on those in the community with special problems: children with special needs, the mentally handicapped, the elderly and those with psychiatric illness.

Finally, we would like to thank Carolyn Richardson of NFER-NELSON and Diana Hilton-Jones, who had a consultative role, for their enthusiasm and close involvement with the production of this volume as well as the numerous individuals who have given their help in other ways.

John R. Beech and Leonora Harding

INTRODUCTION
Historical Considerations in Assessment

Sheila L. Wirz

This volume is written at a time of great changes for speech and language therapy and for the National Health Service which is almost the monopoly provider of speech-and-language-therapy services. In such a period of change it is timely to reflect on the assessment processes that the discipline of speech and language therapy has developed. The processes have been developed, for different client groups, for a variety of clinical and social purposes and with the view of communicating findings to a range of different colleagues. The procedures that attempt to assess disorders of communication vary from inventories of skills or inventories of deficits, from 'test' batteries that examine (or purport to examine) assets to those that examine weaknesses, from assessment procedures that attempt to examine all the communication skills of a client to those that examine specific skills. A further dichotomy exists between those assessments that can be described as 'client-centred', evaluating the strengths and/ or weaknesses of a particular client, and those that can be described as 'disorder-centred', concentrating as they do on the common features of a particular disorder.

A variety of check-lists or inventories record the communicative abilities of communicatively impaired people. Some of these are designed for specific populations, for example, PIP Charts (Jeffree and McConkey, 1976), a check-list designed for learning-disordered children; others are less disorder-specific in their use; some are designed to examine the skills of children, for example, Portage (Bluma *et al.*, 1976), and others the skills of adults who have acquired disorders of communication, for example, the Functional Communication Profile (Sarno, 1975). The range of these check-lists is wide and their common feature is to record the communicative ability of an individual in as near normal settings as possible.

1

In contrast to check-lists, a range of tests has also been developed, either examining what an individual can do, for example, the Test for Reception of Grammar (Bishop, 1982) and the Western Aphasia Battery (Kertesz, 1982), which look at developing or acquired disorders, respectively; or examining what an individual is unable to do, for example, the Milan Token Test (De Renzi and Vignolo, 1962).

Both inventories and tests, both asset-based and deficit-based procedures have their value with different clients.

This chapter will explore how early assessment procedures measured changes in response between impaired and non-impaired communicators. In other words they concentrated on the target behaviours of an individual. More recently assessment has moved from concentrating on responses, to an examination of the processes involved in communication. Thus twenty years ago, for example, the aim of a speech assessment was to show how the target articulatory behaviour of a speaker differed from the norm (see Fisher and Logemann, 1971); the aim now is likely to be to examine the phonological process underpinning that articulatory behaviour (see Grunwell, 1985); this is a move from describing the symptoms of communicative differences to examining communicative processes.

A further distinction among assessments of communication disorder is between those that concentrate upon specific aspects of communication and those that concentrate upon general communicative abilities; or again, those that concentrate on all communicative media, contrasting with those that examine a particular communicative medium, for example, sign or facial expression.

The richness of choice available to therapists is both daunting and exciting. The therapist must determine from a matrix of possibilities which type of assessment is suitable:

- an inventory of assets or one of deficits
- a test battery designed to determine levels of achievement or those of failure
- a procedure with eclectic or specific application
- a procedure examining behaviours or processes
- a procedure designed for all media of communication or only some.

This introduction will explore some ways in which these different assessment processes have developed in the past years and try to forecast some changes that may develop over the next stage in our understanding of communication disorder.

Any introductory chapter of this nature must define first the boundaries of the subject matter under consideration and therefore the first section is an epidemiological account of disorders of communication. Second, the chapter will outline some historical perspective in the rationale regarding the assessment of communication disorder. Finally there will follow an attempt to classify the different assessment processes. Subsequent chapters describe in some detail assessments with specific client groups; this chapter explores the process of assessment with the communicatively impaired population.

EPIDEMIOLOGY

Who are the communicatively impaired, what do speech and language therapists and others wish to assess and how do they implement these assessments? These are questions that providers of speech-and-language-therapy services are being asked with increasing ferocity in the current climate of 'clinical audit', 'commissioned services' and the 'quality assurances' of our newly constituted National Health Service. They are also questions that have been asked by good practitioners for many years and are not as novel as may appear at first sight.

The chapter headings of this volume go some way to enumerating groups of communicatively impaired people. Chapter headings such as 'Assessment of receptive language', 'Assessment of articulation and phonology', 'Assessment of mentally handicapped individuals', 'Assessing the older communication-impaired person' are all labels with slightly different emphases. This list begins to answer the question 'Who are the communicatively impaired?' However, the list also provides a vivid illustration of how the labelling of communication disorder uses concepts from a range of disciplines.

Any assessment of language structure refers to measurable differences between the language behaviour of some communicators as compared with others. Assessment of this nature has a kinship with the assessment of other behaviours in psychology. *Mentally handicapped* or *Geriatric* are labels borrowed from social services and illustrate an attempt to ascribe common symptoms of communicative behaviour to groups with a very wide range of different symptoms. *Psychiatric patients* is a clear example of taking a wide medical disease label and ascribing possible communication features to people so labelled, and by using the word 'patient' to imply a dependency/ illness element through the label.

Any attempt at an epidemiological consideration of communication disorders must first consider how the communicatively impaired population is described. Is it described by using labels which refer to symptoms, social-group labels or disease labels?

Use of a classification system based on measurable symptom deficits may be possible for some areas of communication disorder, but in others would only serve to show how little we know of the normalcy from which such measurements are made. For example, work over the last fifty years from Jesperson (1922) to Grunwell (1985), from Wendell Johnson (1948) to Crystal (1976) has told us something of the way in which children learn to produce intelligible speech and use the structures of the adult language; additionally each has suggested ways in which disordered speech can be assessed. As our knowledge of the process has improved, so our assessment techniques have become more refined and hopefully more useful. More importantly for the current argument, the building of the knowledge base has led to the assessment of children with unintelligible speech being based on clinical linguistic theory and not some related but inappropriate theory. The same cannot be said for all disorders of communication. Some assessments 'measure' behaviours about which we know very little in either the ordered or the disordered population.

In the early part of this century both researchers and practitioners became absorbed with particular groups of communicatively impaired people and there was little attempt to estimate either the size or the extent of the communicatively impaired population. Epidemiological information was almost non-existent. In this account of how assessment has developed in speech and language therapy it is deemed useful to have some idea of the size of the problem. The author has looked at those studies that have tried to determine size. They are of course methodologically dissimilar and in an attempt to facilitate comparison the author has calculated simple percentage incidences from the data reported in the studies. These percentage incidences are not always the preferred reporting method of the individual surveys.

One of the earliest attempts to establish guidelines as to the extent of the language-disordered population in childhood was undertaken in Newcastle in the 1940s and 1950s by Muriel Morley (1965). Her study was part of a larger investigation into child development and disease following the development of 1,142 children born in May or June 1947 in Newcastle. In Morley's study, children's speech was investigated at 3 years 6 months, 4 years 9 months, 6 years 6 months and 9 years 6 months. Morley categorized children into four groups:

1   those with delayed development of speech and language
2   those with 'resolving difficulties of articulation'
3   those with 'persistent defects of articulation' and
4   stammerers.

In common with contemporary thinking, Morley's study used a disease-based medical model and introduced a taxonomy to childhood disorders of speech and language. Of epidemiological interest is Morley's finding that at 6 years 6 months, 3.7 per cent of the children in her study had persisting difficulties with speech.

The impact of Morley's study was not only to suggest the size of the problem, but also to heighten awareness of the need to separate those children with slower from those with aberrant development of speech. This heightened awareness was reflected in assessments in the next few years;

the Edinburgh Articulation assessment, for instance (Anthony *et al.*, 1971), for the first time attempted to show not only whether children's responses to an articulation test showed them to be delayed but whether the responses were typically delayed or abnormal.

The first comprehensive account of the incidence of communication disorder in the United Kingdom was undertaken by the Royal Commission chaired by Randolph Quirk (Quirk, 1972). The aim of the Quirk report was to determine the numbers of speech and language therapists required to provide a speech-and-language-therapy service for the National Health Service; it did not aim to determine the size of the communicatively impaired population. As a consequence of the commission's efforts to determine the former (numbers of therapists required), they did of course give a clearer picture of the latter (the size of the communicatively impaired population) than had hitherto been available. This commission estimated that around 0.6 per cent of the population had a communication disorder of such severity as to need the help of a speech and language therapist.

The next relevant study was one by Enderby and Phillipp (1986) who estimated the incidence of communication disorder in the subpopulations of various disease and developmental groups. Their methodology attempted to determine the size of the communicatively impaired population which they did at 2.3 million (or 4.2 per cent of the population), 800,000 (or 1.5 per cent of the population) of whom they estimated had a disorder of sufficient severity to merit the help of a speech and language therapist.

More recently Enderby and Davies in a further study (1989), supported by the Department of Health, attempted to ascertain the size of the population with a need for speech and language therapy. They posited the incidence of a variety of communication disorders ranging from 0.7 per cent of the population having a communication disorder related to learning difficulties to 0.04 per cent of the population having a communication problem because of a cerebral trauma. They did not provide a total picture of incidence, rather they have attempted to show incidence in subpopulations, within their stated objective to 'estimate the number of speech therapists required to service this [communicatively impaired] population' (p. 301).

Their methodology, based on a mixture of empirical data and conjecture, has caused some concern (Bryan *et al.*, 1991) but their figures none the less provide the most recent published information about the size of the communicatively impaired population. What is equally important from their study is their evidence of involvement with a much wider range of communicatively impaired people, for example, the communication problems associated with progressive disease. Enderby and Davies estimate the incidence of communication disorder related to progressive disease at 0.15 per cent.

These indications of incidence, which many would say are only broad estimates, do give an important perspective to our understanding of communication disorder. It remains a problem that is relatively small in relation to the total population but a problem of devastating effect on the clients so affected and on their families. In recent years much attention has been directed in the social services to the needs of the carers of dependent people. In considerations of the communicatively impaired, while recognizing in therapy the importance of carers and families in the management of communication disorder, no study has estimated the impact of disordered communication on the families. In relation to some disorders, notably stuttering and communication problems related to severe and profound deafness, an assessment of communication would always include an assessment of the close family's communicative strategies with the client. The language behaviour of the family is seen to be of equal importance to that of the client in a full assessment preceding any intervention. However, this contextual assessment of the family unit is, it seems to the author, far less common in relation to other disorders of communication. Assessment practices with other groups of communicatively impaired clients would do well to look at the way in which therapists working with stammerers and deaf clients do not restrict themselves to assessment of the client.

HISTORICAL PERSPECTIVE

There is a long tradition of interest in communication disorder. From Demosthenes with his pebbles, from Leonardo da Vinci with his drawings and models of the vocal tract, from Pedro Ponce de Leon with his early version of 'total communication' in sixteenth-century Spain, and from the divergence of opinion of L'Abbé de L'Eppée and Heineke in the eighteenth century, students of speech pathology know that the inability of some to use communication normally has always fascinated. However, this historical review will be restricted to a very brief outline of changes in emphases of assessment over the twentieth century.

In the early part of this century, speech and language therapists fell broadly into two groups. The first was concerned with the mechanics of speech and embraced the new knowledge derived from phonetics (e.g. Aiken, 1910). Aiken's preface to the second edition of his book *The Voice* states that 'it has become necessary to remodel and rewrite the whole work and to regard it as an introduction to the practical science of phonology' (p. 1). The second group concentrated more on the psychological behaviour of 'speech-disordered' people. Researchers in speech pathology, notably in Berlin following Gutzman, in Vienna following Froeschels, in London and in the United States, notably at the University of Columbia, following Scripture, were fascinated by four problems: those of stuttering, of voice, of 'dyslalia' and of dysphasia, almost to the exclusion of any awareness of other disorders. Similarly the remedial practitioners, who in the early part of the century came from a range of backgrounds, became remedial specialists for specific client groups.

One can look at the aphasia assessments proposed by Head (1926), by Jackson (1898, 1932) and later by Zangwill (1960) and see both how their practice influenced assessment procedures for half a century, and how some of their ideas are still retained in current practice. They attempted to assess their clients' language until they found specific areas of breakdown either in terms of the nature of the task or in the complexity of the task. Assessment of aphasia was rooted in the concept of breakdown caused by neurological damage. Practitioners concerned with aphasia were for the most part neurologists following the German tradition of localization with a continued fascination in determining loci for different functions. Those therapists who worked with the early aphasiologists were rooted in the same traditions.

Generations of British therapists educated in the third quarter of the century were influenced in their assessments by *Butfield's Notes*, an unpublished document derived from the work which Butfield had followed in Bangor Hospital during the early 1940s when she was the speech and language therapist working with Zangwill. The purpose of these assessment notes was to determine the 'type' of dysphasia; 'type' being determined in strongly localizationist terms. As the work of Russian aphasiologists became better known in the West, this emphasis on assessment of responses to tasks in aphasia assessment shifted more to assessment of language function.

The assessment of voice disorder was, like aphasia, strongly influenced in the earlier part of this century by medical practice. Froeschels and other Austrian researchers determined assessments that looked at the dysfunction of different parts of the vocal assembly. They were, as became educated Austrians in the early quarter of the twentieth century, knowledgeable of music and song, and following Garcia's tradition some thirty years earlier, they derived some ingenious early instrumental techniques for looking not only at the larynx and resonators but also at ways to measure functions such as respiration (Froeschels, 1922). As some medical practitioners developed their thinking about how best to assess not only the larynx but also the product of the larynx, namely voice, so too did some phoneticians become interested in how to assess voice. Bell (1916) tried to establish some of the links between anatomy and acoustic output by manipulating the larynx of his dog, and other phoneticians followed in his tradition. Aiken, as early as 1910, outlined an assessment that would be recognizable today: 'a threefold process in the following order. The capacity and conscious control of the breath, the positions and movements of the resonators and the free and unhampered use of the vocal vibrator' (p. 11). Other voice therapists were interested in the relationship between disturbances of the psyche and voice disorder (e.g. Stein, 1942).

What is of note when considering the assessments of early voice therapists was that they integrated knowledge from at least two very different disciplines, that of anatomy and that of phonetics, combined with skills from singing and/ or voice production. It is surely this integration of knowledge from different disciplines that has been vital in the emergence of speech and language therapy as an independent speciality, and the confidence of speech and language therapy to take from the knowledge base of other disciplines without being restricted by their limitations has marked the maturity of the speciality.

Therapists of stuttering have surely benefited most from the field of behavioural psychiatry. They were among the first speech and language therapists to recognize the need to assess the person with the speech disorder and not only the speech symptoms. In 1862, with the publication of 'Heilung des Stotterns', Klenke wrote of the need to treat the whole of a stammerer's personality. Scripture studied the value of psychoanalytic assessment for stammerers, and throughout the long history of interest in this most ill-understood disorder lies a belief that assessment of the speaker, not just the symptoms, is required.

But fewer therapists worked with aphasics, voice-disordered clients and stutterers together, compared with the numbers of therapists working with children. The way in which the assessment of children with disordered speech was undertaken drew on contemporary understanding of child development coupled with a knowledge of segmental phonetics. Assessments were a two-fold attempt to describe how children's development of speech sounds differed in relation to those of their peers and also how their production of speech could be described using simple place, manner and voicing parameters. There was in the earlier part of the century no interest in the use children made of speech nor of the way their speech may have reflected a wider linguistic incompetence.

At their simplest the assessments of speech at this time were an inventory of 'sounds', usually commenting on vowels and consonants but sometimes pitch changes and rhythm changes as well. It was usual to determine how the child responded to a naming task of a word list containing a range of consonant and vowel sounds. The child's responses were then evaluated in terms of how many 'omissions, substitutions or elisions' were contained in his or her responses and if the assessment were to be more specific than this, or, rather, to be influenced by phonetic thought, the responses would then be analysed into 'errors' of place, manner and voicing. This influence of early analysis persisted until the 1960s with assessments of articulatory function, for example, that of Fisher and Logemann (1971), which assessed errors of place, manner or voicing in the speaker's responses. There was no attempt to define error in developmental terms. Errors were simply seen as non-adult form. It was not until Morley (1965) that assessments separated delayed from disordered speech.

One of the biggest differences between speech-and-language-therapy assessment in the first and second halves of the century was the emphasis by early therapists on evaluating the individual client as they strove to establish their all-important differential diagnoses. This was, of course, no mean task when the diagnostic categories that they had available to them were so non-specific. Stein writes little of assessment of speech disorder but rather writes eloquently about

the importance of 'diagnosis' of speech disorders from 'gnonia' the Greek verb 'to know' and 'dia' the Greek prefix 'between'.

It may be noted that Diagnosis consists of a mass of perceptions all having a meaning. But it is more than a mere collection of notions. Diagnosis thus means the act and result of identifying a disease through the knowledge of its history, symptoms and signs and their relation.

(Stein, 1942: 65)

It seems that these early therapists were rooted firmly in the medical model of seeking diagnostic categories, although one has the impression from reading accounts of their therapy that they remained imaginative and creative in their therapy practice despite the constraining force of their diagnoses.

In the 1940s and 1950s two important developments had a great impact on speech and language therapy. One was the improvement in audiological assessment and, with transistors, the growth in efficacy of personal hearing aids bringing a whole new dimension of accuracy to speech assessment by enabling the receptive skills to be carefully examined. The second was, in Britain, the merging of the professional bodies for speech therapists. The remedial section of the Association of Teachers of Speech and Drama together with the Association of Speech Therapists and the British Society of Speech Therapists merged in 1944 to form the College of Speech Therapists. This enabled easier pooling of skills and knowledge from the slightly divergent groups and allowed them to enrich each other and further strengthen knowledge about communication disorder and the remediation of such disorders.

In the 1960s a third important change was that speech and language therapy could now look to a new discipline of linguistics which, although grounded in the bases of philology, grammar and etymology, was to develop concepts that greatly enhanced speech pathology and notably enhanced the development of new assessments.

Until the 1950s, assessment, or the search for a diagnosis, had been client-centred; in the 1950s and early 1960s there were many attempts to provide speech-and-language-therapy assessments with norms based on group data. This was, of course, a reflection of how psychologists were developing child-development norms at that time. Milestones became the markers for assessment, the fixed points against which children's development and progress could be ascertained. It became common for assessments to express their scores in terms of 'language age' or 'articulation age'; furthermore there was a resurgence of interest in grouped data, such as had been collected from aphasic people in the early 1920s. With this emphasis both on milestones and on grouped data there emerged a series of screening tests that aimed to show vulnerable children as those whose skills should be more specifically assessed.

In the early 1970s the application of linguistic knowledge developed in two especially interesting directions for speech and language therapy. First, the developing study of cognitive psychology and the application which this had to our understanding of communication breakdown, and second, growth in pragmatic theory, led to greater understanding of the use of communication. The impact which cognitive psychology has upon speech therapy is a developing force, a force which has demanded a reappraisal of our understanding and management of language disorder, both developmental and acquired. Coltheart's group at Birkbeck College had a profound effect on aphasiology just as the Boston school had done ten years before. Together the work of the Boston school in the mid-1970s and that of the Birkbeck school in the mid-1980s completely changed thinking about assessment of aphasics. Not only did this change affect assessment and management procedures but it also gave speech and language therapy increased confidence to move away from sole dependence on large group studies to prove efficacy. The growth of single case-study design as an investigative approach to the study of aphasia as well as being an assessment tool for individuals has been especially evident for the past eight years (Byng and Coltheart, 1986).

Cognitive psychology gives speech and language therapy the possibility of assessment based on a problem-solving approach either, instead of, or in conjunction with, standardized assessments. This move from scores on a standardized tool to a problem-based assessment for dysphasic clients has occurred at the same time as an increase in use of functional assessment of the retained communicative function in these people. Thus cognitive psychology and pragmatics have contributed to the change in dysphasia assessment away from deficit-based assessment towards a climate where the therapist assesses both the retained communicative assets and, using appropriate tasks, investigates which language processes are affected by the trauma. This is a move from scoring responses to tasks, to the observation of retained abilities and the investigation of the processes that have broken down in a dysphasic person's language system. While the impact of cognitive psychology has had its most immediate influence upon the assessment and management of dysphasia, there is no doubt that its effects are felt throughout speech-and-language-therapy practice.

The brief account above sketches some of the ways in which assessment in speech and language therapy has developed during the twentieth century. It is clear that under the influence of the medical model of seeking diagnostic categories, early assessment was constrained by this search. In their attempt to understand more clearly the phenomena of communication breakdown, therapists sought to refine their diagnostic categories into ever more specific subgroups. Having established such categories they were, not surprisingly, drawn to the practice of describing deviant symptoms – deviance, in such a framework, meaning that the communicative behaviour did not fit the diagnostic categories that had been established.

Following this emphasis on diagnosis as the aim of assessment came the practice of comparative assessment. Here the aim of assessment was to determine how individuals' communicative behaviour compared with that of their peers. Such comparative assessments used developmental milestones derived from studies of the acquisition of a particular skill by groups of children, or normative data derived from standardization procedures where groups of healthy people's answers to tasks are recorded and used as a baseline for comparison. These standardized assessment procedures took little account of the fact that the client may not want to jump through the communicative hoops of the assessment. Communication, perhaps more than any other behaviour, has – as a vital prerequisite – the need to communicate, and if that need is absent one must ask how representative the resulting behaviour really is.

Finally, the historical sketch has suggested how the impact of cognitive psychology has been to move away from symptoms and diagnostic categories towards an examination of processes.

CURRENT PRACTICE

This historical sketch has, however, said little about why assessment is undertaken. It may have been to provide the all-important diagnosis, it may have been data collection to increase the body of knowledge about a particular disorder, or it may have been driven by a search for a remedial programme. Assessment preceding remedial intervention falls into two categories: descriptive and prescriptive. Descriptive assessment describes, often in very great detail, the communicative behaviour of an individual either in terms of how he or she differs from peers or in terms of his or her idiosyncrasies. The therapist must then determine which aspects of this description illuminate the therapy-planning process. In contrast, prescriptive assessment concentrates on an assessment of those behaviours where remediation is possible and pinpoints possible starting points for the therapist.

In all cases where assessment enables the planning of intervention, it is important that the type of intervention is clearly understood. For example, is the aim to follow a re-educative programme of therapy, or a compensatory programme? It is clear to the experienced therapist that the assessment that would be undertaken before a programme of re-educative therapy would be very different from one preceding a programme of compensatory therapy. In the former the assessment would need to show the range of possible skills that the client has retained as well as those that are lost, whereas in the latter the therapist would be concentrating in his or her assessment far more on case-history information as to the communicative need of the client and his or her family. The principle behind this example can be duplicated in the planning of any assessment, and should be considered before any assessment is undertaken.

Although it is axiomatic that the choice of assessment should meet the therapist's need for a procedure that is appropriate for the client's disorder, age, interests, cognitive ability, psychosocial needs and the remedial approach of the therapist, it is clear that this is not always so. Fashion, familiarity, availability, ease of administration and even the salesmanship of publishers' agents, are too often the rationale behind the choice of assessment tool.

Assessment may then be undertaken to advance the remedial planning process. Other reasons for assessment may be to provide baseline measures before therapy, outcome measures of therapy or indeed to do both in studies of the efficacy of intervention. Speech and language therapy has a less than favourable history in terms of the way in which efficacy studies have been accepted by other professionals. One very important reason for this is that attempts at large group studies are fraught with the problems of comparability of results in populations where perforce there is great variation in the communication disorder, in underlying aetiological factors, in the use which clients make of their communication, and in the therapy which is given. These difficulties of interpretation of results from large group studies have been explored in detail elsewhere. Howard and Hatfield (1987) give a comprehensive discussion of the difficulties of using group data in efficacy studies, and review the assessments that have been used in such studies. They point out that efficacious therapy must effect a real change in the aphasic's life, but that few assessments do so. 'If a test is a valid measure there should only be improvement in test scores where there is real improvement in communication and conversely where in reality the aphasic experiences no change, test scores should not change' (p. 114).

Another reason why studies by speech and language therapists are not always favourably received by other professionals is that therapists frequently explain neither the rationale for the choice of assessment tool nor the assessment design. For example, a therapist may choose to use a tool that has a prescriptive basis to its design (e.g. 'Vocal profiles analysis scheme', Laver et al., 1981), and illustrate change over time using such a tool for either individuals or groups of clients. A medical practitioner might seek diagnostic implications, which have never been claimed by the assessment procedure. It is unclear if therapists spend enough time explaining to their colleagues the design of their assessment tools and, as a result, are pilloried in error by people who expect the diagnostic-based assessment tools of the medical model or the standardized assessment, based on group data, of the psychologist. Perhaps in the past therapists have used assessment models borrowed from other disciplines and have not had the confidence to use other more appropriate ones. As suggested above, the work of the Birkbeck group in exploring hypothesis-driven assessments rather than standardized assessments has gone a long way to redress this imbalance.

Assessments based on cognitive-processing theory, on knowledge of language development, on psycholinguistic theory or on neurobiologic theories of speech production, are all measures of language behaviour in one form or another. There is a whole raft of assessments that use instrumental measurement as the basis for the assessment. These instrumental assessments are sometimes given the misnomer 'objective' assessment. It is a misnomer because any assessment is only as good as the practitioner undertaking the assessment and the skill of that practitioner in interpreting the results. It is possible that an inexperienced practitioner can misread the measures provided by an instrumental assessment and be less accurate than the more experienced colleague using non-instrumental procedures. Assessment by instrumental techniques is particularly developed in the field of voice analysis. It was noted above that salesmanship can play too great a part in determining which assessment procedures are available to a practitioner. Nowhere is this more evident than in the choice of instrumentation where unfortunately practitioners may end up with tools that are far from appropriate for their assessment needs.

When choosing an instrumental assessment procedure there are some basic questions that the therapist must ask. First, it is important to determine what type of speech sample is to be assessed. Will it be steady-state vowels, or does the therapist wish to assess a longer sample of connected speech? A tool that can do the former may be quite incapable of the latter. What level of analysis does the therapist seek, is it, for example, information about laryngeal activity or about resonance or about breath support? Again, a tool designed to give information about vocal-fold activity will not help with the assessment of breathing or resonance balance. The therapist must have confidence not only in the choice of assessment but also have the ability to integrate information from the instrumental procedure into the total assessment of the client's needs.

Speech and language therapists have become increasingly aware of the need to assess not only the spoken and written language of their clients but also other media of communication. In considering different media it has been commonplace to assess writing and reading, which are considered to be different facets of the same language. But therapists have, with some exceptions, been slower to examine systematically the pantomime skills, signing ability, facial expression or drawing skills of clients in either the receptive or expressive domain. The assessment of the communication skills of severely and profoundly deaf people is an area where speech and language therapists have developed tools to assess communication through a multimedia approach. Speech and language therapists working with this client group commonly carry out assessments in both British Sign Language and Sign Supported English as well as in spoken English in an attempt to ascertain the language skills of their clients (Parker and Irlam, 1983). In dysphasia assessment, too, therapists seek information in their assessments from a range of different media (Wirz et al., 1990).

With advances in computer technology and speech synthesis a small but significant group of disabled people have come to depend on computer-aided communication. The assessment which precedes the choice of aid, the selection of an appropriate interface by which the disabled person can use the aid, and the acceptability of the aid to clients and their families is a new and exciting area of specialized assessment.

This form of assessment illustrates with great clarity a principle that should be followed in the investigation of all client groups, namely the need to ensure that any testing is carried out in the context of full case-history information. Without detailed information about individuals and their needs, any assessment becomes the analysis of data rather than the assessment of the communication of an individual. One of the characteristics of therapists is that they consider these needs and do not become wooed into thinking of clients as data-producing mechanisms. It is the complexity of the communication process and the idiosyncrasies of each client that challenge the clinician in the assessment and interpretation of findings in each assessment that is undertaken.

It is this richness of variety that offers the speech and language therapist the challenge in any assessment undertaken. Whether the assessment is undertaken as a measurement tool to establish a baseline for therapy, an investigatory procedure leading to a diagnosis of need, an evaluation of the efficacy of intervention, or as a screening procedure to pinpoint areas for further investigation; with whichever client group, using whatever media of communication and measurement, a therapist's value to a client with disordered communication will only be as good as the assessment that precedes the planning of an intervention programme and the assessments that evaluate efficacy throughout the implementation of that programme.

REFERENCES

Aiken, W. A. (1910, 1960). *The Voice.* London: Longman.

Anthony, A., Bogle, D., Ingram, T. and McIsaac, M. (1971). *Edinburgh Articulation Test.* Edinburgh: Churchill Livingstone.

Bell, A. G. (1916). *The Mechanism of Speech.* New York: Funk & Wagnall.

Bishop, D. V. M. (1982). *Test for Reception of Grammar.* Abingdon: Thomas Leach.

Bluma, S. M., Sheaves, M. S., Frohman, A. H. and Hilliard, J. M. (1976). *Portage Guide to Early Education.* Wisconsin: Co-operative Education Service Agency.

Bryan, K., Maxim, J., McIntosh, J., McClelland A., Wirz, S., Edmundson, A. and Snowling M. (1991). 'The facts behind the figures: a reply to Enderby and Davies 1984'. *British Journal of Disorders of Communication* 26, 253–61.

Byng, S. and Coltheart, M. (1986). 'Aphasia therapy research requirements'. In E. Hjelmquist and L. Nilsson (eds) *Communication and Handicap.* Amsterdam: Elsevier.

Crystal, D., Fletcher, P. and Garman, M. (1976). *The Grammatical Analysis of Language Disability.* London: Edward Arnold.

De Renzi, E. and Vignolo, L. (1962). 'The Token Test: a sensitive test to detect receptive disturbances in aphasia'. *Brain*, 85, 665–78.

Enderby, P. and Davies, P. (1989). 'Communication disorders: planning a service to meet the needs'. *British Journal of Disorders of Communication*, 24, 301–31.

Enderby, P. and Phillipp, R. (1986). 'Speech and language handicap: towards knowing the size of the problem'. *British Journal of Disorders of Communication*, 21, 151–65.

Fisher, H. B. and Logemann, J. A. (1971). *Test of Articulation Competence*. Boston: Houghton Mifflin.

Froeschels, E. (1922). 'Ein Apparat zur Feststellung van wilder Luft'. *Zeitschrift für Hals-, Nasen- und Ohrenheilforschung*, 1, 303–13.

Grunwell, P. (1985). *Phonological Assessment of Child Speech*. Windsor: NFER-NELSON.

Head, H. (1926). *Aphasia and Kindred Disorders of Speech*. Cambridge: Cambridge University Press.

Howard, D. and Hatfield, F. (1987). *Aphasia Therapy: Historical and Contemporary Issues*. London: Erlbaum.

Jackson, H. (1898, 1932). *The Characteristics of Aphasia*. Bristol: Taylor & Francis.

Jeffree, D. M. and McConkey, R. (1976). *PIP Developmental Charts*. London: Hodder & Stoughton.

Jesperson, O. (1922). *Language – Its Nature and Development*. London: George Allen & Unwin.

Kertesz, A. (1982). *The Western Aphasia Battery*. New York: Psychological Corporation.

Klenke, A. (1862). 'Heilung des Stotterns'. In M. Eldridge (ed.), *A History of the Treatment of Speech Disorders*. Edinburgh: Churchill Livingstone.

Laver, J., Wirz, S. and Mackenzie, J. (1981). 'Vocal profiles analysis scheme'. *Work in Progress*, Edinburgh University.

Morley, M. E. (1965). *The Development and Disorders of Speech in Childhood* (2nd edn). Edinburgh: Churchill Livingstone.

Parker, A. and Irlam, S. (1983). Unpublished paper, CST/British Association of Teachers of the Deaf conference and MSc thesis. London: City University.

Quirk, R. (1972). *Speech Therapy Services*. London: HMSO.

Sarno, M. T. (1969, 1975). *The Functional Communication Profile*. New York: Institute of Rehabilitation Medicine.

Scripture, D. (1968). In M. Eldridge (ed.), *A History of the Treatment of Speech Disorders*. Edinburgh: Churchill Livingstone.

Stein, L. (1942). *Speech and Voice – Their Evolution, Pathology and Therapy*. London: Methuen.

Watts, A. F. (1944). *Language and Mental Development of Children*. London: Harrap.

Wendell Johnson, J. (1948). *Speech Handicapped Schoolchildren*. New York: Harper.

Wirz, S. L., Skinner, C. and Dean, E. L. (1990). *The revised Edinburgh Communication Profile: communication skill builders*. Tucson, Arizona: Communication Skills Builders.

Zangwill, O. (1960). *Cerebral Dominance and its Relation to Psychological Function*. Harlow: Oliver & Boyd.

1

ASSESSMENT OF RECEPTIVE LANGUAGE

Janet A. Lees

When faced with the need to assess a child's language development in order to produce a profile of strengths and weaknesses that can be used to plan intervention, most therapists begin by investigating receptive-language abilities. Receptive language is the human ability to understand and process symbols, particularly verbal ones, as part of the communicative act (Cooper, Moodley and Reynell, 1979). Thus, it includes the development of pre-linguistic receptive abilities; for example, the understanding of prosodic features or symbolic noises such as animal sounds, as well as the comprehension of complex grammar or lexical items. From this definition it is clear that the clinical task of receptive-language assessment is quite a broad one. However, in practice it is informed by several basic questions as well as our understanding of the development and cerebral organization of receptive language. The basic questions that a clinician needs to consider during the assessment process are:

1. What is the present status of the child's receptive language?
2. If it is mismatched with the rest of the child's development and/or the child's age, is intervention required and if so what?
3. What is the prognosis for further development?

These questions will form the basis of the discussion of the assessment of receptive language in this chapter. The clinical population will be considered in three main age bands; preschool (under 5 years), school-aged (5–10 years) and teenage children (11–16 years). In addition there will also be some consideration of the needs of children with unusual receptive problems including the Landau-Kleffner syndrome (Landau and Kleffner, 1957).

WHAT IS THE PRESENT STATUS OF THE CHILD'S RECEPTIVE LANGUAGE?

The clinician's judgement of a child's receptive-language abilities is informed in two ways: a knowledge of the usual process of language development and a model of the way in which children process language. These two ideas are fundamental to all assessment procedures, both formal and informal. In order to make appropriate decisions during the assessment process a clinician needs to consider new developments in those two fields. The majority of assessment procedures for children are based on developmental levels or stages, and a minority take a view of language-processing. For the valid assessment of a particular child these two notions need to be kept in balance. The choice of particular assessment techniques will depend on a knowledge of the way in which these two ideas are related in any one assessment procedure.

LANGUAGE DEVELOPMENT

It is recognized that language development, along with other aspects of development, has both individual variability as well as general population trends. It is not the intention of this chapter to provide an overview of modern studies in language development. Rather, the clinician's attention is drawn to three particular aspects of the study of language development that are important to receptive abilities: the prelinguistic stage, the age-related or skills-related models of development and the concept of critical period in our understanding of language development.

The importance of the prelinguistic stage for the later development of language has been increasingly recognized in research studies (see Martlew, 1987 for a review). Subsequently, some new assessment procedures have also focused on this area (Gerard, 1986; Dewart and Summers, 1988). Where the child has a severe communication problem it will be particularly important to establish the presence of even the most basic prelinguistic skills. The importance of development of this stage should not be overlooked in retrospect, as in the taking of a case history in an older child. Evidence of very early impairment in communication skills will be significant for predicting prognosis. On-going evidence of impairment in basic skills like turn-taking or the use of gesture will affect the choice of management strategies.

It is usual to refer to a model of so-called 'normal' development when assessing a child's progress. By this means, children's performance is related to the expected average progress of their peers. Two different, but related, approaches are used: the age-related or skills-related models. In an age-related approach the child's development is compared to the expected age level at which a certain skill is generally achieved. The approach is straightforward and is the basis of most developmental screening (Sheridan, 1973). It can be used in check-lists which indicate whether or not a child has been observed to demonstrate a particular skill (Bzoch and League, 1970).

In the skills-related approach, the age at which the child achieves the skill is not as important as the sequence in which the skills are achieved, and the way in which skills in one area relate to other areas of development. Thus, certain preliminary symbolic skills are required before the child can be expected to move on to the first level of verbal comprehension. In the 'normal' model the development of the content, form and use of language (Bloom and Lahey, 1978) are seen to be related to each other. When one aspect of development falls behind others, then a mismatch in development results. This mismatch is generally referred to as a delay in development but this simple idea can be misleading. All aspects of development may be delayed such that the child appears to be functioning as a younger child. This may be the long-term effect of prematurity or a manifestation of general learning difficulties. Where only one aspect of development appears to be delayed in relation to others, this may be described as specific delay, as in specific developmental language delay. This name suggests that all other aspects of development are normal and that language development is just slower. Further, it suggests a belief that the child can catch up this delay. In a longitudinal study to look at the relationships between the development of motor and language skills, and to test the hypothesis of maturational lag, Bishop and Edmundson (1987) found that for the majority of children in their sample the evolution of their development could be accounted for in terms of maturational lag. However, for a small group of children the presence of persisting deficits were difficult to account for using this model. It is the small group of children who present with mismatched development in respect of language to other skills, who are usually referred to as disordered or deviant.

For those children with a persistent mismatch between language and other skills the use of the term deviant or disordered development removes an emphasis on the idea that they will catch up eventually. It has been postulated that there are critical periods in language development; times by which certain stages need to have been reached if full potential is to be realized. Mogford and Bishop (1989) summarized the evidence of studies of language development in relation to the notion of critical period. They concluded that current data are inadequate to answer all the questions about the possibility of prolonged learning in children who have persistent language deficits.

MODELS OF LANGUAGE PROCESSING

It is clear that a range of factors influences the language development of a particular child. This is related to the input of language, the way in which it is processed in the brain and its output. In order to develop language it seems likely that children have to hear and experience its complexities, have an adequate language-processing mechanism and the necessary equipment to be able to produce their own language usually, but not exclusively, in the form of speech. The major organ of language input is the ear. What we hear is conveyed to the brain by the auditory mechanisms of the middle and inner ear and along the auditory nerve (VIII cranial). The efficiency of this mechanism may be impaired by congenital damage (Rubella syndrome, hereditary congenital hearing loss, etc.). However, the commonest form of interference to the competence of the auditory mechanism in childhood is otitis media; infection of the middle ear. This often results in fluctuating conductive-hearing loss, but its implications for language development are not agreed. Klein and Rapin (1989) reviewed over fifty studies of language performance in children with otitis media and concluded that 'the cause–effect relationship between early recurrent otitis media and later cognitive and language development remains uncertain' (p. 108). They concluded that there may be a transient effect on language skills but that this was unlikely to be of long-term significance in children who were otherwise normal. However, they further stated that in sub-optimal conditions for development, like environmental deprivation or cognitive deficiencies, the additional effects of otitis media may be greater.

What is received by the ear and transmitted through the auditory nerve is processed by the receptive-language components of the brain. However, it is not possible to trace the direct path that each 'piece' of receptive language takes within the brain. It is thought that an area of the temporal lobe of the dominant cerebral hemisphere, usually the left, plays a major part in the reception of language information. Called Wernicke's area, this function has been attributed here predominantly on the basis of the analysis of deviant language behaviour in adults who sustain damage to it. One of the main features of Wernicke's aphasia in adults is a loss of verbal comprehension. Despite it being recognized that similar damage sustained in childhood does not have the same consequences (Bishop, 1989), and that even in adults the pattern may be more variable than originally supposed (Marshall, 1986), there has been little progress in the development of a more child-centred model for our understanding of the cerebral organization of language-processing. Evidence from a longitudinal study of acquired aphasia in childhood (Lees, 1989) confirmed that severe receptive problems occurred in the majority of the children, not all of whom had demonstrable damage to Wernicke's area.

A better model for receptive language in children will need to consider clinical data carefully, as Bishop and Mogford (1989) have demonstrated. The way in which factors like neurological development, genetic components, environment and auditory competence interact in the development

19

of receptive language in childhood has only recently started to be addressed. The importance of this approach for the clinician is that rather than take the exclusive view in the diagnosis of language impairment, in which the problem is seen to be the effect of one unknown cause, a more inclusive view which promotes a holistic understanding of the child and his or her language needs should inform practice.

Box 1.1

Factors affecting language input

Environmental factors:
    environmental deprivation
    hearing impairment (otitis media)
    twin or other family factors
    bilingual background
    family are not users of verbal language

Genetic factors:
    inherited hearing loss
    congenital learning disorder, general or specific

Neurological factors:
    disorder of cerebral development
    acquired lesion/s

If we take the view that language is a complex process of many stages which begins with the received signal and ends when the appropriate response has been correctly received by another, we can see that there are many points where the system may break down or become vulnerable to interference. An impairment in an early stage of the process may affect the development of a later stage while a problem at a later stage can affect an earlier part of the process. Bishop (1987) calls these interferences 'bottom up' and 'top down' influences respectively. She considers their importance for the assessment of the child's receptive language. It is clear that a problem of the auditory perception of speech sounds may lead to the confusion of two sentences like:

    he rode the bicycle
        and
    she rode the bicycle

where the two are distinguishable only to someone who correctly differentiates the initial minimal pair. A failure to comprehend these two sentences correctly could not immediately be attributed to a grammatical deficit. Equally, a high-level problem in auditory perception, of the kind where background noise interferes with the efficiency of auditory-verbal processing, could be interpreted as a failure in grammatical comprehension unless this factor is also considered in the assessment process. We are all too familiar with examples of assessment data which fail to consider such environmental effects as classroom noise or the advantages, which may appear rather artificial, of the soundproofed clinical environment.

Bishop (1987) concludes that we may not be in a position to exclude such influences in clinical assessment situations. Therefore we must be prepared to measure them where possible and, at the very least, document them. She takes the point further when she advocates the analysis of results not just to look for correct or incorrect responses, but also for comprehension strategies which the child may employ. The analysis of responses during assessments has been considered by others. Porch (1972) developed a sixteen-point multidimensional scoring system which described responses in considerable detail. Some are daunted by such a system. Lees and Urwin (1991) propose a simple analysis that can be used in a clinical setting which has five different response categories: correct, and four other classes including delay, repetition, self-repetition and self-correction. Some assessment procedures do include multidimensional scoring or the analysis of errors, but most do not, leaving this to the clinician's experience.

Lees (1989) concluded that both were an important part of under-standing the long-term changes in receptive-language skills. It would appear to be useful to develop a more formalized approach to the recording of clinical observations in this respect, such that both long-term and cross-child comparisons can be made more readily. These data will also be vital to the planning of appropriate treatment strategies as they will ensure that the strategies that the child already uses form a part of the management plan.

FORMAL AND INFORMAL ASSESSMENTS OF RECEPTIVE LANGUAGE

Clinicians take two basic approaches to assessment: formal and informal. Formal measures usually have a particular format, are standardized in terms of procedure and make normal data available for peer comparison. Informal measures are much more descriptive, often based on naturalistic observations and do not require the use of standardized procedures or normal data. The range of measures available is wide and once the clinician has clarified the questions being asked, further informal measures can often be developed in the clinical setting. The measures available can be thought of as ranging along a spectrum with the extremes occupied by the most formal and the most informal types of measures. Most of the middle ground will be occupied by those measures which contain some elements of both such that there might, for example, be some choice about the setting, the equipment or the procedure.

Busy clinicians need to make informed choices. Therefore, it is important to remember what the advantages and disadvantages of the formal or informal approaches to assessment may be in a particular setting.

Box 1.2

Advantages and disadvantages of formal and informal assessment

Formal	Informal
Advantages:	
carefully structured;	open-ended;
equipment specified;	free choice of material;
conditions specified;	carried out anywhere;
norm-referenced behaviour.	observations can be freely interpreted.
Disadvantages:	
cannot always respond to specific child's needs;	too little structure, may result in chaos;
equipment may be inappropriate;	child may be distracted by choice;
child may not respond in formal situation;	may be difficult to assess the effects of the specific environment;
norms may be too narrow.	may be difficult to relate observations to peer group.

The clinician needs to consider which procedures may most appropriately provide a profile of the child's receptive skills. This does not mean that any number of check-lists or tests should be administered until the child becomes bored or the clinician's repertoire is exhausted. Rather, the choice will depend on the age of the child, the amount of information already available and the questions being asked of the present assessment. Age will influence the choice from a very practical point of view: most of the procedures are dependent on age to some degree. Even the structure of an informal assessment will be age-dependent. We expect certain things from children of certain ages, as discussed earlier. An older child will be more likely to be able to co-operate with a range of formal measures. Where the clinician is the first to see the child the assessment may proceed differently from a second opinion or a reassessment over a number of months or years. Previous assessment information and the response to therapy or education may suggest that some tests are likely to be more or less useful.

The sharing of information from one assessment to another is an important part of building up a full picture of the child's needs.

The child's receptive-language skills should not be considered in isolation. They should form part of the whole language profile. Equally they will need to be viewed alongside the child's development in other areas, particularly other non-verbal skills. The clinician should work as part of a team, sharing information with others and viewing his or her assessment results alongside the information gained by others. This may include information about hearing and other aspects of cognitive ability as well as motor skills and physical health. When all this information is put together, an informed opinion about the child's development can be made. If there is a mismatch between language and other skills, then this can be clearly seen. However, that is not all that will be shown by such a thorough assessment. The child's strengths will also have been documented alongside his or her needs and these will have important implications for the planning of management.

ASSESSING RECEPTIVE LANGUAGE IN PRESCHOOL CHILDREN

From the general we move to the specific and begin by considering appropriate assessment for the preschool age group. The preschool child's main environment is centred on the family and home life, however that exists in each situation. It is not the clinician's role to enter this environment and prescribe the ways in which it should be ordered. Rather, the clinician should see himself or herself as a partner with the family concerned with furthering the child's development. Thus, the assessment does not begin with questions about the way this family is failing to meet the child's needs. It focuses, rather, on the progress the child has made so far with basic language skills, how these were achieved and over what time-span, as well as the strategies used by child and family to communicate now. These should form the basis of the case history, which is the first stage of the information-sharing exercise. They may be supplemented by the use of check-lists (Bzoch and League, 1970; Gerard, 1986) and informal observations in the home or other environments. Underlying this period of assessment is the question 'What is the child understanding now?' as the clinician works alongside the child and tries to answer this from the latter's perspective. When the twenty-month-old toddler fails to turn to her parents' call in a room in which the television is on and three other people are speaking, the clinician is alerted to trying the same thing later in a quieter situation, as well as asking parents what they have noticed about such a skill.

The clinician will also want to look at a wider range of skills than just the child's comprehension of the spoken word, especially where this is at the very basic stages. An assessment of attention will be important, giving an idea of the child's ability to attend to activities and to communicate with others. Reynell's attention levels provide a useful framework for observing attention skills (Reynell, 1980). It will be important to see how other symbolic skills are progressing and this can be usefully carried out in the context of play. The way in which the child uses familiar and unfamiliar objects needs to be observed and the style of play with a range of toys should be recorded (Sheridan, 1977). Where more formal assessment of these skills is appropriate the use of the Symbolic Play Test (Lowe and Costello, 1976) can be considered. For the child who is still at a very basic level of communication, particularly if entirely non-verbal, some assessment of prelinguistic skills is vital. This should include eye contact, turn-taking and the understanding of gesture, particularly. Whilst this can be done informally, the Pragmatic Profile of Early Communication Skills (Dewart and Summers, 1988) may also be an appropriate tool.

It is unlikely to be possible to carry out the entire assessment procedure at the child's home. Where the child attends a preschool group the value of a period of observation there should be considered. There the clinician can observe how the child's receptive skills aid social functioning and involvement in group activities. These will be important in considering the skills required for a successful transition to the school environment such that learning will continue. Equally, it may be that circumstances dictate that much of the assessment is carried out in the clinical situation. The clinician must be alert to the constraints of such a situation when dealing with the preschool child. Not every small child settles easily into the clinical environment and responds to structured activities set out in a limited time-frame. Any failure to do so does little for the confidence of child or parent/s and may not just be the result of receptive-language problems.

Box 1.3

Assessing receptive language in preschool children

1 Review child's history, family history, etc.
2 Check hearing acuity, the development of auditory perception and other aspects of development as necessary
3 Establish level and extent of attention control
4 Observe level and extent of play development
5 Observe level and extent of symbolic and conceptual development
6 Establish language profile using formal and informal means as appropriate, but remember the advantages of a recording method that makes long-term comparison possible
7 Use continuous observation and reassessment as appropriate to monitor response to treatment and progress

---

However, the clinical situation does present good opportunities for more formal assessment and this may be helpful, particularly when considering the development of verbal comprehension and concepts. Where a formal assessment is used, like the Reynell Developmental Language Scales (Reynell, 1985), it is important to record the results accurately and clearly for later comparison. A record sheet for assessment data on each child can be a useful time-saving device. This means that any future assessment can be easily compared with earlier ones, particularly when these were done by another clinician. Most assessments allow for the child's score to be interpreted in a number of ways. Choosing the most appropriate way to record the results is important for the view it gives of the child. Many give a figure which allows the raw score to be converted to an age-equivalent score, suggesting what age level this score reflects from the standardized sample of the test population. If this method is used the clinician must be sure that the child can reasonably be compared with the test population. Where the test was not standardized in this country, or used a small and unrepresentative sample, this is questionable. It may also present problems for children from bilingual or multilingual backgrounds or those with obvious additional learning difficulties. The other effect of using the age-equivalent score is that where a mismatch between the child and the test population occurs it suggests that the child's development is delayed in respect of the norm. In the early stages of language development it may not seem unreasonable to make this a preliminary suggestion. Indeed, research discussed earlier (Bishop and Edmundson, 1987) supports this view for the majority of children. However, it should not be considered as the only explanation, particularly if the mismatch persists as the child gets older. Other ways of interpreting the test score include a standard score or centile level. The advantages of these two methods is that they allow for a peer-group comparison. The child's place within the range of ability for that group can demonstrate how likely it is that he or she could cope with similar types and levels of activities.

A wide range of informal assessment tasks are outlined by Lees and Urwin (1991). They conclude their discussion of assessment procedures by emphasizing that the clinician must continually ask why the child has failed to carry out the required task. It is not always adequate to attribute this to a failure of verbal comprehension in a general way. They propose six reasons why a child's receptive abilities may prove inadequate for the task:

1 the child may not be attending
2 the child may not be attending for long enough
3 the child may be distracted by the choice of items offered
4 the child may be distracted by the language used
5 the child may not comprehend the content of the language
6 the child may not have understood the form of the request

Of course, several of these factors may be operating in combination. In order to rule out any of them the clinician will need to consider assessing the child in a less distracting environment, choosing a task within the child's attentional capacity or modifying the level of language content and form which he or she uses.

Box 1.4

Receptive language problems in Rapin and Allen's language-disorder subtypes

Verbal auditory agnosia: also called word deafness, no auditory-verbal comprehension

Semantic pragmatic deficit: key word and literal-verbal comprehension with echolalia

Lexical-syntactic deficit: limited comprehension of syntax and lexical classes

Phonological-syntactic deficit: higher-level problems with comprehension of morphological markers and phonological distinctions

Phonological programming deficit: higher-level problems with phonemic distinctions

Verbal dyspraxia: in its pure form this syndrome is not thought to have a receptive component

---

It is clear that not all preschool children who present with language impairment have the same pattern of receptive skills. Rapin and Allen (1987) proposed that the patterns of disordered language development in this population fell into six subtypes. Whilst their description of one of these, verbal dyspraxia, suggests an almost exclusively expressive problem, all of the others include some degree of receptive-language difficulty whether at the phonemic, grammatical, lexical or pragmatic level. In one group, those with verbal auditory agnosia, there is no comprehension in the auditory-verbal channel. Building up a profile of a child's receptive-language skills requires that the assessment procedure should sample as many of these abilities as possible. The Rapin and Allen model can then be used to suggest the likely course of the disorder which is helpful when dealing with the questions of management and prognosis.

ASSESSING RECEPTIVE LANGUAGE IN SCHOOL-AGE CHILDREN

By the time the child enters school at five years the preliminary stages considered to be so important to the potential for language development will be well under way in the majority. However, it is not unusual for problems to persist or even to present during the early school years. The demands that are placed on the child's receptive-language skills change at school entry. The environment is widened such that family and home are no longer the only considerations. For the child with difficulty in receptive-language development the transition to school can be a considerable hurdle. Receptive-language problems may also be accompanied by problems of social maturity or even impairment of social interaction which can further impede progress at school. It will continue to be important to monitor the hearing of children with receptive-language difficulties. These may also create problems in other areas of learning, particularly in reading and concept development. Once again a thorough assessment is required that determines strengths and needs and in which information is shared between parents and professionals.

Box 1.5

Assessing receptive language in school-age children

1 Review previous language history
2 Check aural skills, including hearing acuity, and attention control
3 Establish a language profile, including comprehension of basic concepts, using formal and informal measures
4 Share information when planning for child's needs
5 Include formal and informal measures, as well as parent and teacher reports, in the treatment programme to monitor progress

---

As the classroom becomes a major environment for the child at this stage, we need to consider ways in which receptive language may be assessed there. One of the things that the clinician needs to know is how much information a child has extracted from an instruction. The concept of information-carrying words which is found in the Derbyshire Language Scheme (Knowles and Masidlover, 1982) can be a useful tool in this respect. The system considers the number of such words in an utterance in a step-wise progression and is readily usable in the classroom situation. Other aspects of receptive language which are important in the classroom, particularly for reading and writing, are considered in the Aston Index (Newton and Thompson, 1976).

Assessment in the clinical situation may also be required. With increasing maturity, the child should find it easier to co-operate with formal testing, especially for second-opinion assessment. Lees and Urwin

(1991) discuss a number of assessment procedures which can be used to build up a language profile in children aged 4–12 years. On the receptive side they recommend the Test for Reception of Grammar (Bishop, 1983) for auditory-verbal comprehension. This well-structured test also has the advantage of offering an analysis of errors as discussed earlier. Other aspects of receptive language which need consideration include vocabulary and the accessibility of lexical skills. The Test of Word Finding (German, 1986) includes a number of useful receptive subtests in this respect. Some receptive skills may require informal assessment; auditory discrimination, sentence repetition, the concept of rhythm, ambiguity in language. These auditory-processing skills are among those that contribute to the wide range of skills that are required by the school-age child. Once again, such a profile should be recorded over time to aid discussion of management and prognosis as shown in the example which follows.

Box 1.6

A language profile of a child with a receptive-language disorder

This is the history of a boy who was first referred for speech and language therapy at age three by his health visitor as being slow to talk. There was no family history of speech and language problems. He had had two febrile convulsions between twelve and twenty months of age. Initial assessments suggested a moderate language delay but by the age of five years it was clear that he had made insufficient progress to enter a mainstream school. There were also some problems with his behaviour and his parents were advised by the child-guidance service. His major area of difficulty seemed to be with understanding. He often behaved as if he did not hear properly but all hearing tests were normal. Attention was poorly controlled for his age and he was easily distracted. When he did not understand what was said to him he would frequently repeat or perseverate previous sentences. He attended a language unit attached to a mainstream school for eighteen months where a language programme centred around the Derbyshire Language Scheme was used. He made good progress there and was placed back into a mainstream primary school.

Between the ages of five and seven years he was assessed at regular intervals, to monitor progress, using the following tests:

– for auditory-verbal comprehension: Test for Reception of Grammar (1)

– for naming: Word Finding Vocabulary Test (2) and Auditory Association subtest of the ITPA (3)

– for short-term auditory-verbal memory: Sentence Repetition subtest of the Spreen-Benton tests (4)

The profile of his language abilities demonstrated on these tests is shown in the following figure:

Box 1.6 cont.

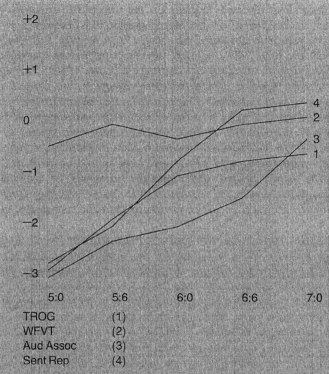

TROG (1)
WFVT (2)
Aud Assoc (3)
Sent Rep (4)

At the age of 6 years 3 months another test for auditory-verbal memory and recall was introduced: the Dog Story Test. He was told the following story, without pictures or other clues.

There was a dog who had a piece of meat and he was carrying it home in his mouth. On the way home he had to cross a bridge across a stream. As he crossed he looked down and saw his reflection in the water. He thought it was another dog with another piece of meat and he wanted to have that piece as well, so he tried to bite the reflection but as he opened his mouth his piece of meat fell out, dropped into the water and was never seen again.

He produced the following response:

He went in the puddle. He seed a face in the puddle. He drop the chop in the water...drop it...a chop...again. He seed a chop again and he opened his mouth and...and...chop went in his mouth...and...the the water...and he didn't seed it again.

And one year later this had improved to:

Once upon a time a dog got a piece of meat...at a traffic light...he had to cross over. He seen a shadow in a water and er...a piece of meat in a water and he went and snap in a water and the meat fall...mouth...he didn't see it ever again.

29

ASSESSING RECEPTIVE LANGUAGE IN TEENAGERS

There have been few research studies of the receptive language of teenagers either in the normal or disordered populations. However, it is clear that severe receptive problems can persist into teenage and young adult life (Ripley and Lea, 1984) and that others can suffer from persistent high-level deficits despite otherwise good progress (Lees, 1989). This age group rarely receives specific clinical attention except in the context of special education so that generalist clinicians will often be unfamiliar with their needs. There are two main considerations for the assessment of this group in particular: the demands of the secondary school environment, and the future needs of the child as an independent adult. Both of these factors will mean that, while appropriate formal measures should be used, these will need to be supplemented with informal measures of everyday receptive-language abilities in the classroom, the family and the outside world if they are to produce a realistic profile of the child's strengths and weaknesses.

Where a teenager appears to have recovered substantially from a long-term language problem it is not unusual to find residual high-level problems with the speed and volume of auditory-verbal processing. This may mean that the child requires or requests more repetitions than others in the group, or just requires longer to complete a task for which complex verbal instructions were given. This may show up on formal assessment, particularly if an analysis of errors is made on a test like TROG, for example. Some teenagers complain of other high-level residual problems, like a deterioration in efficiency of auditory-verbal processing when background noise is high, particularly where that noise is verbal as it often is in a mixed-ability mainstream secondary classroom. Others will require the opportunity to 'think out loud' for certain activities as they have difficulty carrying out the processing aspects of the receptive task internally. It is clear that many of these problems will not show up on formal tests

---

Box 1.7

Assessing receptive language in teenagers

1 Review previous language history
2 Check aural skills: acuity, perception, discrimination as appropriate
3 Establish profile of receptive abilities at all language levels: syntax, morphology, semantics, speed and volume of auditory-verbal processing
4 Share information when planning for educational and life needs
5 Build informal measures into treatment/management plans, including self-evaluation, to monitor progress

---

unless a careful method of error analysis is used. Careful discussion with the individual, the class teachers and the family will also be required to obtain a clear view of the problem.

PARTICULAR RECEPTIVE LANGUAGE PROBLEMS

The ideas outlined above should address the most commonly encountered clinical situations. However, the following are some groups of children for whom the assessment of receptive language requires particular consideration.

Cerebral palsy

Where the child has a severe spastic quadriplegia and no verbal expression, assessment of receptive language and other cognitive functions may take some time to establish. The modality of response will be limited by the motor deficit such that neither play nor pointing as generally used will be possible. Receptive-language assessment may become a series of questions to which the child responds by eye-pointing. Some tests, including the Reynell Development Language Scales, include a modification that can be used this way. However, this can have limited appeal to the child and less experienced clinicians may find eye-pointing difficult to judge. Once again it is important to consider what the child needs to understand in his or her environment. Time spent watching the child and family interact is very valuable in establishing commonly used strategies as well as informal levels of comprehension. Some formal assessments can be adapted to the eye-pointing technique, including the Test for Reception of Grammar (Bishop, 1983). Recent developments in micro-technology are changing the assessment of children with cerebral palsy. Such technology is available at a number of national centres as well as some local ones.

Landau-Kleffner syndrome

This is possibly the rarest and most puzzling language disorder of childhood. First described by Landau and Kleffner in 1957 it is also called acquired receptive aphasia and acquired aphasia with convulsive disorder. Both of these two names point to what is considered the major language problem and the accompanying seizure disorder. In its severest form a prolonged deterioration in receptive language, which may or may not be accompanied by a seizure disorder, persists for many years. Some of the children in the follow-up study by Ripley and Lea (1984) continued to have this into adulthood. In children who have acquired written language skills before losing auditory-verbal comprehension, assessment of inner language through reading and writing will be an important consideration.

31

Fluctuating receptive language problems

This is a puzzling group of disorders that seems to be related to the Landau-Kleffner syndrome as part of the spectrum of acquired convulsive aphasias. These children may be described as lazy or inattentive and the possible presence of organic pathology is often overlooked. Where a child is suspected of having fluctuating receptive language, neurological examination will be an important part of the overall assessment. If epilepsy is diagnosed it may be necessary to monitor the child's receptive language in association with the prescription of anticonvulsant medication. Such monitoring will probably have to be done at fairly frequent intervals, at least during the initial stages of treatment, and therefore it is important to remember reassessment restrictions when choosing language tests for this task. Often informal tasks relating to speed and volume of auditory processing like sentence repetition or association-naming are more useful than lengthy formal tests. The way in which epilepsy interferes with receptive language is not fully understood, but careful assessment of receptive language in children with complex epilepsy and special educational needs is recommended so as not to overlook these.

Box 1.8

Assessing receptive language in acquired childhood aphasia

1 Remember this is not a developmental disorder; however, where possible, establish a profile of child's previous language history

2 Hearing Test: aural competence is just as important in rehabilitation as in initial learning

3 Work in a team where possible: these children have complex needs

In the acute period:
The situation may change rapidly. Therefore screening tests or informal measures are probably more useful. However, as the child begins to stabilize, a formal measure of verbal comprehension can provide a useful reference point for later discussion of prognosis.

In the period of steady recovery:
Make regular and sensitive reassessments to plot progress. This will be important for educational placement. Use formal measures with good peer-group comparison data.

In the period of plateau:
Use a wide range of measures to establish residual deficits and strengths. Build informal measures into treatment programmes to evaluate effectiveness and direction of therapy.

In a fluctuating condition:
Use both formal and informal measures to determine extent of fluctuations and monitor response to medication.

Acquired traumatic aphasias

Children who sustain traumatic cerebral injury, whether diffuse as in head injury or localized as in cerebrovascular accidents, are probably uncommonly encountered in general paediatric practice. Longitudinal studies suggest that they can have both acute and residual receptive problems (Lees, 1989). In the long term these most often affect speed and volume of auditory-verbal processing which can make classroom learning difficult if they are not fully assessed and understood.

CONCLUSIONS

The multifactorial model of childhood language impairment which has been discussed here emphasizes that the assessment of receptive language is fundamental to our understanding of a child's needs. A holistic understanding of these needs recognizes that receptive-language skills are related to other aspects of language and cognitive development and that none of these should be viewed in isolation. The importance of long-term monitoring of receptive language for children with special educational needs has also been addressed. Children's receptive language should always be assessed in relation to their environment and the demands that this places on comprehension. In preparing the language-impaired child for independent living the emphasis needs to be on useful language skills and the assessment process must be built on this condition.

REFERENCES

Bishop, D. V. M. (1983). 'The test for reception of grammar'. Available from the author at MRC APU, 15 Chaucer Road, Cambridge CB2 2EF.

Bishop, D. V. M. (1987). 'The concept of comprehension in language disorders'. *First International Symposium: Specific Speech and Language Disorders in Children.* London: AFASIC.

Bishop, D. (1989). 'Language development after focal brain damage'. In D. Bishop and K. Mogford (eds), *Language Development in Exceptional Circumstances.* Edinburgh: Churchill Livingstone.

Bishop, D. V. M. and Edmundson, A. (1987). 'Specific language impairment as a maturational lag: evidence from longitudinal data on language and motor development'. *Developmental Medicine and Child Neurology, 29,* 452–9.

Bishop, D. and Mogford, K. (1989). *Language Development in Exceptional Circumstances.* Edinburgh: Churchill Livingstone.

Bloom, L. and Lahey, M. (1978). *Language Development and Language Disorders.* New York: Wiley.

Bzoch, K. R. and League, R. (1970). *Receptive and Expressive Emergent Language Scale.* Baltimore: University Park Press.

Cooper, J., Moodley, M. and Reynell, J. (1979). *Helping Language Development.* London: Edward Arnold.

Dewart, H. and Summers, S. (1988). *The Pragmatic Profile of Early Communication Skills.* Windsor: NFER-NELSON.

Gerard, K. (1986). 'The Checklist of Communicative Competence'. Available from the author at 3 Perry Mansions, 113 Catford Hill, London SE6.

German, D. J. (1986). *National College of Education Test of Word Finding (TWF)*. Allen, TX: DLM Teaching Resources.

Klein, S. K. and Rapin, I. (1989). 'Intermittent conductive hearing loss and language development'. In D. Bishop and K. Mogford (eds), *Language Development in Exceptional Circumstances*. Edinburgh: Churchill Livingstone.

Knowles, W. and Masidlover, M. (1982). 'The Derbyshire Language Scheme'. Education Office, Grosvenor Road, Ripley, Derbyshire.

Landau, W. and Kleffner, F. (1957). 'Syndrome of acquired aphasia with convulsive disorder in children'. *Neurology*, 7, 523–30.

Lees, J. (1989). 'A linguistic investigation of acquired childhood aphasia'. MPhil. thesis (unpublished), London: City University.

Lees, J. and Urwin, S. (1991). *Children with Language Disorders*. London: Whurr.

Lowe, M. and Costello, A. (1976). *The Symbolic Play Test*. Windsor: NFER-NELSON.

Marshall, J. (1986). 'The description and interpretation of aphasic language disorder'. *Neuropsychologia*, 24, 5–24.

Martlew, M. (1987). 'Prelinguistic communication'. In W. Yule and M. Rutter (eds), *Language Development and Disorders*. Oxford: McKeith Press/Blackwell.

Mogford, K. and Bishop, D. (1989). 'Five questions about language acquisition considered in the light of exceptional circumstances'. In D. Bishop and K. Mogford (eds), *Language Development in Exceptional Circumstances*. Edinburgh: Churchill Livingstone.

Newton, A. and Thompson, M. (1976). 'The Aston index'. Learning Development Aids, Wisbech.

Porch, B. (1972). *The Porch Index of Communicative Ability in Children*. Palo Alto, CA: Consulting Psychologists Press.

Rapin, I. and Allen, D. A. (1987). 'Developmental dysphasia and autism in preschool children: characteristics and subtypes'. *First International Symposium: Specific Speech and Language Disorders in Children*. London: AFASIC.

Reynell, J. (1980). *Language Development and Assessment*. Lancaster: MTP Press.

Reynell, J. (1985). *The Reynell Developmental Language Scales* (revised), Windsor: NFER-NELSON.

Ripley, K. and Lea, J. (1984). 'Moor House School: a follow-up study of receptive aphasic ex-pupils'. Moor House School, Oxted, Surrey.

Sheridan, M. (1973). *Children's Developmental Progress from Birth to Five Years: the Stycar Sequences*. Windsor: NFER-NELSON.

Sheridan, M. (1977). *Spontaneous Play in Early Childhood, from Birth to Six Years*. Windsor: NFER-NELSON.

2

ASSESSMENT OF EXPRESSIVE LANGUAGE

Elspeth McCartney

THE PROBLEM OF CLINICAL ASSESSMENT

Clinicians who assess children's expressive language usually do so with two questions in mind – is there a problem, and if so what can be done about it? Behind these questions lie the assumptions made by clinicians about the normal language performances of children of different ages in a variety of social contexts. The answer to the first question depends upon deciding if an individual child's language output lies within the parameters described as normal for children of the same age. Assuming the answer is no, the answer to the second question depends upon the speech and language therapist further defining the nature of the problem by drawing up a detailed picture of the child's language skills in a variety of linguistic domains, in order to decide where intervention might take place and exactly where change might be targeted. It is possible to get very detailed answers to both of these questions, using current assessment procedures and therapeutic expertise. However, just as the child must be seen in a social context, so must the speech and language therapist. Clinical practice and the pressures of case loads mean that speech and language therapists have to answer the first question very quickly indeed, in order to ascertain if any further action is needed. The answer to the second question is also pressing, as action to improve the child's functioning is obviously required as soon as possible after a problem has been identified. Clinical assessments of language should provide accurate information upon which intervention can be based as quickly as possible in order to fulfil a useful function.

Unfortunately, language is complicated, and does not lend itself to simple assessments. Not only does it involve intrinsically complex patterns, whose regularities take much effort to unravel, but language ability can only be assessed through performance. And performance, perhaps especially where children are concerned, is subject to a large amount of contextual variance that has received much theoretical attention. Sampling manageable chunks from this varied performance is far from simple, and making assumptions about a child's ability from even a large corpus of language data can be misleading and inaccurate. When clinical time pressures are added the tensions increase, and the need for accuracy and thorough investigation of language parameters comes up against the conflicting need for a fast result – the old 'quick and dirty' versus 'clean and careful' assessment problems are writ large in the therapy clinic. The problems of balancing accurate assessment procedures against the imperatives of clinical practice were raised almost ten years ago by Crystal (1982a) and remain as acute as ever, despite a certain amount of refinement of assessment procedures.

THE PROBLEM OF 'EXPRESSIVE' LANGUAGE ASSESSMENT

There are difficulties inherent in linguistic and psychological measurements that must try to assess an assumed underlying language ability using examples of language performance. Even the most accurate, life-like assessment of a child's expressive language can only give data on which inferences about a child's language ability can be made. Skehan (1989) in discussing second-language assessment comments that 'performance in any one situation may draw upon component competencies unpredictably and in compensatory manner' (p. 7), and although common sense dictates that a wide collection of naturally occurring utterances will give a clearer measure of ability than more limited, experimentally induced utterances, competencies may remain undisclosed. Wells (1985) discusses this problem in relation to nautralistic versus experimental methods of gaining language data, and notes:

> No method has privileged access to a child's linguistic ability and ... each has its strengths and limitations. With their different emphases, they are best seen as complementary: the naturalistic approach leading to hypotheses concerning specific aspects of development which may be tested by a more experimental approach, or supporting evidence being sought for findings obtained under experimental conditions in an investigation of naturally occurring situations in which similar behaviour is expected to occur.
>
> (Wells, 1985, p. 128)

These two main methods of assessing children's language output will be discussed in this chapter, and their relative strengths and weaknesses reviewed. First, however, it is necessary to consider what principles underlie the assessment process, in order to give a framework against which language assessments can be measured.

CHARACTERISTICS OF A 'GOOD' ASSESSMENT

For any assessment to be worth the time it takes to administer, meaningful results must be obtained. In the context of measuring children's expressive language, this means that at the end of the battery of assessments the therapist should have a realistic picture of what the child can do, and be certain that this picture would not alter when the child left the clinic, or conversed with another person, or woke up the next day. An assessment procedure that fulfils these criteria is said to be valid. One of the most important prerequisites of validity is that the assessment should be reliable, which means that the child would achieve the same result on the assessment on two occasions closely related in time, and that the person scoring the test would respond and make the same scoring decisions on each occasion; without this it is difficult to see how the result obtained could be a meaningful representation of the child's language skills. The problems that arise when validity criteria are not met are obvious – different therapists will get different results when considering the same child, and misleading, untypical results can be obtained.

Unfortunately, reliability and other measures of validity have not always been tackled well in clinical assessments of child language, and therapists cannot rely on test-writers or publishers to have disseminated only good instruments. One reason for this may be simply innocence, but the other is the fact that assuring reliability and the complex matter of validity is difficult. Language performance will certainly show variation according to context, and it is incumbent upon an assessment to take this into account, and to measure the amount of variance that might normally occur in the language features under investigation. It is easier to locate and record typical examples of language features for which there are few variables, such as syntactic structures or phonological processes, than it is to measure the range of output of vocabulary or aspects of language use. Good assessments make their underlying assumptions clear, and relate their measures to careful descriptions of normal child-language performance.

VALIDITY

The problem of collecting 'representative' examples of child-language output has always been of concern to clinicians, and indeed to child-language research in general, and is in the end a problem of validity. Data-collection methods that sample utterance in a variety of social contexts, often at home and in nurseries and schools, have been developed involving audio and video recordings, sometimes using concealed microphones and remote switching devices to attempt to ensure as natural and representative a recording sample as possible (Wells, 1985). Therapists seldom have such sophisticated technology available, and have relied on tape recordings of play and conversation in clinics, if possible with relatives, friends and carers as well as therapists, supplemented by recordings in other settings to collect language for analysis. There has been little research on the type of language that may be collected in such contexts, although aspects of language forms, such as the variety of structures recorded, fortunately provide fairly robust measures, and are likely to be collected in a similar way at home and in a clinic (Scott and Taylor, 1978).

Therapeutic measures of such aspects were relatively early to develop. However, as interest shifts to the actual use of particular structures it cannot be expected that similar performance will occur across contexts. Crystal, Fletcher and Garman (1989) observe that their study of children interacting with a previously unknown adult female produced fewer child interrogatives than would be expected in a home setting. Such factors affect clinical assessment practices, and therapeutic procedures that allow for such variance and try to build a more complete picture are now common-place.

Types of validity

As well as considering the validity of the language database obtained, assessment procedures, whether naturalistic or standardized, should consider several types of validity. *Face* validity concerns what the test appears to measure, even to the psychometrically naïve observer. *Content* validity concerns the specified areas of language skill which the assessment is measuring, as agreed by best practice in the field. For example, an assessment of syntax would have to allow the child to use syntactic structures in a way appropriate to children of the same age in order to measure such usage. *Criterion*-related validity concerns the way in which the assessment relates to an independent measure of a similar task. When the independent measure is carried out at the same time as the original assessment, the measure is of *concurrent* validity; an example would be where a syntax assessment based on a fifteen-minute language sample was seen to correlate highly for most children with an assessment based on much longer recordings. When the independent-criterion measure is carried out later, a measure of *predictive* validity is obtained, which indicates how far the assessment predicts performance on the future measure: a language assessment at the age of three might attempt to predict reading development at the age of six, for example. *Construct* validity refers to the degree to which an assessment measures the theoretical construct it is intended to measure, and the content of the assessment should be related to the author's theoretical statements about language abilities and the relationship between measured performance and abilities. Determining construct validity is a research exercise, which can help to refine theoretical approaches to language acquisition and development, but the assessment-user should at least know what assessment-constructors had in mind in developing the instrument.

Although all of these aspects of validity are important in the therapy clinic, some are at present curiously underused in language assessment. Face validity is usually high, in order that therapists and others will purchase and use tests, but this is the least important aspect of validity. Content validity is obviously relevant, and an assessment should, and usually does, specify which aspect of language performance is being measured and the basis for the measures taken. Virtually all current measures of expressive language use research from studies of normally developing children as the basis for sampling and comparing utterances.

Any assessment is used by practitioners to give a rapid reflection of reality, and to represent accurately the aspects of talk that cannot be collected and analysed. It should be possible to rely on the fact that an assessment, whether a test or a principled analysis of a language sample, gives a measure that correlates well with the range of the child's performance. Thus, criterion-related validity is most important. Criterion-related validity measures should be included at the design stage of assessment procedures. Construct validity has been problematic in the field of language assessment. Muma (1983) reviews this issue, and concludes that descriptive approaches to language may provide more valid constructs than psycholinguistic normative test models, and hence descriptive assessment procedures are necessary.

A good assessment should take account of each of these aspects of validity.

RELIABILITY

One of the most important factors in making a valid assessment is that the procedures adopted should be reliable. This refers to the need for measures to be replicable. Two major areas are often controlled – the ability of the assessment to get the same (or very similar) results if it is used twice at close time intervals with the same people; and the reliability of the scorers, so that two different scorers would come to the same conclusion about the same set of responses and of course any one scorer would agree with him- or herself over time. In fact slight variations do always occur, and the typical size of these (the error of measurement) of any assessment should always be known.

Clearly it is easier to establish reliability when responses can be predicted, and when scorers do not have many decisions to make. For this reason some language assessments have attempted in the interests of reliability to force language behaviour into a set of predictable responses which could be scored using a simple 'right–wrong' system. There has been a clinical backlash against this approach, arguing that the interests of reliability must serve validity, and that there can be tension between achieving high reliability and obtaining a valid sample of communicative language. Much of the antipathy encountered among speech and language therapists to standardized tests is based on this difficulty. However, reliability cannot be ignored and any good assessment procedure must take it into account, while achieving an acceptable trade-off with other measures of validity.

ASSESSMENT PROCEDURES

The two questions with which we opened this chapter have, broadly speaking, been answered in the therapy clinic using two types of assessment procedure – standardized tests, and descriptive profiles. Well-constructed standardized tests, used as screening or investigative tools, are rather good at comparing the child with other similar children, and correlating performance on the test with performance in other related areas. This lets the speech and language therapist know, within the limits of statistical probability, how the child compares with other children and helps to answer the question of whether or not there is a problem. Such tests are perhaps less good at answering the question of what is to be done once a problem is identified. For this, detailed linguistic description is needed. Both types of assessment require that the principles outlined above relating to a 'good' assessment be adhered to in the construction stage.

Standardized tests

Standardized tests are here taken to comprise a set of carefully controlled tasks and materials used in a predetermined and consistent manner to gain a result that allows comparison between an individual child and his or her peers. If the test is so constructed, the child's performance and result on the test can be assumed on a sound statistical basis to compare with his or her performance in real-life conversations. The extent to which the test can carry out these functions should be stated clearly in the test manual. A properly constructed test is therefore very useful to the therapist as a quick, valid and reliable measure of expressive language output.

None the less, in parallel with some other disciplines, speech and language therapists have moved away from standardized tests in clinical settings in recent years. There are probably several reasons for this. One has already been touched upon – tests are good at identifying a problem (Lund and Duchan, 1983, p. 284 ff.) but other assessment procedures give better guidelines for intervention. But among the main reasons for the decline in test use must certainly be the factor of psychometric inadequacy. This has not been discussed greatly in the therapeutic literature in Britain, but McCauley and Swisher (1984a) looked at a range of preschool language tests (not all tests of expressive language) commonly used in America, and concluded that none met all of their eight basic criteria of psychometric excellence. Criteria related to validity and reliability, which are amongst the most important criteria but ones which are relatively time-consuming and expensive to ensure while constructing tests, were met least often; and none of the tests investigated showed evidence of predictive validity or of adequate inter-examiner reliability. Most failures to show good psychometric practice were due to a lack of information about a test's construction rather than to demonstrably poor construction, but this cannot serve to increase the users' confidence in the instruments discussed.

Similar points can be made regarding many tests of expressive language commonly used in Britain (see detailed Test Reviews, this volume). The essential purpose of a language test, to control variance and provide an accurate measure of performance, may not be fulfilled in such cases.

Not all tests are so inadequate, and test-users are advised to scrutinize individual test packages carefully to decide on their usefulness. There are recent examples of authors paying close attention to psychometric principles and clinical experience when constructing tests, such as the Test of Word Finding (German, 1986) described by German (1989).

Some aspects of validity, such as predictive validity, can only be measured over a period of time, and reviews and reports often appear in the literature before they are incorporated into test manuals. A review of commonly used British tests is that by Bishop and Edmundson (1987) which showed that 'good' outcome among individual language-impaired children at the age of 5 years 6 months, defined as having no score below the third centile and no more than one score below the tenth centile on a variety of tests, could be predicted from their test per-formance at four years with 90 per cent accuracy. The best predictor of performance, at least for the narrow age group studied, was the infor-mation section of the story-retelling task, the Bus Story (Renfrew, 1969), which measures the child's ability to relate the main events of a story in the correct sequence. Much further empirical work of this kind is needed to provide useful diagnostic and prognostic assessments of a standardized nature.

As well as being criticized along dimensions usually associated with test construction, some language tests have also been criticized for linguistic anomalies. The scoring of tests often demanded clear-cut right or wrong decisions, not all of which could be justified in terms of normally developing child language. Furthermore, any test that requires the child to respond to materials such as pictures in a systematic way cannot be carried out much below the age of three – younger than that, the child cannot be relied upon to pay attention for a sufficiently long period to obtain results. Many language skills are acquired before the age of three, and therapists are interested in assessing children who are much younger, including pre-verbal children, and also in comparing older children with limited language skills with the language of normally developing children in their early years. For therapists interested in very young children, only a few tests are available, and other measures have to be sought.

However, the most serious challenge to the notion of a formalized test of expressive language came in relation to the control of variance. The major difficulty in assessing expressive language lies in gaining a representative sample of utterance, one which is able to predict performance in as many non-sampled situations as possible. Child-language research and socio-linguistics have shown that some aspects of children's expressive language respond to context and vary according to the situation in which children find themselves, the people to whom they speak and the topic they talk about. The test situation, where the child talks to strangers and conforms to a predetermined response pattern which often requires elicited or imitated utterance, was thought by many clinicians to be less than ideal in gaining information about a child's abilities. Forcing the child into making test responses was seen as imposing unnecessary distortion on the very behaviour that was being measured: 'tests by their very nature and purpose present language removed from ordinary intentionality' (Lund and Duchan, 1983, p. 283).

Reliability, which should serve validity, had been bought at too high a price. Therapists wanted to know what children could do in a communica-tive context, and turned to naturalistic, descriptive measures to help them find out.

NATURALISTIC ASSESSMENTS

Naturalistic assessments are concerned with noting a piece of 'real life' behaviour, in an unstructured and naturally occurring context, and coding it against a predetermined analysis framework. To assess expressive language a representative sample of a child's utterance is recorded, in as realistic a manner as possible, and the transcribed data coded for language features. To be 'representative' the sample must of course contain a complete range of examples of the language features that are to be analysed. The validity of descriptive measures is increased where regular sequences (or stages) of development have been documented, as for aspects of language form such as young children's use of syntax (Ingram, 1989), and where it can be predicted that even relatively brief snatches of child conversation will contain examples that are typical of the child's performance in other contexts. Aspects of language form are therefore routinely analysed using naturalistic, descriptive profiles. LARSP, reviewed in the Test Reviews at the end of this volume, is probably the most commonly used naturalistic analysis of syntax in British speech-and-language-therapy clinics (Baker, 1988).

Moves into profiling other areas are taking place as theoretical frameworks develop. There are now profiles of semantics (see, for example, PRISM, Crystal, 1982b) and of aspects of pragmatics and discourse developed as coding taxonomies that gain useful information from detailed study of small amounts of language data. An example of the analysis of semantics, syntax and pragmatics for preschool children would be BLADES, reviewed in the Test Reviews. There are also 'semi-formal' assessments such as that used by the Derbyshire Language Scheme (see review, this volume) which elicit language in partly structured contexts, and compare it with the stages of normal language acquisition, without providing standardized norms *per se*. This assessment leads directly into a teaching programme, and was devised for use with people at an early developmental stage of language skill.

Other aspects of interest that are investigated using naturalistic and profiling methods are preverbal and to some extent non-verbal behaviours and 'social' skills (Rustin and Kuhr, 1989) – see, for example, the review of the Pragmatics Profile of Early Communication Skills in the Test Reviews. These aspects of communication are so context-sensitive that the be-haviours to be assessed cannot readily be elicited outside the situations in which they naturally arise. The opportunities for collecting examples in a clinical context are limited, and so it is common to ask those concerned with the child in real-life settings, such as parents and other care-givers, to record examples that occur naturally. This is intended to enhance validity, by ensuring that the full range of a child's performance is considered, giving a highly realistic picture of overall ability, although it can be difficult to ensure reliability. Naturalistic assessments can be very useful in providing a detailed picture of a child's communication patterns, which can be used to suggest targets for change. In some cases, the stage reached by a child can be compared with normally developing children sufficiently accurately to allow an approximate age rank to be assigned.

Whereas standardized tests have largely been criticized for rigidity, and for enforcing reliability at the expense of validity, criticism of naturalistic measures can, by and large, be made in the opposite direction. Because data are collected, transcribed and analysed in great detail, or observed in real-life contexts and profiled using structured-interview techniques, the possibility of errors creeping in at any (or indeed each) stage is high. A great deal of decision-making is required from the person doing the profiling, especially at the transcription and coding stage.

This is recognized by many authors of naturalistic assessment profiles – see, for example, comments by Fletcher and Garman (1988) concerning LARSP and by Wells about the reliability problems encountered in his study of normal children, upon which BLADES was based (Wells, 1985, p. 45 ff.). None the less, the clinical assessments themselves do not usually give details of trial periods and revisions based upon attempts to increase reliability when used in the field. This is partly due to the pioneering nature of many of the naturalistic profiles which have attempted to get rapidly developing research-based information and practice incorporated into clinical assessments as swiftly as possible, often in new areas of clinical interest and as a response to a lack of appropriate assessment procedures. The authors frequently, and sensibly, wanted to check that procedures based on the language behaviours of normally developing children were actually useful in coding speech therapists' data in order to test their usefulness, which meant getting into the field as soon as possible. Most acknowledge the 'first approximation' (Crystal, 1982b) nature of the profiles devised, and have made their assumptions very clear about what they are measuring and how it is being done, and the compromises and decisions that have been made. Description of the authors' background thinking is often much more explicit than in the case of many standardized tests, and content validity is good. It is partly because naturalistic assessments recognize the complexity and subtlety of child expressive language and attempt to take this on board that assessment problems have arisen. It is probable that attention to psychometric principles would show the quality of the assessments, and that only a little statistical work would demonstrate the usefulness of many procedures. Such work is needed urgently, and indeed is under way in the case of LARSP (Johnson, 1986). Other authors (Adams and Bishop, 1989; Bishop and Adams, 1989) have recognized the need to establish reliability and validity and to take aspects of good assessment construction into account in areas as complex as conversational analysis for children with language disorders, and there is nothing in the notion of a naturalistic assessment which prevents this. Indeed, the relative neglect of traditional parameters of assessment construction and trials by producers and publishers of naturalistic assessments is rather odd, and may be a peculiarity of the assessment of disordered child language. Parallel fields, such as second-language assessment, have shown no similar lack of concern for validity and reliability, although the problems and difficulties of constructing natural and representative procedures are no less: second-language learning assessment has recently been characterized by statistical innovation in such areas as test development and item analysis (Skehan, 1989). It is probable that future work that builds upon the early clinical profiles will seek to demonstrate their psychometric credibility.

CLINICAL ASSESSMENT

Despite the limitations of many clinical assessment procedures outlined above and reviewed in the Test Reviews clinicians are left with the problems discussed at the beginning of this chapter, and with the difficulty of answering important questions about an individual child's performance using a combination of less than perfect measures – many assessments may be sound, but we do not really know! This is clearly an unsatisfactory state of affairs: clinicians deserve better.

Those who disseminate assessment procedures should ensure that basic validations and reliability measures are carried out before publication, and that results are presented in the assessment manuals. If a procedure is published at an earlier stage of development, in a preliminary form as a pilot measure, this should be made clear to potential users, and a clear intention to check on its application should be stated.

Reviews of assessment procedures sometimes appear in the scientific literature, although not all expressive language assessments have received this kind of attention. Where they are available, reference should be made to them in assessment manuals as these are revised. It is probably too much to hope that procedures that prove unreliable or of doubtful validity would be taken off the market, but a knowledgeable group of clinicians evaluating assessment procedures in themselves incorporate a solid market force.

Speech and language therapists who meanwhile must use the instruments available have their principal responsibilities to their clients. It is important, therefore, that therapists know the limits of the measures they are using and the confidence that can be placed in them when reporting on individual children's language skills and in decision-making. This information could be presented much more clearly in test manuals; then therapists can evaluate what is presented. Scores must be presented in meaningful ways: standard scores and age scores have different meanings, and misapprehensions about test interpretation can arise (McCauley and Swisher, 1984b). It makes clinical sense to choose the best possible assessment procedure for the language factor being measured.

Most therapists probably use both standardized and naturalistic measures of expressive language, using tests to determine the existence of a language problem, then making detailed linguistic analyses to describe the problem and to suggest areas for intervention. A clinical example of such an integrated approach is given by Kelly and Rice (1986) who describe how the combination of standardized assessments and descriptive profiles allows speech therapists to capitalize on the strengths and minimize the weaknesses of each approach. The ability to do without any standardized measures at all depends to some extent upon the information that can be elicited from normal profiles. Where there is a good, research-based description of normal child performance in the skill being assessed, a naturalistic assessment may give information about stages (or even comparative ages) reached by an individual child, as well as showing the patterns of language used. If, however, the 'normal' use of a language behaviour is not known, therapists are thrown back upon standardized tests; as when ascertaining word-retrieval rates, as tested by the TWF (Test of Word Finding), and when assessing many aspects of older children's and adolescent language and 'high-level' language skills such as processing relationships and ambiguities (see *Clinical Evaluation of Language Functions (CELF)*, Semel and Wiig (1981), reviewed by Spekman and Roth (1984), Muma (1984), and Lieberman *et al.* (1987)). Structured and standardized tests are commonly used, if only for want of alternatives, in such cases.

Such a mix of assessment practices relates to the earlier quotation from Wells (p. 36), where the need to balance experimental and naturalistic assessments was stressed. However, experimental investigations can also take place without the use of standardized assessments, as instanced by exploratory therapy sessions that test out the child's ability to use a particular structure, word or conversational device. Because naturalistic measures can only record what was said, not what might have been said, it is not possible to infer that a child cannot use a particular language skill simply because it was not heard in the sample recorded. Most therapists planning therapy therefore check any 'gaps' in the initial profile by providing opportunities for the child to produce the missing items. This usually involves setting up a controlled exploratory elicitation interaction where content and context are skewed so that the child has every opportunity to use the particular item. If it still does not appear, it does not mean that the child cannot say it, but the probabilities that it is not in his or her repertoire are greater. Such a check is recommended as good practice in BLADES and implied in LARSP (Crystal, Fletcher and Garman, 1989, pp. 113, 115). Therapists using this strategy are acting upon Wells's advice, and using assessment as hypothesis-testing, with results being checked against further data. Time-consuming though this appears, it is much less so than spending time preparing therapy materials that prove not to be needed when the child shows instant mastery of the skill the therapist sought to teach! Where deficits are real, a more detailed 'micro' profile of an area of particular clinical interest can be drawn.

Therapists will also check their decisions and inferences against parents' and others' ideas of an individual child's typical performance, and be willing to update the picture presented as further examples of talk become available. But most therapists would want to have a sufficiently detailed picture by the end of the second assessment period to begin intervention if necessary, reassessing later to evaluate progress and the effectiveness of therapy. Therapists who are thinking ahead to that time might take extra baseline measures of language skills that are not to be the focus of change, and continue to take these at reassessment intervals. The specific effects of therapy-targeted change can be measured against general growth and language development in non-targeted areas (Hesketh and McCartney, 1987).

Rather than being seen as a one-off procedure, assessment as a way of drawing a current picture of a child's expressive-language status and of exploring areas and methods for change continues throughout the therapeutic process.

ACKNOWLEDGEMENT

With thanks to my colleague, William Ramsay, who commented upon a previous draft of this chapter.

REFERENCES

Adams, C. and Bishop, D. V. M. (1989). 'Conversational characteristics of children with semantic-pragmatic disorder. I: exchange structure, turntaking, repairs and cohesion'. *British Journal of Disorders of Communication*, 24, 211–39.

Baker, L. (1988). 'The use of language analysis – results of a questionnaire'. *CST Bulletin*, May 1988, 2–3.

Bishop, D. V. M. and Adams, C. (1989). 'Conversational characteristics of children with semantic-pragmatic disorders. II: What features lead to a judgement of inappropriacy?' *British Journal of Disorders of Communication*, 24, 241–63.

Bishop, D. V. M. and Edmundson, A. (1987). 'Language-impaired 4-year-olds: distinguishing transient from persistent impairment'. *Journal of Speech and Hearing Disorders*, 52, 156–73.

Crystal, D. (1982a). 'Terms, time and teeth'. *British Journal of Disorders of Communication*, 17, 3–19.

Crystal, D. (1982b). *Profiling Linguistic Disability*. London: Edward Arnold.

Crystal, D., Fletcher, P. and Garman, M. (1989). *Grammatical Analysis of Language Disability* (2nd edn). London: Cole & Whurr.

Fletcher, P. and Garman, M. (1988). 'LARSPing by numbers'. *British Journal of Disorders of Communication*, 23, 309–21.

German, D. (1986). *Test of Word Finding*. Allen, TX: DLM Teaching Resources.

German, D. (1989). 'A diagnostic model and a test to assess word finding skills in children'. *British Journal of Disorders of Communication*, 24, 21–40.

Hesketh, A. and McCartney, E. (1987). 'Evaluating the effectiveness of therapy'. *CST Bulletin*, 418, May 1987, 1–4.

Ingram, D. (1989). *First Language Acquisition*. Cambridge: Cambridge University Press.

Johnson, M. (1986). 'Transcription and computer analysis of child language'. *Proceedings of the Child Language Seminar*. Durham: University of Durham.

Kelly, D. J. and Rice, M. L. (1986). 'A strategy for language assessment of young children: a combination of two approaches'. *Language, Speech and Hearing Services in Schools*, 17, 83–4.

Lieberman, R. J., Heffron, A. M. C., West, S. J., Hutchinson, E. C. and Swem, T. W. (1987). 'A comparison of four adolescent language tests'. *Language, Speech and Hearing Services in Schools*, 18, 250–66.

Lund, N. J. and Duchan, J. F. (1983). *Assessing Children's Language in Naturalistic Contexts*. Englewood Cliffs, NJ: Prentice-Hall.

McCauley, R. J. and Swisher, L. (1984a). 'Psychometric review of language and articulation tests for preschool children'. *Journal of Speech and Hearing Disorders*, 49, 34–42.

McCauley, R. J. and Swisher, L. (1984b). 'Use and misuse of norm-referenced tests in clinical assessment: a hypothetical case'. *Journal of Speech and Hearing Disorders*, 49, 34–42.

Muma, J. R. (1983). 'Speech-language pathology: emerging clinical expertise in language'. In T. M. Gallagher and C. A. Prutting (eds), *Pragmatic Issues in Language*. San Diego, CA: College-Hill Press.

Muma, J. R. (1984). 'Semel and Wiig's CELF: construct validity?' *Journal of*

47

Speech and Hearing Disorders, 49, 101–4.

Renfrew, C. E. (1969). 'The bus story: a test of continuous speech'. Available from the author at North Place, Old Headington, Oxford, England.

Rustin, L. and Kuhr, A. (1989). *Social Skills and the Speech Impaired.* London: Taylor & Francis.

Scott, C. M. and Taylor, A. E. (1978). 'A comparison of home and clinic gathered language samples'. *Journal of Speech and Hearing Disorders*, 43, 482–95.

Semel, E. and Wiig, E. H. (1981). *Clinical Evaluation of Language Function (CELF)*. Columbus, OH: Charles Merrill.

Skehan, P. (1989). 'Language testing – part II'. *Language Teaching*, Jan. 1989, 1–13.

Spekman, N. J. and Roth, F. P. (1984). 'Clinical Evaluation of Language Function (CELF) diagnostic battery: an analysis and critique'. *Journal of Speech and Hearing Disorders*, 49, 97–111.

Wells, G. (1985). *Language Development in the Pre-school Years*. Cambridge: Cambridge University Press.

3

ASSESSMENT OF ARTICULATION AND PHONOLOGY

Pam Grunwell

A traditional and essential component in the clinical practice of speech pathology and therapy is the assessment and evaluation of an individual's speech. As the title of this chapter indicates, there are two parameters to be investigated in the assessment of speech; for speech is spoken language. Assessment procedures must therefore evaluate an individual's ability to produce different types of speech sounds and to use them appropriately to communicate through spoken language. An individual who mispronounces, or who has a 'speech defect', is readily identified by fellow members of the linguistic community. It is the speech pathologist who has the skills to discover the nature of the pronunciation problem and to assess its effect on communication.

Assessment of articulation and phonology involves the investigation of four dimensions of speech production:

- anatomical and physiological dimension
- phonetic dimension
- phonological dimension
- developmental dimension

The *anatomical and physiological dimension* of speech assessment is concerned with the structure and function of the organs of speech production. For the purpose of this chapter, consideration will be focused on the vocal organs as shown in Figure 3.1. This diagrammatic representation shows the vocal tract and the location of the organs used to produce speech sounds. In speech production, sound is created by movements of these vocal organs which modify or impede the expiratory phase of the respiratory cycle. Controlled respiration is essential for normal speech production. None the less, it is customary to describe the vocal organs as being those structures above and including the larynx. This chapter adheres to this custom and there will therefore be no further consideration of respiratory function. Many of the organs for speech production are observable *in situ* and in action without invasive techniques of investigation. It is this type of routine examination that will be examined below.

The *phonetic dimension* of speech assessment is concerned with the description and classification of the sounds produced by the movements of the vocal organs. In carrying out this assessment the speech pathologist employs the techniques of articulatory phonetics. The continuous flow of movements that produces the continuous flow of speech sound is segmented into a sequential series of positions (or postures) in which each particular type of speech sound is produced. Each speech sound is produced at a particular *place of production* by an *active* and *passive articulator*. The active articulator moves to a position close to or touching the passive articulator; this relationship being the *stricture* or *manner of articulation*. The presence or absence of vocal-fold vibration (i.e. phonation) determines whether a sound is voiced or voiceless. The most common pronunciation problems involve the production and use of consonants. This chapter therefore concentrates on consonant production. The active and passive articulators and places of articulation are identified in Figure 3.1.

The *phonological dimension* of speech assessment is concerned with describing and evaluating the use of speech sounds in spoken language. Every language is spoken using a unique range of pronunciation patterns. Phonological analysis involves the description of these patterns. It identifies the sound differences that signal meaning differences; for example, the presence or absence of phonation (voicing) is distinctive – that is, it signals a meaning difference – in certain types of English consonants, thus *mate* /meɪt/ and *made* /meɪd/ are different words; but voicing is not distinctive in all types of consonants, thus *mail* might be pronounced [meɪl] which would sound unusual but the word is still recognizable. Phonological analysis also describes the order and combinations of sounds that occur in pronunciation patterns, thus *stay* /steɪ/ is an English word, but *[tseɪ] is not; *blue* /blu/ and *brew* /bru/ are words but not *[bwu]. From these examples it will be evident that speech assessment must go beyond investigation of an individual's ability to produce speech sounds; it must analyse the individual's use of speech sounds in spoken language by comparison with the pronunciation patterns of the language.

The *developmental dimension* of speech assessment is essential in the evaluation of children's pronunciation abilitis. As these are the focus of this chapter the developmental dimension must be given equal consideration alongside the preceding three dimensions. In fact a comprehensive developmental assessment would evaluate anatomical, physiological, phonetic and phonological factors in learning to pronounce. Most assessments, however, concentrate on the phonetic and phonological factors, drawing upon research into the order of development of different types of

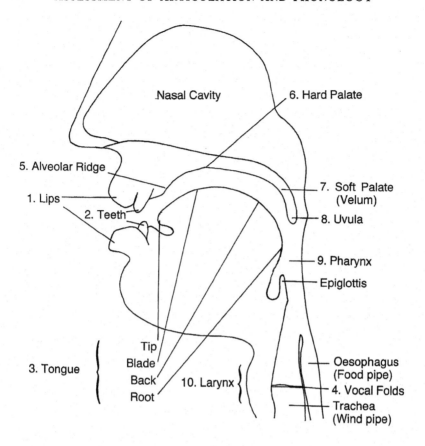

Active articulators		Passive articulators (places of articulation)	
1	Lips: bilabial	1	Lips: labial
2	Lower teeth to upper lip: labiodental	2	Upper teeth: dental
3	Tongue: lingual	5	Alveolar ridge: alveolar
	Tip: apical	6	Hard palate: palatal
	Blade: laminal	7	Soft palate (velum): velar
	Front: anterodorsal	8	Uvula: uvular
	Back: posterodorsal	9	Pharynx: pharyngeal
4	Vocal folds: glottal	10	Larynx: laryngeal

Figure 3.1 Diagrammatic representation of vocal organs

pronunciation patterns and the nature of the process of learning to talk. Physiological maturation is an important factor in this process and therefore should not be overlooked in routine clinical assessment. The purpose of the developmental assessment is to discover whether a child's pronunciation patterns are appropriate for his or her age or whether they are delayed or different from the expected patterns. If there is evidence of delay or difference, then it will be necessary to investigate the possible causes of the child's learning difficulties. Assessment of articulation and phonology in all four dimensions is only of value to the speech pathologist when all the information is brought together and interpreted. The interpretation is an explanatory evaluation that will inform and guide subsequent clinical management, especially treatment-planning.

ANATOMICAL AND PHYSIOLOGICAL ASSESSMENT

Pronunciation problems may be associated with anatomical anomalies and/or physiological restrictions. It is therefore advisable, as a matter of routine, to carry out an examination of the vocal tract. Space does not permit detailed description of the procedures that can be included in such an examination (see Newman, Creaghead and Secord, 1985; St Louis and Ruscello, 1981). An outline of these types of procedures is given below. An examination of the vocal tract involves an examination of oral structures and an assessment of the mobility and movements of the articulators.

The speech pathologist can observe directly the overall proportions of the face, the alignment of the lower jaw, the presence of dentition, the dental occlusion, the size and appearance of the tongue, the length of the frenum, the structure and appearance of both the hard and soft palates. Detailed investigation of palatal structures, the pharynx and the larynx, using endoscopy and laryngoscopy will be carried out by the Ear, Nose and Throat (ENT) consultant in collaboration with the speech pathologist. An oral examination may reveal an anomalous structure such as a short frenum or an undetected submucous cleft palate which may, in part, account for an individual's pronunciation problems. Even when an anomaly is known and has been treated, an oral examination should be undertaken to evaluate the current state of the oral structures; for example, with a repaired cleft palate there may be irregular dental growth that may contribute to pronunciation difficulties.

Assessment of articulatory mobility and movements focuses primarily on the lips, the tongue and the soft palate. Lingual mobility and control of movements will be affected by conditions such as dysarthria and dyspraxia. In dysarthria, all types of movements may be affected both for speech production and for vegetative functions such as sucking and swallowing. In dyspraxia, movements to command will probably evidence struggle while automatic movements for eating and drinking will be accomplished easily. Assessment of rate as well as accuracy of movements is important. Diadochokinetic rate is usually measured by rapid repetition of [pətəkə]. Assessment of palatal mobility may be difficult without the assistance of ENT-investigative techniques such as endoscopy and video-fluoroscopy. A number of protocols have been developed for the assessment of the movements and abilities of the vocal organs; for example, Enderby, 1983; Huskins, 1987; Milloy, 1985; Robertson, 1982. These provide detailed frameworks in which to investigate the functioning of the organs that are used in speech production.

PHONETIC ASSESSMENT

The primary purpose of a phonetic assessment is to investigate the type and range of speech sounds used by an individual in speech production. In order to carry out this assessment, a sample of the individual's speech production needs to be obtained. This type of data sample requires careful consideration. In order to ensure that the sample contains all the possible types of sounds in the pronunciation patterns of the language, some assessment procedures involve the individual in reading a piece of prose or list of words aloud or in naming pictures or retelling a story (e.g. Anthony, Bogle, Ingram and McIsaac, 1971; Goldman and Fristoe, 1972). While ensuring a comprehensive sample these procedures do not provide a natural situation for speech production. Therefore, the sample obtained may not be representative of the habitual pronunciation patterns of the individual. The most natural sample would be obtained in a situation where an individual was engaged in spontaneous conversational speech. Although preferable to controlled elicited samples, this type of sample has potential shortcomings as it may not contain occurrences of all the possible types of sounds. A compromise needs to be reached in which the contents of the sample are at least partially controlled but the context of the sample allows for spontaneous speech. PACS Pictures (Grunwell, 1987a) represent an attempt to achieve that compromise through a set of composite pictures designed to elicit narrative and descriptive utterances rather than single-word naming responses.

Assessment of speech production based on a speech sample provides information about individuals' use of speech sounds. It does not necessarily reveal their full range of ability to produce speech sounds. Assessment of modelled speech-sound production or stimulability should therefore be a routine clinical procedure. Whether or not a child is able to repeat a modelled consonant in isolation or in a nonsense syllable, when he or she is not currently using that consonant in speech, is important information for assessment, diagnosis and treatment-planning. If a child has the articulatory ability to produce a sound then his or her pronunciation problems

53

are probably not attributable to physiological or phonetic restrictions and so phonological investigations should be instigated.

Reliable phonetic assessment is dependent upon the recording of the data sample. An audio recording and, if possible, a video recording should be made of the whole of the speech sample, including any stimulability testing. Ideally, a phonetic transcription should be made 'live' and the audio recording be used to check this transcription. In practice, continuous simultaneous transcription is difficult to achieve since, as is usually the case, the speech pathologist is interacting with the child at the same time. In this situation the practicable compromise is to note any articulatory phenomena or phonetic features that may be difficult to detect from an audio recording such as silent co-occurring articulations or dental articulations, which can be seen but not easily heard.

A phonetic assessment can be made using instrumental techniques of investigation. These are not as yet in general use but they are available in some centres. ENT techniques have already been mentioned. In addition, instrumentation developed for phonetic research has been applied in clinical assessment. Spectrography has made possible acoustic analysis of disordered speech (Code and Ball, 1984). Electropalatography enables clinicians to investigate the placement and movements of the tongue in the mouth and thus to describe precisely the characteristic of misarticulations (Hardcastle, 1989). These techniques can provide useful additional information and insights. They cannot, however, replace the standard phonetic assessment procedures based on an audio-recorded speech sample.

The first stage in routine phonetic analysis and assessment is to transcribe the recording using phonetic transcription. A clinical phonetic transcription should record the pronunciation of the speaker in as much detail as possible. The conventions of the International Phonetic Alphabet (revised in 1989) should be used, supplemented if necessary by additional phonetic symbols and diacritics devised for the representation of disordered speech (*PRDS*, 1983). Seemingly minor details should be recorded as they can prove to have considerable importance in subsequent analysis. For example, a child may not be articulating any word-final consonants but may be consistently nasalizing the vowel in a word ending in a nasal in the adult pronunciation, lengthening the vowel in a word ending in a voiced plosive and adding a palatal vowel off-glide to the vowel in a word ending in a voiceless fricative; thus:

bun [bʌ̃] bud [bʌː] bus [bʌj].

The child is clearly signalling the differences between these words, in forms which can be phonetically related to features in the target pronunciations. The remedial implications of this assessment are that phonetic training to facilitate orthodox signalling of existing contrasts is required.

Once a phonetic transcription has been made, the phonetic analysis and assessment can follow directly, since transcribing a data sample entails identifying in auditory–articulatory terms the segments that occur in the sample. In some assessment procedures (e.g. Weiner, 1979; Shriberg and Kwiatkowski, 1980) analysing a child's phonetic inventory involves recording the presence or absence of target English consonants in the data sample. While this information is necessary, such an analysis does not necessarily provide a complete description of the range of consonants used by a child in his or her habitual pronunciation patterns. A more useful format for a phonetic inventory is to record all the different types of consonants that are present in the sample classified in a matrix according to place and manner of articulation (e.g. Grunwell, 1985). In this descriptive framework not only can the occurrence of target consonants be recorded but also any other types of consonants whose presence may be indicative of the nature of the child's speech disorder. For example, the occurrence of lateral fricatives and lateralization is frequently associated with dental and occlusal anomalies secondary to a cleft palate (Albery and Russell, 1990).

As well as a phonetic inventory, an analysis of the distribution of the inventory in different positions in word and syllable structure provides further valuable information. This would reveal any restrictions in the occurrence of consonants at certain positions and thus indicate goals for treatment.

The phonetic assessment, while being an important procedure in the clinical evaluation of an individual's speech production, is incomplete. It does not provide any information about the use of the different types of sounds in spoken language. This information is essential for evaluation and appropriate intervention for children with pronunciation problems and is provided by a phonological assessment.

PHONOLOGICAL ASSESSMENT

The primary purpose of a phonological assessment is to investigate an individual's linguistic usage of the speech sounds occurring in his or her phonetic inventory. To this end, a comparison needs to be made between the individual's pronunciation patterns and those of his or her linguistic community. The functional consequences of any differences between these two patterns are then assessed in regard to any failures to signal meaning differences. As with the phonetic assessment, careful consideration needs to be given to the data sample upon which the phonological assessment is based. The same prerequisites apply: the sample must be representative of the range and distribution of the sounds in the target pronunciation patterns and representative of the individual's habitual pronunciation patterns. In addition, the sample must be large enough to reveal any variability in the realizations of target pronunciations. Finally, in order to carry out a phonological assessment the utterances that constitute the sample must be glossable; that is, the target words must be identifiable. Thus, a compromise between a controlled and completely spontaneous sample has to be found and the sample size needs to be at least 200 words (see Grunwell, 1985, 1987a). As illustrated in the preceding section a detailed phonetic transcription is as important for phonological assessment as it is for phonetic assessment.

The phonological assessment itself has to fulfil a number of criteria:

1   it should provide a description of the patterns in an individual's pronunciation of the language
2   it should identify the differences between the expected target patterns and those used by a speaker with pronunciation problems
3   it should analyse the functional consequences of these differences by identifying the phonological contrasts that are not signalled in the speech of the individual with pronunciation problems
4   a phonological assessment of a child's pronunciation patterns should also include an evaluation of the developmental status of the child's speech.

These four criteria apply the principles of phonological analysis to the clinical context. Assessments that fulfil these criteria will enable the speech pathologist to identify in what ways an individual's pronunciation patterns systematically differ from the target patterns. The implications of these differences can also be evaluated in terms of their likely effects upon the intelligibility or communicative adequacy of the individual's speech. This information is highly relevant to the formulation of a prioritized treatment programme. When assessing children's speech, however, it is also important to take account of the developmental assessment. This will provide a complementary set of treatment guidelines based upon indications of the developmental normality and/or delay in a child's pronunciation patterns. Using these types of assessments, changes in an individual's pronunciation patterns that occur following intervention or after a period of time has elapsed can be identified and evaluated both in terms of functional improvements and developmental advances.

Several different types of phonological analyses have been devised for clinical assessment (see Grunwell, 1987b for a detailed discussion and examples). The traditional approach was *error analysis*. This involved identifying the differences between the target pronunciations and the different realizations or mispronunciations as one of four types of error:

–   *substitution* of one sound (phoneme) for another; e.g. *key* /ki/ pronounced [ti]
–   *omission* of a sound; e.g. *spoon* /spun/ pronounced [pun]

- *distortion* of a sound (phoneme) such that its pronunciation is not acceptable; e.g. *shoe* /ʃu/ pronounced [çu]
- *addition* of a sound (phoneme) to a word; e.g. *pram* /pram/ pronounced [pəram]

This type of approach has certain major shortcomings, the main one being that it does not lead to the identification of patterns in the data. Each different pronunciation is analysed as an isolated error. Nor does this approach straightforwardly provide for a functional assessment of the error pronunciations. Notwithstanding these inadequacies the influence of this approach is evident in many of the procedures in use at the present time, even though they are apparently derived from a much more sophisticated theoretical background.

The approach to phonological assessment most widely used is *phonological process analysis*. This involves descriptive statements characterizing the systematic correspondences between the individual's pronunciation patterns and the target pronunciation patterns. These relationships generally occur between classes of sounds that share phonetic properties or features in common, i.e. natural classes. They can also involve types of structures that have features in common. Process analysis thus identifies patterns rather than isolated instances of differences.

There are a number of published assessment procedures which focus primarily on phonological process analysis. They are:

- Weiner (1979) *Phonological Process Analysis (PPA)*
- Shriberg and Kwiatkowski (1980) *Natural Process Analysis (NPA)*
- Hodson (1980) *Assessment of Phonological Processes (APP)*
- Ingram (1981) *Procedures for the Phonological Analysis of Children's Language (PPACL)*
- Grunwell (1985) *Phonological Assessment of Child Speech (PACS)*

These five procedures each provide a different set of processes for the phonological analysis. Close scrutiny of the procedures, however, reveals basic similarities between the descriptive framework. The differences result mainly from different terminology and from the amount of detail given in the specification of the processes. Reviews of each of these five procedures are given in Grunwell (1987b; 1989). Here, the framework of description they share in common will be outlined.

Three general types of phonological processes can be identified:

- *substitution processes* which analyse replacement relationships between natural classes of sounds
- *syllable structure processes* which analyse omission- and transposition-type relationships between natural classes of sounds
- *assimilation processes* which analyse interactive relationships between sounds

57

Frequently occurring processes in each of these three types are given below.

Substitution processes

Fronting of target velar consonants to the alveolar place of articulation:

$$\begin{bmatrix} k \\ g \\ \eta \end{bmatrix} \rightarrow \begin{bmatrix} t \\ d \\ n \end{bmatrix}$$

Stopping of target fricative and affricate consonants to homorganic plosives:

$$\begin{bmatrix} s \\ \int \\ t\!\int \end{bmatrix} \rightarrow [t]$$

$$\begin{bmatrix} z \\ d_3 \end{bmatrix} \rightarrow [d]$$

Gliding of target liquids /rl/ to glides [wj].

Syllable structure processes

Final consonant deletion, i.e. omission of word-final consonants:

e.g. *comb* [koʊ]   *five* [faɪ]

Cluster reduction, i.e. omission of one or more consonants from a target cluster:

e.g. *spoon* [pun]   *train* [teɪn]

Assimilation processes

Consonant harmony where one consonant is assimilated to or harmonized with another consonant in a word:

e.g. *duck* [gʌk]   *dog* [gɒg]

Context-sensitive voicing where the voicing characteristic of consonants is determined by their position in word structure: word-initial consonants are voiced, being assimilated to the voiced following vowel; word-final consonants are voiceless being assimilated to potential silence that follows:

e.g. *tub* [dʌp]   *pat, bad* [bat]

As is evident from these definitions and examples, phonological processes closely resemble the traditional error-analysis categories. The important difference between the two frameworks is that process analysis describes patterns of relationships and identifies the errors in terms of natural classes of sounds.

A further major advantage of phonological process analysis is that it enables the speech pathologist to carry out a developmental assessment of a child's pronunciation patterns. Research into children's phonological development during the last twenty years has for the most part been reported using the framework of phonological process analysis (e.g. Ingram, 1976; 1989; Stoel-Gammon and Dunn, 1985). It is therefore possible to identify whether a process is characteristic of normal development and at what stage and age it would normally be evidenced in a child's pronunciation patterns. This type of assessment will be discussed further below.

Unfortunately, phonological process analysis fails to meet in a direct way the third criterion for a phonological assessment; namely, that it should provide an analysis of the functional consequences of an individual's pronunciation patterns. Indirectly, of course, one can deduce that fronting of velars to alveolars entails a loss of contrast between /k/ and /t/ etc. Deducing the implications of other processes, however, may not be so simple. A different type of phonological procedure provides a straightforward framework for this type of assessment.

Contrastive analysis and assessment involves comparing the child's pronunciation system directly with the adult pronunciation system. Figure 3.2 presents a display of the English systems of consonants in word-initial and word-final positions (see Grunwell, 1985; 1987b for detailed discussion of this procedure). Figure 3.3 exemplifies the use of this procedure to analyse and assess the pronunciation patterns of a child with pronunciation problems. It shows both the matches and mismatches between the target and the child's consonants. The functional consequences of Lisa's patterns are clearly evident. For example, in word-initial position she fails to signal the contrasts between /t/d/ʧ/ʤ/k/g/f/s/ʃ/, all these target consonants being realized, at least in some words, as [d]. In the word-final position she fails to signal contrasts /t/k/g/; these three targets all being omitted in some words. The restrictions and inadequacies of the child's pronunciation patterns are thus presented in a succinct and explicit format.

This framework is not complete as no analysis is made of structural differences between the target patterns and the child's realizations of clusters and multisyllabic words. Additional procedures are required to investigate these aspects of pronunciation. Space does not permit consideration of these in this chapter; detailed descriptions are provided in Grunwell (1985).

Ideally, a phonological assessment should provide a profile of a child's pronunciation patterns in regard to both their functional and developmental

59

Syllable initial word initial

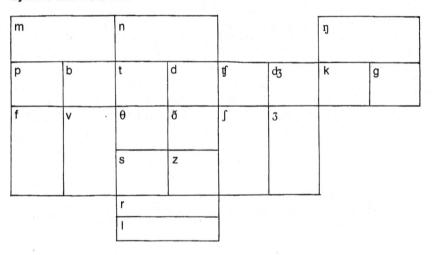

Syllable final word final

Figure 3.2 English consonant systems in word-initial and word-final positions

Name .. Lisa .... 4 YEARS 5 MONTHS ......

Syllable initial word initial

m m	n n				
p b	b b	t d	d d	tʃ d	dʒ d	k d g	g g d
f d b	v w	θ b	ð j	ʃ d	
		s d	z w		
w w b	r w	j w n	h h	
	l w		

Syllable final word final

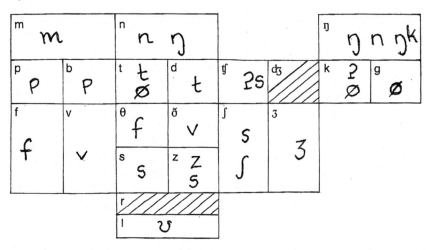

m m	n n ŋ		ŋ ŋ n ŋk
p p	b p	t t ∅	d t	tʃ ʔs	dʒ ///	k ʔ ∅	g ∅
f f	v v	θ f	ð v	ʃ s ʃ	ʒ 3
		s s	z z s	
		r ///	
		l ʊ	

Figure 3.3 Contrastive assessment of word-initial and word-final consonants: Lisa, 4 years, 5 months

61

status. Such a profile is available in the PACS set of procedures (Grunwell, 1985) and is reproduced here as Figure 3.4. This profile is primarily a developmental assessment. It displays on the left-hand side of the chart the gradual emergence of the adult system of consonant contrasts. At each stage, or age range, a different system of consonants is evidenced with more contrasts being signalled. The arrangement of the consonant system follows the display presented in Figures 3.2 and 3.3, so that direct comparisons can be made between the contrastive assessment and the developmental assessment. Indeed, this part of the developmental assessment can be derived from the contrastive assessment procedure. On the right-hand side of the chart the chronology of phonological process occurrence is displayed. As can be seen in the early stages all of the processes described above occur; gradually these processes disappear completely or become limited in their occurrence until finally at Stage VII the target consonant system is almost complete and there are virtually no major error patterns or processes. Figure 3.5 exemplifies the use of the profile to carry out a developmental assessment of Lisa's pronunciation patterns.

Using the contrastive analysis figure, given a knowledge of the definitions of the different types of phonological processes, it is possible to identify the occurrence of processes and thus complete both parts of the chart. While functional implications can be deduced from the co-occurrence of processes alongside the system of consonants, it is preferable to use the contrastive assessment for this. It will be noted that Lisa's pronunciation patterns cannot be mapped directly on to the developmental assessment chart. This does not mean that the chart is inadequate; it is a clear indication that Lisa's pronunciation patterns are developmentally different from those one would normally expect. In other words it suggests a diagnosis of a developmental phonological disorder.

Phonological and developmental assessment of pronunciation patterns complete the range of investigations a speech pathologist would undertake into an individual's speech production. Assessments, however, are not carried out for their own sake; they are undertaken in order to provide the information required for diagnosis and management.

EVALUATION

Interpretation of the results of articulatory and phonological assessments involves an evaluation of the information provided by these investigations having regard to information obtained from other investigations, such as the case history, medical notes, cognitive and intellectual tests, audiological assessments, socioenvironmental factors, and so on. Such considerations are beyond the scope of this chapter. Interpretation here is confined to a discussion of the results obtained from the investigations of speech

Developmental Assessment

PACS
© Pamela Grunwell 1985

Name ....

		Labial	Lingual				Protowords and First Words:
Stage I (0;9–1;6)	Nasal						Show phonetic variability and all phon processes. *Examples*
	Plosive						
	Fricative						
	Approximant						

Stage II (1;6–2;0)	m		n				Reduplication / Consonant Harmony / FINAL CONS. DELETION / CLUSTER REDUCTION	FRONTING / STOPPING / GLIDING / C.S. VOICING
	p	b	t	d				
	w							

Stage III (2;0–2;6)	m		n		(ŋ)		Final Cons. Deletion / CLUSTER REDUCTION	Fronting / STOPPING / GLIDING / C.S. VOICING
	p	b	t	d	(k	g)		
	w				(h)			

Stage IV (2;6–3;0)	m		n		ŋ		Final Cons. Deletion / CLUSTER REDUCTION	STOPPING/v ð z tʃ dʒ/ / FRONTING/ʃ/→[s] / GLIDING / C.S. VOICING
	p	b	t	d	k	g		
	f		s					
	w	(l)		j	h			

Stage V (3;0–3;6)	m		n		ŋ		Clusters used: obs. + approx. /s/ + cons.	STOPPING/v ð z/ / FRONTING/ʃ tʃ dʒ/ / GLIDING / /θ/→[f]
	p	b	t	d	(tʃ)	k	g	
	f		s		(ʃ)			
	w	l		j	h			

Stage VI (3;6–4;6)	m		n		ŋ		Clusters used: obs. + approx. /s/ + cons.	/ð/→[d] or [v] / PALATALIZATION/ʃ tʃ dʒ/ / GLIDING / /θ/→[f]
	p	b	t	d	tʃ	dʒ	k	g
	f	v	s	z	ʃ			
	w	l	(r)	j	h			

Stage VII (4;6 <)	m		n		ŋ		Clusters used: obs. + approx. /s/ + cons.	/ð/→[d] or [v] / /r/→[w] or [v] / /θ/→[f]
	p	b	t	d	tʃ	dʒ	k	g
	f	v	θ	s	ð	z	ʃ	(ʒ)
	w	l	r	j	h			

Comments and Notes

_____
_____
_____
_____
_____
_____

Figure 3.4 PACS developmental assessment

63

Developmental Assessment

PACS
© Pamela Grunwell 1985

Name ....**Lisa   4;5**..

		Labial		Lingual		Protowords and First Words: Show phonetic variability and all phon processes. *Examples*		
Stage I (0;9–1;6)	Nasal							
	Plosive							
	Fricative							
	Approximant							
Stage II (1;6–2;0)	m		n			Reduplication	FRONTING	
	p b	t	d			Consonant Harmony	STOPPING	
						FINAL CONS. DELETION	GLIDING	
	w					CLUSTER REDUCTION	C.S. VOICING	
Stage III (2;0–2;6)	m		n	(ŋ)		Final Cons. Deletion	Fronting	✓
	p b	t	d	(k g)		CLUSTER REDUCTION	STOPPING SIWI	✓
							GLIDING	
							C.S. VOICING	
	w			(h)			Gliding of WI Frics	✓
Stage IV (2;6–3;0)	ⓜ		ⓝ	ⓖ		Final Cons. Deletion ✓	STOPPING/v ð z ʧʤ/	
	ⓟⓑ	ⓣ	ⓓ	✗ ⓖ		CLUSTER REDUCTION ✓ invariably SIWI	FRONTING/ʃ/→[s] SFWF	✓
	ⓕ ⓥ	ⓢ	ⓩ ⓢ ⓩ				GLIDING	✓
	ⓦ	⅋		ⓛ	ⓗ	Glottal Realizations ✓	C.S. VOICING	✓
Stage V (3;0–3;6)	m		n	ŋ		Clusters used:	STOPPING/v ð z/	
	p b	t	d	(ʧ)	k g	obs. + approx.	FRONTING/ʃ ʧʤ/	
	f	s		(ʃ)		/s/ + cons.	GLIDING	
	w	l		j	h		/θ/ → [f]	
Stage VI (3;6–4;6)	m		n	ŋ		Clusters used:	/ð/ → [d] or [v]	
	p b	t	d	ʧ ʤ	k g	obs. + approx.	PALATALIZATION/ʃ ʧʤ/	
	f v	s		z	ʃ	/s/ + cons.	GLIDING	
	w	l	(r)	j	h		/θ/ → [f]	
Stage VII (4;6 <)	m		n	ŋ		Clusters used:	/ð/ → [d] or [v]	
	p b	t	d	ʧ ʤ	k g	obs. + approx.	/r/ → [w] or [v]	
	f v	θ s	ð z	ʃ	(ʒ)	/s/ + cons.	/θ/ → [f]	
	w	l	r	j	h			

Comments and Notes

Lisa gives evidence of many immature patterns. Yet she has within her pronunciation system the potential to signal many target consonant contrasts. There is a combination of persistent processes, chronological mismatch, a few unusual patterns, systematic sound preference for [d] in SIWI position and some variability.

Figure 3.5 PACS developmental assessment: Lisa, 4 years, 5 months

production. Within the context of these articulatory and phonological assessments, evaluation of the phonetic and phonological findings should be made in the light of the anatomical and physiological investigations. As indicated by Harris and Cottam:

> the term natural when used in the context of clinical phonology is in principle at least, independent of the term normal. Measures of normality versus deviance in speech assessment are made with reference to adult or developmental norms. The naturalness of particular phonological phenomena, on the other hand, has to do with the extent to which their occurrence can be accounted for by reference to external factors whose domain is the natural world rather than language itself. In connection with phonology, the relevant factors are generally supposed to derive from such areas as articulatory physiology, acoustic phonetics or perceptual psychology. It is thus perfectly possible for a child's speech to exhibit phonological patterns which are deviant but which are none-the-less natural to the extent that they are attributable to external phenomena of this type.
>
> (Harris and Cottam, 1985, pp. 73–4)

For example, the occurrence of 'Backing', that is the replacement of target alveolar consonants by velar consonants (i.e. the opposite of fronting), is an unusual, if not to say deviant, pattern. It is, however, a pattern that would naturally occur if a child had a short frenum (or tongue tie), since such a condition restricts the mobility and range of movement of the tongue tip (see Grunwell, 1985; 1988). Furthermore, this pattern may persist after surgery has corrected the condition because the pronunciation pattern has become habituated. The occurrence of patterns that involve discoordination between phonation and articulation, such as devoicing and prevocalization, prolongation of articulations and within-word pauses may be associated with dysarthria and these patterns too may persist if the child is unable to achieve motor control of the articulators (Milloy and Morgan-Barry, 1990). In the instance of an identifiable anatomical and/or physiological disability, therefore, it is likely that characteristic patterns associated with the condition will be evident from the phonetic and phonological assessments.

It must also be borne in mind, however, that children with articulatory disabilities are engaged in the process of learning to pronounce. It is, therefore, probable that a number of the patterns characteristic of normal phonological development will be evidenced in their speech. It may also be found that they are experiencing difficulties in the learning process. This will be indicated by the occurrence of one or more of the characteristics of a developmental phonological learning disorder. These have been identified as:

Persisting normal processes normal patterns that remain in the child's pronunciation patterns long after the age at which they would normally have disappeared; e.g. the presence of fronting in Lisa's speech (see Figure 3.5).

Chronological mismatch the co-occurrence of some of the earliest patterns with some patterns characteristic of later stages of development; e.g. the co-occurrence of the early pattern of fronting and the presence of final fricatives in Lisa's speech.

Unusual processes the occurrence of patterns rarely attested in normal development; e.g. the occurrence of gliding of fricatives in Lisa's speech.

Systematic sound preference one type of consonant being used for a large range of target consonants; e.g. in Lisa's speech word initials /t/d/tʃ/ dʒ/k/g/f/s/ʃ/ are all realized as [d].

Variable use of processes more than one simplifying process being used for the same target consonants; e.g. in Lisa's speech variability is particularly evidenced in the occurrence of very different patterns in word-initial and word-final position for the same target consonants. (For further discussion of these characteristics see Grunwell, 1985; Stoel-Gammon and Dunn, 1985).

These five characteristics suggest delayed, uneven and disordered learning of pronunciation patterns. They may occur in the absence of any articulatory disability, of which Lisa's case is an example.

The evaluation of the articulatory and phonological assessments is not only relevant to diagnosis; it is also important in planning treatment strategies. Information about the nature of a disabling condition or about specific problems learning particular target sounds or structures enables the speech pathologist to define treatment goals and decide upon appropriate treatment techniques. Another important factor that must also be taken into account in treatment-planning is the functional consequences of any phonetic and phonological deviations. The prime aim of any treatment strategy must be to enable an individual to communicate more effectively.

Phonological assessment, in particular, has brought into central focus the functional or communicative dimension of all types of disorders of speech production (see, for example, Grunwell, 1990). In clinical practice, the speech pathologist should, therefore, integrate traditional articulatory assessments with phonetic and phonological procedures as demonstrated in this chapter. This type of explanatory evaluation leads to a more insightful understanding of the nature of children's speech disorders and their developmental disabilities.

REFERENCES

Albery, E. and Russell, J. (1990). 'Cleft palate and orofacial abnormalities'. In P. Grunwell (ed.), *Developmental Speech Disorders*. Edinburgh: Churchill Livingstone.

Anthony, A., Bogle, D., Ingram, T. T. S. and McIsaac, M. W. (1971). *The Edinburgh Articulation Test*. Edinburgh: Churchill Livingstone.

Code, C. and Ball, M. (1984). *Experimental Clinical Phonetics*. London: Croom Helm.

Enderby, P. (1983). *Frenchay Dysarthria Assessment*. Windsor: NFER-NELSON.

Goldman, R. and Fristoe, M. (1972). *Goldman-Fristoe test of articulation*. Circle Pines, Minnesota: AGS.

Grunwell, P. (1985). *Phonological Assessment of Child Speech (PACS)*. Windsor: NFER-NELSON.

Grunwell, P. (1987a). *PACS Pictures*. Windsor: NFER-NELSON.

Grunwell, P. (1987b). *Clinical Phonology*. London: Croom Helm.

Grunwell, P. (1988). 'Phonological assessment, evaluation and explanation of speech disorders in children'. *Clinical Linguistics & Phonetics*, 2, 221–52.

Grunwell, P. (1989). 'Assessment of phonology'. In K. Grundy (ed.), *Linguistics and Clinical Practice*. London: Taylor & Francis.

Grunwell, P. (ed.) (1990). *Developmental Speech Disorders*. Edinburgh: Churchill Livingstone.

Hardcastle, W. (ed.) (1989). Clinical Applications of Electropalatography. Special Issue of: *Clinical Linguistics & Phonetics*, 3, 1.

Harris, J. and Cottam, P. (1985). 'Phonetic features and phonological features in speech assessment'. *British Journal of Disorders of Communication*, 20, 61–74.

Hodson, B. W. (1980). *The Assessment of Phonological Processes*. Danville: Interstate Inc.

Huskins, S. (1987). *Working with Dyspraxics*. Bicester: Winslow Press.

Ingram, D. (1976, 1989). *Phonological Disability in Children*. London: Edward Arnold (1st edn); Cole Whurr (2nd edn).

Ingram, D. (1981). *Procedures for the Phonological Analysis of Children's Language*. Baltimore: University Park Press.

International Phonetic Alphabet (1989). *Journal of International Phonetic Association*, 19, 81–2.

Milloy, N. R. (1985). 'The assessment and identification of developmental articulatory dyspraxia and its effect on phonological development'. Unpublished Ph.D. thesis, Leicester Polytechnic.

Milloy, N. R. and Morgan-Barry, R. (1990). 'Developmental neurological disorders'. In P. Grunwell (ed.), *Developmental Speech Disorders*. Edinburgh: Churchill Livingstone.

Newman, P. W., Creaghead, N. A. and Secord, W. (1985). *Assessment and Remediation of Articulatory and Phonological Disorders*. Columbus: Charles Merrill.

PRDS (1983) *The Phonetic Representation of Disordered Speech: final report* London: King's Fund.

Robertson, S. (1982). *Dysarthria Profile*. Private publication.

Shriberg, L. D. and Kwiatkowski, J. (1980). *Natural Process Analysis (NPA)*. New York: Wiley.

St Louis, K. O. and Ruscello, D. M. (1981). *The Oral Speech Mechanism Screening Examination*. Baltimore: University Park Press.

Stoel-Gammon, C. and Dunn, C. (1985). *Normal and Disordered Phonology in Children*. Baltimore: University Park Press.

Weiner, F. F. (1979). *Phonological Process Analysis (PPA)*. Baltimore: University Park Press.

4

ASSESSMENT OF VOICE PROBLEMS

H. Fiona Robinson

By nature, voice variety is limitless and the standards for voice adequacy are broad (Aronson, 1990). Moore says:

> it is obvious that there is no single sound that can be called 'normal voice', instead there are children's voices, girls' voices, boys' voices, women's voices, men's voices, voices of the aged and so on. In each of these types of voice both the normal and the abnormal can be recognised ... and the threshold which separates the one from the other is judged by each listener on the basis of his cultural standards, education, environment, vocal training and similar factors but ... it is obvious that each individual has acquired concepts of normalcy and defectiveness.
>
> (Moore, 1971)

A voice disorder exists when the loudness, pitch, quality and functionality such as voice projection and prosody differ from the voices of others of the same sex, similar age, build, dialectal and cultural group, or when the voice has changed from that which was previously deemed normal for this particular speaker.

In assessing a pathological voice, it is vital that the clinician is familiar with the components which are necessary for normal voice production.

- normal extrinsic laryngeal structure
- normal intrinsic laryngeal structure and function
- normal vocal tract
- adequate velopharyngeal closure
- good breath support and control

The assessment of voice cannot be undertaken by the presentation of a set of clear-cut tasks and exercises scored against normative data. The complex aetiology of a voice disorder – potentially a combination of organic and psychological factors with situational variables – necessitates a broad-based and methodical assessment process.

The aim of the assessment process is to elicit data which will enable the clinician to:

1 identify and confirm the aetiology of the dysphonia
2 describe its type and severity
3 document the onset and course of the disorder
4 interpret the data for differential diagnosis
5 identify prognostic indicators
6 make decisions about appropriate management and intervention, for example, advice, referral on, monitoring, review, therapy or discharge

The assessment process follows a defined outline, the weighting of which will be determined by the bias of the clinician and his or her initial perceptions about the patient, as well as the availability of resources, but will include the following:

-   laryngologic investigation
-   interviewing
-   observation
-   case-history taking and 'diagnostic counselling'
-   physical and neurological assessment
-   acoustic-perceptual voice assessment
-   comparison of data with standard or normal phonation

The data are then open to interpretation. The clinician's own skills, qualities, expectations and judgements contribute to the success or failure of the assessment process in eliciting the data necessary for successful interpretation and recommendation.

OBTAINING DATA

Referrals for voice assessment and speech-and-language-therapy opinion are made to clinics from a variety of agencies, clinical and non-clinical. The information given will naturally be indicative of its source; for example, Ear, Nose and Throat, neurology, respiratory medicine, cardiothoracic clinic, nurses, physiotherapist, and psychiatrist and other non-hospital sources such as teachers, singing teachers, drama schools, and indeed self-referrals.

Obtaining the relevant data from outside sources can be a lengthy process of letter-writing, telephone calls and face-to-face discussion. The medical background from medical notes and the referrer's full information should be to hand prior to the speech-and-language-therapy evaluation in an ideal world, but any delay should not deter the clinician from instigating his or her own evaluation procedure. However, it is vital that a laryngoscopic report is available as soon as possible, as the presence or absence of organic aetiology will determine the assessment route, or even the relevance, of the speech and language therapist's involvement at all.

LARYNGOLOGIC INVESTIGATION

In most centres, the ENT staff refer the majority of patients by letter, which outlines the laryngoscopic findings. Some centres have organized joint-assessment clinics where the speech and language therapist is present to gain a first-hand view of the larynx (Simpson, 1971). It is of paramount importance that a good view of the larynx is obtained and the report should make reference to the appearance of the structures viewed; for example, redness, dryness, the structure and the function, such as glottic closure, apparent neuropathy. The speech and language therapist should be familiar with the viewing method employed and discuss appropriate alternatives with the laryngologist should he or she need further or different information from that provided.

Mirror laryngoscopy

This procedure, carried out usually by the ENT doctors, is more commonly known as indirect laryngoscopy (IDL) because the view is obtained indirectly via a laryngeal mirror. The warmed (to prevent misting) mirror is guided posteriorly into the oropharynx. The examiner, who wears a head mirror, is able to reflect a beam of light on to the laryngeal mirror, which illuminates the interior of the larynx. The appearance, structure and function of the larynx is assessed during quiet breathing and vowel prolongation. The usual vowel used is [i] which encourages laryngeal elevation and pharyngeal dilation, enabling a wider field to be viewed. This method of examination of the larynx is by far the most common in the average ENT department in this country. If the patient can co-operate without gagging, and the procedure is carried out confidently yet considerately, an experienced laryngologist is able to elicit much of the necessary information about the organic factors contributing to the dysphonia. Occasionally, IDL is not possible and other investigations may need to be carried out.

Fibrescope

A flexible fibre-optic bundle is introduced through the nasal passages to overhang the larynx and thus provide a free view of the larynx. The tip of the fibrescope provides its own light source and there is no gagging. The laryngologist is able to evaluate the structure, function and appearance of the larynx at rest, in vowel prolongation and also in connected speech. Because of the increased tolerance of the patient, the speech and language therapist can participate in the evaluation, not only by suggesting phonatory tasks but also in viewing the structures in action through the eyepiece. The patient may also be permitted to view his own larynx, thus reinforcing the assessment findings. Although tolerated by a majority of patients, there may be some difficulty in introducing the bundle nasally in cases of deviated septum or other structural problems. The fibrescope can be introduced orally. However, a bite inhibitor needs to be placed intra-orally to prevent the patient from biting down on the bundle, and this precludes evaluation of the larynx in connected speech.

Laryngostroboscopy

This technique is simply a combination of the use of a flexible fibrescope coupled with a flashing light source, which is often integral to the system. Prytz states that, in stroboscopy, an optical illusion is produced that arises from persistence of vision. In short, each light admission to the retina leaves a positive after-image lasting 0.2 seconds. A sequence of individual frames, presented at intervals shorter than 0.2 seconds, appears as a con-tinuously moving picture. This gives a life-like impression of movements but what is seen are only fragments of the complete movement. The frequency of the flashing light may be altered so that a particular phase is in 'freeze-frame' for detailed examination, or the whole cycle appears to be in slow motion so that a detailed evaluation of the appearance and function of the vocal folds and mucosa can be made. He describes how the stroboscope may be used for phase measurements and indicates the actual position of the vocal folds, enabling exact measurements to be made of the individual vibratory phases, such as opening, closing and glottic closure. In addition to the basic movement, a glottic or travelling wave of the overlying mucosa of the vocal fold is apparent. The glottic wave is a particularly sensitive indi-cation of pathological changes and is not detectable with the naked eye. The stiffer the mucosa, the less marked the mucosal wave. If the wave stops travelling at a specific portion, there is indication of fixed mucosa as in a cancer lesion or benign tumour.

A video camera may be attached to the laryngoscope and thus the image is stored for re-viewing and comparison. This expensive equipment is not routinely available in every ENT department. However, it is a valuable assessment tool for patients with persistent dysphonias, complicated post-surgical recovery after removal of benign tumours, or complicated histories. The detailed examination afforded, especially of the mucosal wave, may reveal an otherwise unseen aetiology for the dysphonia.

Direct laryngoscopy

This procedure is carried out when the patient is under a general anaesthetic. It may be indicated for patients who cannot tolerate any other laryngeal examination in the conscious state (because of gagging or apprehension), where only a poor or limited view of the larynx was possible (commonly in children, and patients with awkard dentition or an overhanging epiglottis) or for whom it is vital that a longer and more detailed evaluation of the larynx and surrounding structures is necessary.

If possible, the speech and language therapist should be present when the larynx is being viewed. He or she will be able to reinforce the findings to the patient who will perceive him or her as an integral team member, and the therapist will have no doubts about the organic aetiology.

INTERVIEWING

The initial interview sets the scene for both the patient and the therapist. The structure, format and setting of the early assessment interviews are important to build trust and to provide the sort of environment in which to elicit the maximum amount of information and allow the patient to feel at ease with any instrumentation and the performance of assessment tasks. Ideally, the setting is a private and quiet room with comfortable furniture and easy access to instrumentation. Adequate time should be allocated with no unplanned interruptions. The clinician may wish to tape-record the session, with the permission of the patient, or make notes, but any method of recording should be as unobtrusive as possible to encourage co-operation and disclosure.

Should the patient or the therapist begin to tire, the session should be drawn to a close, a summary explained and a further time arranged.

OBSERVATION

During the initial interview, the clinician will have a valuable opportunity to observe and assess the patient's non-verbal behaviour, general communication skills and any tendency to excessive musculo-skeletal tension of the whole body or specifically the laryngeal and facial area.

CASE HISTORY

This is arguably one of the most important elements in the assessment of voice disorders. Herein lie many of the clues to the causation of the disorder, the predisposing and risk factors, the onset and course and the reinforcing elements at play (Robinson and Bradley, 1987). Taking the case history can be seen simply as a means of eliciting the factual information, or additionally – and more fruitfully – as an opportunity for exchange of information and reassurance, using the question/answer format as a basis for discussion and explanation. Sometimes this is therapeutic in itself and the patient leaves with insight into the voice disorder and some self-help strategies. A literature search will reveal examples of case-history formats which may be used (see end section).

The clinician should employ all his or her interviewing and counselling skills to elicit information in a structured and non-judgemental way. But rather than asking questions from a prepared sheet, or asking patients to fill it out themselves, it is valuable to use a check-list format as an aid to memory and to direct the interview and allow the discourse to develop and continue in a natural and relaxed manner.

If undertaken sensitively, the clinician will guide and coax the patient to further disclosure, teasing out the relevant facts, discarding irrelevant information and exploring preferred avenues. Here, especially, the clinician should have regard for the patient's discomfiture and should change tack should he or she show signs of resistance.

Most clinics have a standardized form for biographical details and summary of reports from ENT, plus sections for general health and medical history, voice use/abuse, vocal hygiene and personal history. In addition to these factual sections, consideration should be given to more subjective points; for example, the patient's own interpretation and experiences of the dysphonia, remedies which have some effect and his or her emotional well-being prior to or at the time of the onset. This encourages the patient to participate actively in building up the whole picture of the dysphonia and to begin to take some responsibility for the outcome. Information regarding patients' motivation to change and their expectations of outcome can be gleaned which will indicate compliance for therapy, prognosis and outcome (Robinson, Bradley and Heritage, 1990).

Recent life events and changes have been shown to be of real significance in the development of psychogenic dysphonia (Robinson and Bradley, 1987). If the patient is compliant, it is well worth exploring these in some detail in order to ascertain the experiences and responses at the time, the coping strategies employed, and to determine whether the episode and its emotional response is resolved or is still causing residual problems.

The check-list (Box 4.1) is used in our Nottingham practice. Consideration is given to all items, which are expanded or deleted at the discretion of the clinician, according to the needs and expectations of the patient in that particular session. In this way, the check-list becomes a valuable adjunct in assessment, rather than an intrusive and inhibiting questionnaire to be filled out.

PHYSICAL AND NEUROMUSCULAR ASSESSMENT

The physical examination carried out by the speech and language therapist is complementary to the ENT consultant's assessment. This includes the observation of the larynx at rest and on phonation. The laryngeal region should be observed with regard to the position and degree of tension of the suprahyoid muscles, strap muscles, thyroid cartilage and submental

Box 4.1

Check-list for case-history taking (dysphonia)

1 BIOGRAPHICAL DETAILS
   Name, address, date of birth
   Consultant and GP
   Referral date and referee
   Hospital number

2 ENT DIAGNOSTIC IMPRESSION
   Clinical examinations   IDL/DL   date
            oral: tongue, palate, lips, function
            larynx: appearance, function, not viewed
            vocal fold: appearance, function, palsy
            neck, hearing, dentition, reflux
            voice: normal, abnormal
            swallow: normal, aspiration, pooling, consistency problems
            nasal regurgitation
            post-nasal drip, sinus problems, septum, mouth-breathing
            thyroid function tests, endocrine function
            follow-up, review in joint clinic, time-scale, discharge

3 GENERAL HEALTH AND MEDICAL HISTORY
            involvement with other agencies, clinics
            current medical intervention
            current medications, inhalers, thyroxine, controlled drugs
            CVA, MS/DS, MND, myaesthenia gravis, epilepsy, other
            hypo/hyper thyroid
            surgery: pneumonectomy, thyroid, other
            trauma, intubation, tracheostomy
            respiratory problems, asthma, bronchitis
            accident, RTA, arthritis, other
            menstruation/menopause
            constipation, insomnia, allergy
            general well-being, fitness, improving/deteriorating

4 VOICE HISTORY
   Previous episodes
            time-scale, onset, occurrence, associated factors
            intermittent, constant, fluctuating
            resolution, speech therapy, other agency
            family history
   Current episode
            time and mode of onset, associated factors
            sensations: pain, 'lump', location, tightness, raw, gritty
            what helps/what makes it worse
            improving/deteriorating, intermittent, constant, fluctuating
            best/worst time of day, tiring
            what does it prevent you doing?
            patient's theory of cause

5 VOICE USE/ABUSE/MISUSE
Environment
Work/school, noise, machinery, radio, telephone
        dust, dirt, wear filter, mask, fresh air, heating
Home   noise, central heating, bedding type, TV, children
Phonation
        amount, duration, voice rest
        coughing, throat-clearing, productive, habitual, vomiting
        shouting, screaming, baby voice, impressions, cheering
        singing: ageing voice, forcing pitch, volume, duration
        musculo-skeletal, posture
Irritants
        smoking, spirits, spices, dairy products, pollution, aerosols,
        solvent abuse, fabrics

6 PERSONAL HISTORY
        occupation/school, satisfaction, recent change, why?
        marital status and satisfaction
        dependants: children, ageing/infirm relatives
        general niggles
        social life, hobbies, solitary/gregarious
        daily routine

Recent (2 years) life events and changes: significance
    (happy, stressful, planned, unexpected,   timing
    bereavement, weddings, arguments,   emotion
    birth, divorce, holidays, Christmas)   outcome
                                                     coping strategies

© H. Fiona Robinson,
  Nottingham 1990

musculature. The clinician should firmly and gently palpate the area and manipulate the larynx (see Aronson, 1990), making observations and judgements about the resistance and degree of tension exhibited. In the absence of laryngeal disease, a resistance to laryngeal displacement and pain in response to pressure may indicate chronic laryngeal muscle tension (Bless, 1987).

All vocal parameters can be affected if the neurological control of the laryngeal and respiratory systems is impaired. Dysphonia can present as the first sign of a wider presentation of a neurological disease or disorder; for example, CVA (cardiovascular accident), motor-neurone disease, myaesthenia gravis. The clinician must have an awareness of this possibility and if there are other discrete signs; for example, a minimal hypernasality, dysarthria, emotional lability, limb weakness or dysphagia, he or she will assess for a wider neurological impairment of the speech mechanism by oral examination and by using one of the standardized neurological speech assessments available in each clinic; for example, the Frenchay dysarthria assessment (Enderby, 1980). This will provide information to support a referral back to the referrer or to a neurologist, to confirm or deny his or her suspicions. Additionally, any medication being taken currently or prior to the onset should be noted as this may be implicated in the aetiology of the dysphonia (Garvel, 1981).

ACOUSTIC-PERCEPTUAL VOICE ASSESSMENT

In clinical practice, there is a plethora of labels used to describe abnormal voice usually based on the perceptual attributes of the voice. However, a voice described as 'whispery' by one clinician may be described as 'squeaky' by a second and 'quiet' by a third. Even within clinical teams, agreement over labels is difficult, and thus across units and health districts the task is nigh impossible. Indeed the best description of vocal characteristics is a combination of both the aetiological label, relating to the laryngological findings with the acoustic-perceptual label from a standardized format such as the John Laver vocal-profile analysis (Laver *et al.*, 1982); see Box 4.2. This is a perceptual-descriptive system, based on acoustic and articulatory criteria; a revised form has been in use since 1988. Another simple but standardized classification is proposed by Hirano (1981).

VOCAL PARAMETERS

In the assessment of vocal parameters of children, adolescents and adults, a knowledge of the development of the larynx and the effects of these physiological changes is essential.

The assessment of the perceptual attributes of a voice, either normal or pathological, should relate to the numerous, individual components which make up the end product, namely:

- pitch
- prosody
- loudness
- breath support
- quality
- resonance

Box 4.3 outlines informal assessment tasks used to elicit information about these individual parameters used in the Nottingham clinical practice. The therapist should model the target for the patient, who should be assessed on his or her third attempt. The tasks incorporate the parameter in isolation and in connected speech to enable the clinician to identify a specific problem, one associated with the complex interactions of the phonatory mechanism or related to situational variables.

Box 4.2

John Laver vocal-profile analysis protocol

Speaker: .... Sex: .... Age: .... Date of Analysis: .... Tape: .... Judge: ....

I VOCAL QUALITY FEATURES

CATEGORY	FIRST PASS		SECOND PASS						
	Neutral	Non-neutral	SETTING	Scalar Degrees					
		Normal	Abnormal		Normal	Abnormal			
					1	2	3	4	5	6

A. Supralaryngeal Features

1 Labial
- Lip Rounding/Protrusion
- Lip Spreading
- Labiodentalization
- Extensive Range
- Minimised Range

2 Mandibular
- Close Jaw
- Open Jaw
- Protruded Jaw
- Extensive Range
- Minimised Range

3 Lingual Tip/Blade
- Advanced
- Retracted

4 Lingual Body
- Fronted Body
- Backed Body
- Raised Body
- Lowered Body
- Extensive Range
- Minimised Range

5 Velopharyngeal
- Nasal
- Audible Nasal Escape
- Denasal

6 Pharyngeal
- Pharyngeal Constriction

7 Supralaryngeal Tension
- Tense
- Lax

B. Laryngeal Features

8 Laryngeal Tension
- Tense
- Lax

9 Larynx Position
- Raised
- Lowered

10 Phonation Type
- Harshness
- Whisper(y)
- Breathiness
- Creak(y)
- Falsetto
- Modal Voice

II PROSODIC FEATURES

CATEGORY	FIRST PASS			SECOND PASS						
	Neutral	Non-neutral	SETTING		Scalar Degrees					
		Normal	Abnormal		Normal	Abnormal				
					1	2	3	4	5	6

1 Pitch
- High Mean
- Low Mean
- Wide Range
- Narrow Range
- High Variability
- Low Variability

2 Consistency
- Tremor

3 Loudness
- High Mean
- Low Mean
- Wide Range
- Narrow Range
- High Variability
- Low Variability

III TEMPORAL ORGANIZATION FEATURES

CATEGORY	FIRST PASS		SECOND PASS			
	Adequate	Inadequate	Scalar Degrees			
			Inadequate			
			1	2	3	

1 Continuity
- Interrupted

2 Rate
- Fast
- Slow

IV COMMENTS

	Adequate	Inadequate	1	2	3
Breath Support					
Rhythmicality					

Other Comments:

Diplophonia: Present / Absent

'VOCAL PROFILES OF SPEECH DISORDERS' Research Project (M.R.C. Grant No. G978/1192) Phonetics Laboratory, Department of Linguistics, University of Edinburgh.

© 1981

Pitch and prosody

Pitch is the auditory perception of the fundamental frequency of the voice. Generally, the fundamental frequency of the human voice descends with age, relating to the enlargement of the larynx, its descent in the neck, and respiratory development. This lowering of frequency is parallel in the male and the female until puberty when the male voice drops one full octave, due to increased enlargement of the antero-posterior dimension of the male larynx, and the female voice drops 3–5 semitones (Aronson, 1990).

Box 4.3

Vocal-parameters assessment tasks

Use tape recorder. Model task if necessary. Assess third attempt.

TASK	TO ASSESS PRIMARILY
I VOICE IMPRESSION	
Set A	Help identify organic/psychogenic
1 Observe reflex cough	quality of reflexive phonation
2 Cough (ask patient)	voluntary forced vocal adduction
3 Extend cough aa>>	discrepancy /x/ reflex/voluntary phonation
4 Throat clearing	vocal-cord adduction, quality
5 Extend throat clear mm>>	quality of 'mm'
6 Glottal stop	vocal-cord adduction
7 Whistle + 'oo' concurrently	voice quality when distracted
Set B	Gross voicing ability
1 Sustain fricative 'ss'	duration of exhalation, breathing centre, e.g. clavicular
2 shshSHSHshsh	breath support to increase volume
3 Sustain phonation 'aa', 'ee', or 'mm'	duration, consistency, quality, pitch, voice-onset time, loudness
4 Days of week, months	Voice-onset time, breath support
5 Reading passage or conversation	phrasing, breath support, overall impression of vocal ability and suitability, breathing centre

II PITCH	
1 Conversation ask re: own perceptions of pitch and any changes	appropriateness of pitch to speaker, overall prosody
2 Reading passage (standardized)	prosodic features, ability to adapt to dialogue
3 Siren	gross pitch movement ability, laryngeal movement
4 Battlements (no phonation breaks)	pitch/phonation breaks, associated changes in voice quality
5 Sing a scale up/down	discrete pitch movements, check face/neck tension, laryngeal movement, vulnerable points, pitch breaks
6 Further neuromuscular assessment indicated	

III LOUDNESS	
1 Conversation ask re: own perceptions any changes, difficulties	appropriateness to speaker and environment
2 Reading passage	gross ability to change loudness according to dialogue
3 Shout 'HEY!'	gross ability and functionality
4 Reading passage in quiet voice	phonation breaks, vulnerable points, compensating for poor quality with increased intensity
5 Count 1 2 3 4 5 on rising loudness	points of difficulty, ability to monitor loudness
6 Further neuromuscular assessment indicated	

© H. Fiona Robinson,
Nottingham 1990

In adulthood, the general trend is for the fundamental frequency to continue to descend. In the ageing population the general trend is for the female mean pitch to continue to descend, whilst in the male, the fundamental frequency will begin to rise (Hollien and Shipp, 1972; Kelly, 1977; Aronson, 1990; Wilson, 1979).

Disorders of pitch refer to high or low voices. Fundamental frequency increases as subglottic air pressure increases, the larynx rises in the neck and the vocal-cord length and tension increase. In low voices, the converse is true.

Prosody or intonation refers to the use of pitch variability to denote meaning, and is a complex interaction of physiological and language processes (Lieberman, 1967). Some neurological diseases disrupt this physiological ability and the reduced pitch variability (monotonous voice) can contribute to reduced intelligibility.

Assessment of pitch should address the appropriateness and the variability so phonatory tasks in isolation and in connected speech are used. Instrumentation (see later section) will give an accurate mean-pitch figure and the spread of formant frequencies. Without instrumentation, an impression about the appropriateness of the pitch used in relation to the patient's hypothetical norm, and the use of the pitch variations to denote meaning can still be gained.

Loudness and breath support

Loudness is the auditory perception of vocal intensity which increases as subglottic air pressure increases. For a constant loudness during speech, subglottic air pressure must be held constant (Aronson, 1990) – a complex interaction of the control of exhalation and the constancy of laryngeal musculature.

Increased loudness should be supported by increased volume and rate of exhaled air preferably by diaphragmatic breathing. Clavicular breathing is adequate for quiet conversational phonation in a quiet environment, but in itself will be inadequate to support increased loudness and compensation by excessive tension of the intrinsic and extrinsic musculature of the larynx and the face, neck, shoulders and thorax will occur. The clinician should observe and note such manifestations as part of the vocal-parameters assessment.

Some neurological disorders have reduced vocal intensity as a feature for which respiratory impairment or impaired vocal-fold adduction may be responsible. And in organic voice disorders due to a mass vocal-fold lesion, such as nodules, or a lower motor-neurone lesion resulting in a specific vocal-fold paresis, the adduction of the vocal folds is impaired so the subglottic air pressure cannot be held constant and the vocal intensity is reduced resulting in the auditory perception of a quiet voice.

Assessment of loudness should include the evaluation of the respiratory mechanism, identification of the type of breath support for phonation, reference to the function of the larynx as well as assessment tasks to expose subtle impairment, in isolation and in connected speech. Instrumentation is available to identify objectively the vocal intensity.

Quality

Quality is the most difficult vocal parameter to quantify. To date there is no instrumentation which will assess and label voice qualitatively. Johnson *et al.* (1965) state that 'quality must be pleasant'. Because of the many labels in use by clinicians it is useful to subscribe to one particular descriptive system, for example the vocal-profile analysis (Laver *et al.*, 1982). Here, the phonation types are defined as modal falsetto, whisper(y), creak(y), harshness. Some of these simple phonation types can occur alone but there is the ability to describe the voice using a combination of phonatory settings. The setting is ascribed a scalar degree – 1, 2 and 3 being normal and 4, 5 and 6 being abnormal. The extreme of each continuum represents the auditory effect corresponding to the most extreme adjustment of which the normal, non-pathological vocal apparatus is physically capable. In Hirano's (1981) classification, the five voice parameters of grade, rough, asthenic, strained and breathy are rated on a four-point scale (0 = normal, 3 = extreme problem).

Resonance

Hypernasality and nasal emission interfere with the aesthetics of speech and can seriously compromise intelligibility, producing serious psychological, educational and occupational consequences (Aronson, 1990). In the evaluation of voice the resonant quality should not be overlooked. There may be organic reasons to account for hypernasality (cleft palate, neurological disease) or hyponasality (obstruction of the nasopharynx or nasal passages) which should be confirmed by the appropriate investigations. However, it is possible that an apparent disorder of resonance can be part of a psychological voice disorder (Robinson, 1990). In these cases, once the dysphonia has recovered, usually dramatically, the clinician finds that the resonance is also absolutely normal. Therefore, the clinician should assess the resonance as a routine part of the dysphonia evaluation, and be sensitive to any changes which may occur, referring on as necessary.

INSTRUMENTATION

In the recent past, the range of electronic instrumentation, developed specifically for, or adapted to, the field of voice assessment has grown. It is beyond the scope of this chapter to analyse critically the products on the market, but there are some notable packages which most voice clinicians should be familiar with and these are noted in the references section. Most equipment in current use is now computer-aided and somewhat more portable than previously. This makes for ease of use in all environments, and the waveforms can be either stored on disc or printed as hard copy for the records or to supplement a report.

The equipment either analyses an acoustic signal with microphone input; for example, Visispeech, Visipitch (King *et al.*, 1982), which gives information about the fundamental frequency and the intensity of the voice as well as the prosodic patterns in use, or a signal from electrodes placed on either side of the larynx which measures the changing electrical resistance during the opening, open, closing, closed phases of the vocal folds in phonation; for example, Laryngograph, ELI (Abberton and Fourcin, 1984; Winstanley and Wright, 1986). Not all clinics are endowed with funding for such instrumentation, and indeed it should not deter the clinician if it is not routinely available for each new patient. Informal clinical assessment carried out using the clinician's trained and experienced ear is valid using the assessment procedures described previously, but access to this equipment is invaluable in selected cases. Cook, Hooker and Webb (1986) note that 'however ingenious, any electronic instrument can only play a limited role in voice work, being almost superfluous for example in the delicate psychological work so often needed with voice problems' (p. 1). However, the voice clinician should be aware of the usefulness of these accurate measurers of frequency (pitch and pitch range) and intensity (loudness) in clinical practice when problems with these particular parameters are specifically indicated, for example, in the assessment of acceptable pitch in the transsexual client, the use of appropriate loudness in vocal-abuse cases and voice function in the deaf client.

Obviously, for research purposes, objective measures are essential and this equipment is useful, despite its limitations. However, no measure of the voice quality in the pure sense is possible, and the interpretation of the waveforms relating to vocal-fold movement is dependent upon the experience of the clinician and the accurate placement of the electrodes.

Greene and Mathieson (1989) include details of instrumentation for objective assessment and biofeedback of vocal-fold function, vocal-tract imaging, acoustic analysis, airflow and volume measurement, as well as nasal resonance and amplification, and this text is recommended for further reading.

SUMMARY

The complex aetiology of a voice disorder necessitates a broad-based and methodical assessment process. The speech and language therapist receives information from the other disciplines investigating the patient and his or her dysphonia. Although it is vital to have these opinions the speech-and-language-therapist assessments contribute the bulk of the information about the functionality of the pathological voice.

But the voice clinician is not the 'end of the line' as far as the assessment process goes. During his or her own evaluation, the clinician is at liberty to seek confirmation of findings and further investigations from the team, whose membership changes according to the requirements of individual cases.

The speech-and-language-therapy assessment process comprises a battery of informal and formal procedures to elicit the necessary data. In the case-history interviews, there is a real opportunity to establish a therapeutic relationship with the patient. Additionally, factors pertaining to both the organic and psychological elements at play can be revealed in an informal but structured way, using a check-list as an *aide-mémoire*.

There may be useful access to instrumentation for voice analysis, but just as important is a clear concept and understanding of the parameters of normal voice for any given speaker. Using a standard acoustic-perceptual format, the pathological voice can be set against the expectations of normalcy for that speaker.

Tape-recordings (and print-outs from computer-aided analysis if available) form an essential part of data gathering and aid subsequent analysis and review.

The assessment process of the dysphonic patient appears lengthy and perhaps piecemeal. However, the speech and language therapist is uniquely placed to bring together the findings of the other disciplines with his or her own, to interpret the data and to differentially diagnose the problem, thus subsequently offering recommendations for intervention and future management.

REFERENCES

Abberton, E. and Fourcin, A. (1984). 'Electrolaryngography'. In C. Code and M. Ball (eds), *Experimental Clinical Phonetics*. London: Croom Helm.

Aronson, A. E. (1990). *Clinical Voice Disorders* (3rd edn). New York: Thieme

Bless, D. M. (1987). 'Voice disorders in the adult: assessment'. In R. Kent and D. E. Yoder (eds), *Decision Making in Speech-language Pathology*. Toronto: Brian Decker.

Cook, J., Hooker, D. and Webb, J. (1986). 'The application of the Visispeech to pathologies of voice'. *Bulletin of the College of Speech Therapists*, 4, 11, July.

Enderby, P. (1980). 'Frenchay dysarthria assessment'. *British Journal of Disorder of Communication*, 15.3.

Garvel, M. J. (1981). 'The effects of drugs on speech'. *British Journal of Disorder of Communication*, 16.1.

Greene, M. and Mathieson, L. (1989). *The Voice and Its Disorders* (5th edn). London: Whurr.

Hirano, M. (1981). *Clinical Examination of Voice*. New York and Vienna: Springer.

Hollien, H. and Shipp, T. (1972). 'Speaking fundamental frequency and chronologic age in males'. *Journal of Speech and Hearing Research*, 15, 155–9.

Johnson, W., Brown, S. F., Curtis, J. F., Edney, C. W. and Keaster, J. (1965). *Speech Handicapped Children*. New York: Harper & Bros.

Kelly, A. (1977). 'Fundamental frequency measurements of female voices from twenty to ninety years of age'. (Unpublished manuscript). Greensboro: University of North Carolina.

King, Parker, Spanner, Wright (1982). 'A speech display computer for use in schools for the deaf'. *IEEE Proceedings*.

Laver, J. (1980). *The Phonetic Description of Normal Voice.* Cambridge: Cambridge University Press.

Laver, J., Wirz, S., Mackenzie, J. and Hiller, S. (1982) 'Vocal Profiles Analysis Scheme'. MRC Grant G/978/1192/N. (Revised 1988.)

Lieberman, P. (1967). *Intonation, Perception and Language.* Cambridge, Mass: MIT Press.

MacCurtain, F., Evans, E., Cassidy, C., Morgan, R., Commins, J. and Valery, M. (1988). 'Computer-assisted voice instrumentation'. Unpublished manuscript.

Moore, G. P. (1971). *Organic Voice Disorders.* Englewood Cliffs, N.J.: Prentice-Hall.

Morgan, D. A. L., Robinson, H. F., Marsh, L. and Bradley, P. J. (1988). 'Vocal quality 10 years after radiotherapy for early glottic carcinoma'. *Conference Proceedings and Clinical Radiology,* 39, 295–6. Southampton: British Institute of Radiology.

Prytz, S. (n.d.) 'Laryngostroboscopy'. ENT Department, Rigshospitalet, Denmark.

Robinson, H. F. (1990). Unpublished case notes.

Robinson, H. F. and Bradley P. J. (1987). 'A joint approach to functional dysphonia'. Proceedings of the College of Speech Therapists' National Conference, Exeter.

Robinson, H. F., Bradley, P. J. and Heritage, M. (1990). 'Total voice rest in a regime of management for vocal nodules'. Proceedings of the International Seminar on Care of the Professional Voice, Ferens Institute of Laryngology, University of London.

Simpson, I. C. (1971). 'Dysphonia: the organisation and working of a dysphonia clinic'. *BJDC,* 6.1, April.

Wilson, K. (1979). *Voice Problems of Children.* Baltimore: Williams & Wilkins.

Winstanley, S. and Wright, H. (1986). 'The portable electro-laryngograph: a further development of its use in the clinic'. *Bulletin of the College of Speech Therapists,* November.

5

ASSESSMENT OF
STAMMERING

Armin Kuhr and Lena Rustin

Traditionally, stammering has been seen as a disorder in which the forward flow of speech is impaired by interruptions. The 'individual knows precisely what he wishes to say, but at the time is unable to say it because of an involuntary repetition, prolongation or cessation of sound' (*International Classification of Diseases*, 9th revision, 1978, p. 1123). For the purpose of a preliminary diagnosis this definition is sufficient. However, if decisions on treatment recommendations are to be made, a full assessment is necessary. This should enable the clinician to obtain a comprehensive picture of the impairment and arrive at a formulation that includes theoretically based hypotheses on the origin and maintenance of the undesired behaviour. The scope of the assessment should be broad, as it has not been possible to establish clear-cut aetiological factors in stammering. No single theory is able to provide a full explanation of the disorder. The position which most researchers in the field adhere to is that stammering is caused by genetic, organic and environmental factors. Thus, any assessment should take account of all these components including overt motorical, biological, cognitive-behavioural and systems components.

This chapter seeks to present a comprehensive structure that allows the therapist to collect data on all relevant dimensions of stammering in order to devise appropriate treatment strategies for children, adolescents and adults.

The information gained during the diagnostic interview should lead to a clear understanding of the speech disorder's relevant dimensions and provide the basis on which the therapist can support or refute hypotheses on the development and maintenance of the stammer and any related problems. The relative importance of the major problem areas is estimated and a rationale for selecting the appropriate intervention can be formulated. The interaction between assessment and therapy should be seen as a continuing process in which therapeutic interventions are re-evaluated and revised as new information comes to light. Any changes in strategy that are necessary would, however, have to be restricted to a minimum in order not to undermine the client's confidence in the therapeutic approach. Box 5.1 illustrates how treatment may have to concentrate on aspects not at first sight relevant to stammering.

> **Box 5.1**
>
> *Treatment of stammering and other problems*
>
> A thirteen-year-old boy was sent to therapy by his parents. He had started stammering for the first time about six months previously. Difficulties at school and conflicts with classmates were concomitant with the onset of stammering. It was decided to concentrate on the modification of his stammering behaviour which proved unsuccessful in his everyday life. However, when he was given help to cope with his school problems and to solve conflicts, his self-confidence improved and the stammer disappeared without any further symptomatic therapy.

At the end of the initial interview the therapist should have the necessary information to decide whether he or she can offer a course of therapy. Preliminary hypotheses on the aetiology of the stammer and its maintainance can be presented, including suggestions for the basic structure and content of therapy: important goals; choice of targets for direct therapeutic work; planning of specific interventions and preliminary order of treatment steps as well as possibly a comment on the prognosis. At this stage the therapist points out that the original plan might be altered as therapy proceeds. This may be due to unforeseeable experiences occurring during therapy which might require goals to be changed. It is important to note that the clinician's ability to present a well structured and acceptable treatment plan can be a powerful beginning to the therapy process.

It is not always possible to obtain all relevant information during the first interview. This is not only due to lack of time but because clients might have difficulty 'opening up' at the first meeting. Some clients have problems discussing their stammer both intellectually and emotionally and the therapist therefore needs to be sensitive to this by creating an atmosphere of mutual respect and understanding, in other words, by meeting clients at their level. This helps to establish a therapeutic alliance and to promote fruitful co-operation.

PRACTICAL CONSIDERATIONS FOR CONDUCTING THE INTERVIEW

In order for the stammerer and/or family to feel as comfortable as possible during the interview, it is advisable to arrange the seating so that therapist and client face each other without a desk between them and not too close or too distant. Apart from the feeling of comfort for the client, it gives the therapist the opportunity to observe the client easily. A description of how the interview will be conducted should be given so that all those involved know what to expect.

Due to the complexity of stammering, a variety of methods may be used to collect the necessary information. Usually, in the first instance, the adult client is interviewed and the therapist will need to set aside ample time

---

Box 5.2

Interview for adults

1 Why did the client come for help (was it a planned decision, or forced compliance); what is their understanding of therapy; what are his or her goals; what time and effort is he or she willing to invest; knowledge of stammering
2 Analysis of dysfluency
3 Factors that affect stammering and general speaking behaviour: what are the reactions to communicative stress (e.g. hurry, interruptions, misunderstanding, listener loss); what situations are feared and why are they feared (e.g. speaking on the telephone or in small groups)
4 Functional analysis: what are the client's attitudes and emotional reactions toward stammering and speech; motivation for therapy; self-image (description of strengths and weaknesses); secondary gains (interpersonal and intrapersonal)
5 History of speech and language development and stammering: time and circumstances of onset (initial characteristics, reactions of listeners, etc.), fluctuations, remissions; former therapies, relapses; awareness and reactions of client over time, related events
6 Environmental considerations: familial stammering; where does the client live, work and socialize; social status; current social network (including spouses and intimate relationships, family); satisfaction with current life (past/present ambitions); how is leisure time spent (of own choosing); what are the limitations and opportunities which might affect therapy; how does he or she respond to his or her environment
7 Social interaction: communication skills (e.g. eye contact, listening, turn-taking – non-verbal cueing)
8 General background: siblings; birth order; parents still alive; intrafamilial relationships (description of siblings, parents); basic educational goals of parents; any other adults; who played an important part in client's life; childhood fears; academic performance; relationships in school and at work; sexual experiences
9 General health: past and present; use of drugs, alcohol; eating habits; physical exercise
10 Exploration of other significant problems which client might have; specific behaviours, actions or habits client would like to change.

Box 5.3

Interview for adolescents and children

1 Present complaint:
   a Why are you here today? Who instigated the visit? Any previous speech therapy? What happens when you stammer?
   b Other problems: with parents, siblings, teachers, etc.
   c First language
   d When is speech really bad/when is it good? When did stammer start? Is there anything you can do to help yourself?

2 School:
   a Attitude – whether they like it or not.
   b Teaching staff – any very good or bad – for what reasons.
   c Subject – favourite, worst, any exams pending?
   d Any academic difficulties?

3 Social interaction:
   a Friends – at home or school? What do you like doing with them? Do you see them out of school?
   b Bullying: does he/she get bullied. Do they bully?
   c Teasing: is this a problem/how do they cope with it?
   d Hobbies.

4 Home/Parents:
   Do parents get on? How does client get on with mother/father? What do you do together as a family or with each parent separately? Do they help you with problems? Position in family, how they get on, which is favourite? How does the stammer affect the family?

5 Interests:
   How do they spend evenings, do they belong to any clubs or organizations, part-time job? Pocket money (how much) and how it is spent. Any pets?

6 Concepts:
   Best thing that ever happened? Worst thing that ever happened? To whom would you go if you had a problem? If you could change one thing in your life what would it be? How would your life be different if you didn't stammer? Do you want help with your speech? Is your stammer recognized and discussed at home?

(60–90 minutes) in order to arrive at sound conclusions. The interview will need to be well structured, without digressions and should not be conducted randomly or aimlessly. It is important that the client has confidence in the therapist's ability and expertise as this will obviously affect the client–therapist relationship. During the interview the therapist is able to observe and make notes of their general interaction. Box 5.2 provides guidelines for the initial interview for adults.

Behavioural check-lists and questionnaires (Brutten, 1973) can be a helpful way of gaining further information, and are available for adults, parents, adolescents and children (Cooper and Cooper, 1985). Some of the forms can be filled in as homework tasks, thus saving therapy time. When dealing with children and adolescents, both parents should be fully involved in the interview as well as the child. If possible, two therapists should be involved with the interview; one to assess the parents and one to assess the child. The assessment should, if possible, be completed in one session which will need to be extended to approximately two and a half hours. If this is not possible the stammerer should be interviewed first and the parents on a separate occasion. Box 5.3 provides guidelines for interviewing the child or adolescent and therapists should select those questions appropriate to the age of the stammerer.

In the event that it is a one-parent family, then only the parent bringing up the child would be involved. We are not suggesting that a standardized approach should necessarily be used for the parental-assessment procedure but hope the following questions formulated in Box 5.4 will be helpful guidelines for the therapist.

Box 5.4

Interview for parents

1 Present complaint:
   a Stammering plus any other problems.
   b Description of stammer including frequency, severity, context, parents' and family's reaction and reason for seeking help.

2 General health and developmental history:
   Child's overall health including eating, sleeping, speech and general development. Antenatal history.

3 Child's relationships:
   With siblings, other family members, and adults. How is affection shown, his or her general sociability and any anti-social trends.

4 Family structure, history:
   How parents relate, occupation, education, general health and emotional state. Any difficulties in their own speech, language and learning development. Discussion of parents' background and any extended family issues including separations. Description of home and financial circumstances.

5 Family life:
   Child's participation in family, parent/child interaction, discipline, pocket money, restrictions within family. How child reacts to problems. How do parents resolve problems within the family? The rate of parents' speech should be noted, as well as any future impending changes. This would include change of school, moving house, any close friends or relations who are very ill or may die.

89

Notes should be taken during the initial interview as the information gained will be quite extensive – it might even be advisable to audiotape or videotape this session for later recall when deciding on therapy strategies, and permission for this should be obtained.

In addition to the interview, the therapist will require a standard assessment of the client's speech and language skills, the basic equipment for this is: cassette recorder, microphone, recording tapes, tally-counter to count stammered syllables, stopwatch, reading material for different age groups, attitude scales and any other speech and language tests that may be required, particularly for children and adolescents.

FUNCTIONAL DIAGNOSIS OF STAMMERING SYMPTOMS

Wingate's (1964) list of the core elements of stammering is widely accepted and many practical measuring systems have been based on his criteria:

1   repetitions (unitary – of one sound or syllable: multiple-unit)
2   silent prolongations or involuntary hesitations
3   audible prolongations
4   interjections
5   broken words
6   speech-related concomitant movements of speech mechanism and/or body
7   associated observable features (tension, strong emotions)

Box 5.5 lists the symptomatic behaviour that will need to be taken into account in the descriptive diagnosis.

A sample of speech should be tape-recorded for analysis of stammered

---

Box 5.5

Symptomatic behaviour in the descriptive diagnosis of stammering

All clients, whether adults, adolescents or children will require an analysis of dysfluency: oral reading, monologue, dialogue. Observation of speech production and associated behaviours – blocks, repetitions, tension, synchronization of phonation, articulation and respiration, initiating phonation, improper co-articulation, symptomatic avoidances like starters, postponements, specific avoidance of sounds, words, people, situations, loci of stammers (sounds, words, position). Associated behaviours or mannerisms. Voluntary efforts to control the stammer. Analysis of speech production: rate, rhythm, stress, pitch, response length, amount of daily output.

syllables (SS%) and rate of syllables spoken per minute (SPM). Stammered syllables should be counted live during the assessment on the tally-counter and all syllables spoken should be counted from the tape-recording. The following calculations should then be made:

$$SPM = \frac{\text{number of stammered and fluent syllables}}{\text{time in minutes}}$$

$$SS\% = \frac{\text{number of stammered syllables} \times 100}{\text{number of stammered and fluent syllables}}$$

The sample of speech that is recorded will vary according to the age and abilities of the client but should take into account a variety of tasks and/or settings. A preschool child would be tape-recorded during a play session with either the parent or the therapist. An older child might be more formally tested on a fluency interview (Rustin, 1987), including samples of automatic and imitative speech as well as reading, monologue and conversation. For adults it could be two minutes' reading, monologue and conversation as well as speaking on the telephone or in any other pressurized situation. From the recorded speech samples the clinician should also note differences in prosody, inappropriate or incorrect patterns of rhythm, inflection or stress, starters or postponements (these are devices that delay the onset of speech if a stammer is expected). Many stammerers, particularly adults, are able to predict problems quite accurately and may employ a wide variety of means to avoid them. These could include:

1   using filler words or syllables (e.g. 'and', 'er') and extraneous movements (struggle behaviour)
2   word avoidance (replacing difficult words by synonyms)
3   generally speaking little or speaking less in difficult situations
4   using cognitive strategies (e.g. self-suggestion including instructions for self-relaxation like 'I can speak, I am quite calm', anti-expectation strategies – 'don't think of it')
5   preparing each conversation intensively

There is considerable evidence from treatment studies (Ingham, 1984), congruent with clinical experience, that the degree of stammering varies markedly between different situations. Therefore, it is important to identify these variables as they have a bearing on the choice of specific therapy targets:

1   social stimuli (presence of conversation partners, especially people in authority, number of communication partners, negative listener reactions)
2   situational stimuli (at home, at school, in the workplace, on the telephone)
3   speech material (reading, picture description, spontaneous speaking)

4   organismic variables (excitement, tension, restlessness, fatigue)
5   cognitive variables (communication intention and responsibility, self-perception)

In order to identify difficult speaking situations efficiently a self-rating system might be used such as Shumak (1955) or Ham (1986).

Having taken samples of the stammerer's speech, the therapist will need to experiment with a variety of speech-modification techniques to establish those that would be easiest for the client to use effectively. The therapist should first model a technique, then repeat it together with the client and finally clients should try it on their own. These may range from reducing the rate of utterance, to altering air flow, making easier articulations, softening hard contacts, prolonging the articulation or any combination of these.

The measurement of severity is usually based on a global assessment to ascertain the degree of impairment in the stammerer's ability to use speech for social and vocational purposes. Different factors are included in such a rating, like frequency and average duration of stammering incidents and rate of speech. There are some assessment instruments that measure severity specifically, for instance the scale by Johnson, Darley and Spriestersbach (1963), which takes into account the amount of stammering, duration of stammer, type of stammer (repetitions being rated less severe than blocks) and tension. Cooper and Cooper (1985) proposed criteria of severity which are: frequency, duration, consistency across speech situations, concomitant behaviours and handicapping reactive attitudes and feelings. Starkweather (1987) has suggested 'that stammering should be assessed in three ways – the rate at which meaningful speech is produced, the ease with which meaningful speech is produced, and the impact of the disorder on listeners' (p. 130). The use of severity scales has declined in recent years; the main reason being that they are cumbersome to administer without providing substantial additional information. Largely, they have been replaced by frequency-count measures which have been shown to correlate highly with severity scales (Ingham, 1984). The relationship of syllable rate to stammering would normally be inverse: the higher the frequency, the lower the speaking rate.

In young children it is very important to determine whether the child is a potential chronic stammerer or in a transitional phase of normal dysfluency. To differentiate between developmental and impending chronic stammering, we use criteria which are derived from the literature (Adams, 1980) and our clinical experience. If any or all of the following are present then it is more likely to be early stammering behaviour:

1   part-word repetitions and prolongations occur on at least 5 per cent of all words spoken
2   part-word repetitions involve more than 2–4 unit repetitions

3 part-word repetitions contain a schwa rather than the target vowel
4 prolongations exceed 25 per cent of dysfluency total
5 concomitant movements (struggle behaviour)
6 observable signs of negative effective reactions to speech with subsequent avoidance
7 parental anxiety

There are cases in which a clear, unequivocal diagnosis cannot be made, and a prophylactic approach is advisable. The parents will need counselling sessions and should continue to be seen at regular intervals for reassessment with the emphasis firmly placed on 'prevention'.

Making the differentiation between stammering and cluttering can sometimes be difficult because in some cases there is evidence of both stammering and cluttering behaviour (Daly, 1986). Clutterers typically present a much broader picture of deficit in speech and language skills. They talk at a fast, irregular rate, slighting or omitting consonants, displaying syllable elisions, ignoring punctuation, neglecting phrasing, omitting or inserting syllables and words, using incorrect sentence structure, breathing at inappropriate points and demonstrating irregular stress patterns. Clutterers have difficulties in self monitoring and are often not fully aware of dysfluencies; they tend to have a short attention span and poor concentration but are carefree and uninhibited in spite of the speech problem. Unlike stammerers, clutterers tend to become more fluent when attention is drawn to the self and are generally better at reading tasks, whereas stammerers in most cases are better in spontaneous speech (Ham, 1986).

There is some evidence that children who stammer seem to differ from their normally fluent peers in terms of overall neuromotor development. Studies done by Conture and his associates – for example, Conture and Kelly (1994) – have confirmed that these differences are subtle and that it is as yet unknown how these disruptions in speech production can be influenced therapeutically. Behavioural neuromotor testing may not be sufficiently sensitive to assess brief disruptions in speech. However, it is advisable to test for the ability to control co-ordination and timing of respiratory, phonatory and articulatory processes. Riley and Riley (1985) published the oral motor assessment scale to evaluate 'correct voicing, smooth co-articulation, proper sequencing and age-appropriate rate of syllables'. They claimed that this test would help detect 'oral motor disco-ordination' in children and enable the therapist to implement appropriate motoric training. Conversely, Wingate (1988) feels that stammering should not just be seen as a disruption of speech motor processes but that it involves more central functions of the language-production system. Linguistic factors which he feels are important and that should consequently be assessed are lexical access (word search and retrieval), stammering in relation to syntax, grammatical class of the stammered words, their length and position in a sentence and propositionality of an utterance. Clients who show signs of neurological impairment such as clumsiness and abnormal tone asymmetry of movement or involuntary movements might need to be referred for in-depth neurological or psychomotoric assessment.

OTHER COMPONENTS

Time constraints demand that in clinical practice the assessment procedures should be as concise and brief as possible and limited to those factors that are judged to be critical for clinical management. Depending on the age of the client, different importance will be attached to different aspects of personality or environmental variables. Even though no general differences in personality traits have been found between stammerers and fluent speakers (Andrews *et al.*, 1983), it is nevertheless of great importance to assess habitual behavioural patterns. This will provide the therapist with insights into the client's generalized reactions to stressful situations, as degree of assertiveness, level of frustration tolerance and achievement motivation, among others, will influence cognitions, emotions and behaviour.

It is well documented (Bloodstein, 1987) that the speech of stammerers is affected by their emotional state, such as social anxiety. According to current models of cognitive processes (Dobson, 1988), clients can be helped to reduce their levels of anxiety by altering their underlying thoughts. To identify negative self-statements and irrational beliefs, clients could produce a verbal or written report of their 'internal dialogue' for discussion with the therapist. In order to identify the self-image of a client, Kelly's self-characterization could be used:

> I want you to write a character sketch of Harry Brown, just as if he were the principal character in a play. Write it as it might be written by a friend who knew him very intimately and very sympathetically perhaps better than anyone could ever really know him. Be sure to write it in the third person. For example, start out by saying 'Harry Brown is ...'

(Kelly, 1955: 323)

The use of more formal methods of assessing personality and emotional state through protocol analysis or structured measures is not necessary unless the assessment is needed for research purposes (Arnkoff and Glass, 1989).

The assessment should include some measurement of social skills. Just being fluent will not necessarily be enough – a fluent person who is unable to interact well will have problems communicating satisfactorily and this poor social interaction could sabotage maintenance of fluency. The importance of social skills has been shown by Rustin (1984) who found that social skills and technique-training, combined on an intensive course for adolescents, was of benefit to the maintenance of fluency. This study also demonstrated that adolescents receiving social-skills training only, did nearly as well as those using only technique-training. Rustin and Kuhr (1989) state 'that the goal of social skills assessment should help to identify necessary changes in the client's social interactions' (p. 57). This is particularly relevant to stammerers as they often have difficulties with appropriate eye contact, initiation of conversation and topic maintenance, interrupting, turn-taking, inappropriate body language and poor listening skills. There are various methods of measuring social skills and the therapist should select the most appropriate. These range from therapist's rating scales on various aspects of the client's social interactions, such as eye contact, posture, topic maintenance and so on. These ratings may be taken from role-plays, video-recordings, or direct behavioural observations in a variety of settings (Rustin and Kuhr, 1989: 65). There are self-report questionnaires to enable the client to rate his or her own performance (Rathus, 1973), as well as questionnaires available for teachers, parents, carers and so on (Walker, 1970) which give additional insight into others' perceptions of the client's social skills.

Many stammerers, both adults and children, have often had a long history of unsuccessful therapies that would affect their view of treatment and themselves negatively. Ultimately, this might have led to very low self-respect and a sense of helplessness and possibly hopelessness. Since the stammerer's attitudes towards communication are obviously an important part of the disorder, it would be useful to measure them effectively. The therapist might use a scale like the S24 (Andrews and Cutler, 1974) to learn about the extent of a stammerer's conviction that he or she is speech-handicapped. The client is presented with a series of statements to which he or she should answer true or false, for instance 'I usually feel that I am making a favourable impression when I talk'; 'I find it hard to make talk when I meet new people'.

As long as the client's abilities appear to fall within the normal or above-normal range, it would not be necessary to carry out a full, detailed IQ assessment. However, if there are doubts, then testing would be advisable as intellectual deficits might influence the choice of treatment. It is of particular importance that children should be identified who have speech and language and/or reading, writing and spelling difficulties as these could cause them serious problems in the school setting (Rustin and Klein, 1989) and would need to be addressed in the therapy process.

Most therapists who work regularly with stammerers have some experience with 'covert stammerers'. These clients have built such an elaborate system of word or sound avoidances, that family, friends or colleagues are not fully aware of the extent of the stammering problem. These interiorized stammerers are so committed to keeping their speech impediment secret that they might show up as mild stammerers during the symptomatic assessment. The evaluation of their cognitions, however, should alert the therapist to the true extent of the problem. In such cases it is sometimes quite difficult to find common ground regarding agreed goals for therapy, as the client often wishes to supress the stammer whereas the clinician normally recommends bringing it into the open. This might be deeply threatening for the client and so jeopardize the therapy process.

A functional analysis of behaviour, based on a behavioural analytic approach that is essentially derived from learning therapy, endeavours to ascertain the explicit environmental and historical variables which contribute to the present stammering. The assumption seems justified that these factors play an important part in how a client, whether child or adult, might achieve and maintain fluency. It is necessary, therefore, to gain information about the stammerer's family and life-style in order to understand the external determinants of current functioning and develop strategies concerning necessary changes that might need to be implemented before training in fluency techniques can begin. When dealing with children or adolescents, the parents obviously play a key role in the initial interview, whereas with adults the family may not be involved until later in treatment. The following elements should be included when interviewing parents:

1 parental perceptions as to the nature of the child's problems, concerns and goals
2 identifying factors eliciting and maintaining stammering and possibly other problem behaviours
3 obtaining historical information about the development of stammering and any previous treatment
4 giving parents information regarding the nature of stammering, in terms of prevalence, prognosis and possible aetiologies
5 providing the parents with a rationale for the proposed intervention and suggesting realistic goals

Much has been written concerning the parents of stammering children. Contradictions persist but these parents tend to be more competitive and perfectionistic, often setting very high standards for their children. Mothers may be less successful in creating or maintaining a well-balanced home environment thereby putting undue pressure on their child's speech development (Bloodstein, 1987). The parents' willingness and ability to help the child with his stammer are of prime importance as they will be required to take an active role in the therapy process. Therapists will also need to look for elements in the family system that could sabotage therapy and consider how to work with the family to prevent this. Additionally it has to be taken into account that young children through to adolescents are not necessarily seeking therapy of their own volition, which might affect their motivation to co-operate in treatment. Adult stammering clients may have partners who want to be involved in the therapeutic process. The degree of involvement will depend on the wishes of the client and the therapist should be sensitive to any changes in role the partners may experience as a result of therapy. Specific problems in work and social situations may need to be explored in order to experiment with alternative coping strategies.

CONCLUSION

Assessment not only marks the beginning of therapy but is an on-going process that should be implemented regularly and consistently throughout the acquisition, transfer, maintenance and follow-up phases of therapy. Assessment as an integral part of treatment contributes to an increasingly detailed picture of the problem, measures progress and directs therapy. This does not mean that therapy is always a 'logically' sequenced series of steps. Even if the functional analysis indicates which basic problems are relevant to the stammering symptom it may not always be advisable to deal with these immediately. Sometimes the client may not be ready to have these specific problems addressed by the therapist. A statement such as 'you need your stammer to explain your professional failure' may lead to resistance on the part of the client and give him or her the feeling that he or she is not being taken seriously. Despite the therapist's feeling that such a hypothesis is highly probable it might be better to proceed from the symptom, thus allowing the client to work at his or her own level. As treatment proceeds, the therapist will discover whether the original assumption was correct.

REFERENCES

Adams, M. R. (1980). 'The young stutterer: diagnosis, treatment and assessment of progress'. In W. Perkins (ed.), *Strategies of Stuttering Therapy*. New York: Thieme & Stratton.

Andrews, G., Craig, A., Feyer, A. M., Hoddinott, S., Howie, P. and Neilson, M. (1983). 'Stuttering: a review of research, findings and theories'. *Journal of Speech and Hearing Disorders*, 48, 226–46.

Andrews, G. and Cutler, J. (1974). 'Stuttering therapy: the relation between changes in symptom level and attitudes'. *Journal of Speech and Hearing Disorders*, 39, 312–19.

Arnkoff, D. B. and Glass, C. R. (1989). 'Cognitive assessment in social anxiety and social phobia'. *Clinical Psychology Review*, 9, 61–74.

Bloodstein, O. (1987). *A Handbook on Stuttering*. Chicago: National Easter Seal Society.

Brutten, G. J. (1973). 'Behavior assessment and the strategy of therapy'. In Y.

Lebrun and R. Hoops (eds), *Neurolinguistic Approach to Stuttering*. The Hague: Mouton.

Conture, E. and Kelly, M. (1994). 'Research regarding the speech production of young stutterers: implications for treatment strategies'. In L. Rustin (ed.), *Parents, Families and Stuttering Children*. Leicester: Far Communications.

Cooper, E. B. and Cooper, C. S. (1985). *Cooper Personalized Fluency Control Therapy Revised*. Allen, TX: DLM Teaching Resources.

Daly, D. A. (1986). 'The clutterer'. In K. O. St Louis (ed.), *The Atypical Stutterer*. Orlando: Academic Press.

Dobson, K. S. (ed.) (1988). *Handbook of Cognitive Behavioural Therapies*. New York: Guilford Press.

Ham, R. (1986). *Techniques of Stuttering Therapy*. Englewood Cliffs, NJ: Prentice-Hall.

Ingham, R. J. (1984). *Stuttering and Behaviour Therapy: current status and experimental foundations*. San Diego, CA: College-Hill Press.

International Classification of Disease, Clinical Modifications. Vol. 1, 9th revision, (1978). Ann Arbor, Michigan: Edwards Brothers.

Johnson, W., Darley, F. L. and Spriesterbach, D. C. (1963). *Diagnostic Methods in Speech Pathology*. New York: Harper & Row.

Kelly, G. A. (1955). *The Psychology of Personal Constructs*. New York: Norton.

Rathus, S. A. (1973). 'A 30-item schedule for assessing assertive behaviour'. *Behavior Therapy*, 4, 398–406.

Riley, G. D. and Riley, J. (1985). 'Oral motor discoordination among children with fluency and phonological disorders'. Paper presented at the annual conference of American Speech and Hearing Association, Washington.

Rustin, L. (1984). 'Intensive treatment models for adolescent stuttering: a comparison of social skills training and speech fluency techniques'. M.Phil. thesis (Unpublished). De Montfort University.

Rustin, L. (1987). *Assessment and Therapy Programme for Dysfluent Children*. Windsor: NFER-NELSON.

Rustin, L. and Klein, H. (1989). 'Language difficulties in adolescent stutterers: some observations'. Paper presented at the conference of the International Association of Logopaedists and Phoniatrists, Prague.

Rustin, L. and Kuhr, A. (1989). *Social Skills and the Speech Impaired*. London: Taylor & Francis.

Shumak, I. C. (1955). 'A speech situation rating sheet for stutterers'. In W. Johnson and R. R. Leutenegger (eds), *Stuttering in Children and Adults*. Minneapolis: University of Minnesota Press.

Starkweather, C. W. (1987). *Fluency and Stuttering*. Englewood Cliffs, NJ: Prentice Hall.

Walker, H. M. (1970). *Walker Problem Behaviour Identification Checklist*. Los Angeles, CA: Western Psychological Services.

Wingate, M. E. (1964). 'Recovery from stuttering'. *Journal of Speech and Hearing Disorders*, 29, 312–21.

Wingate, M. E. (1988). *The Structure of Stuttering: a psycholinguistic analysis*. New York: Springer.

6

ASSESSMENT OF ACQUIRED LANGUAGE PROBLEMS

Jean Kerr

Assessment is one of the primary functions of the speech and language therapist, because of its importance in making a communication diagnosis, guiding subsequent management and treatment, and measuring the efficacy of intervention (Byng *et al.*, 1990; Chapey, 1981). Management that is based on inadequate, irrelevant, poorly constructed or sketchily recorded assessment is unlikely to be efficacious (David, 1990), nor can its effects be demonstrated without accurate baseline measures.

Thus, 'getting it right' is one of the first things the speech and language therapist attempts to do. This task is made difficult by the many aims that need to be served, the wealth of material available, the conflicts between the rationales underlying many assessments and rapid advances in knowledge within a variety of differing theoretical frameworks.

What follows is an attempt to summarize the historical development of the major approaches, outline the aims of testing and describe assessments currently available in the contexts in which they might be used. Due to constraints of space, it is not possible to give detailed accounts of the theory or composition of assessments. Critiques of many published tests are included later in this book; readers are directed to these and to the test manuals themselves. Wherever possible, further reading is suggested that expands on issues raised in the text.

Neither has it been possible to outline the management implications of assessment results, although it is acknowledged that these are of primary importance to the working therapist. Management and suitable treatment techniques are discussed in some detail in much of the literature cited, however, and it is hoped that the reader will refer to them; in particular, attention is directed to Byng *et al.* (1990), Franklin (1989) and Howard *et al.* (1985).

TERMINOLOGY

The starting point for any investigation is a definition of terms. Broadly, assessment may be anything that provides data about the nature of the problem and the patient's performance. Thus, it can include observation and questionnaires, as well as controlled testing of specific skills. The quality and usefulness of the information gathered depends on how it is gathered and how it is interpreted.

The term 'acquired language problems' is usually synonymous with that of aphasia. Definitions vary, but in its pure form this is a difficulty across all language modalities, that is, speech output, auditory comprehension, reading comprehension and writing, that arises due to acquired brain damage, and is not itself caused by motor impairment, sensory problems or intellectual deficits (Head, 1926; Schuell, 1965). In practice, some acquired language problems differ qualitatively from those traditionally labelled 'dysphasia', for example in the case of head-injured patients (Hagen, 1984; Holland, 1982). More importantly, language problems may be confused with other deficits, and frequently coexist with other problems, as has been pointed out by many authors (e.g. Chapey, 1981; Schuell, 1965). Immediately, the importance of differentiating the nature of the presenting problems becomes obvious. Differential diagnosis is one of the main aims of initial assessment, and the need to check the presence, nature and degree of associated problems and discriminate between them and language deficits dictates that such functions as vision, hearing, memory, and orofacial (oral and facial combined) motor skills may also need testing. Brief descriptions of such testing are included later in this chapter, and the need to discriminate between underlying causes of disability is stressed throughout.

PATHOLOGY

Assessment varies with causative pathology, in order to address the particular problems of that group and yield information useful in planning management. This chapter will concentrate primarily on assessment appropriate for cerebrovascular accident (CVA) and head-injured populations, as these are the commonest causes of acquired language problems. Data on the incidence of specific disorder are difficult to collect and analyse accurately, as Enderby and Philipp (1986) have pointed out. Moreover, 'speech' and 'language' problems tend to be lumped together, particularly in the case of adults, and therefore information regarding the incidence of aphasia alone is difficult to extract. Nevertheless, it is clear that CVA is the commonest cause (Chapey, 1981). Enderby and Philipp (1986) calculated that there may be 11,400 new dysphasic patients per year in Britain following CVA, and estimated a 30 per cent prevalence of speech and language problems in the CVA population. In younger age groups, head injury is a major cause of acquired language problems. Field research by the DHSS found that in almost half of the 15 per cent of survivors of head injury who experienced speech disturbances 'the dysphasia was prolonged' (cited in Enderby and Philipp, 1986: 161). Enderby and Philipp estimated 10,500 new cases of persistent dysphasia caused by head injury in England and Wales each year, and pointed out that all figures regarding head injury were probably underestimates.

HISTORICAL PERSPECTIVE

The aims and composition of aphasia assessments have always reflected the theoretical bias of the authors and prevailing wisdom regarding language impairment. Understandably, the construction of tests has also depended upon the current understanding of the methodology of assessment (Byng *et al.*, 1990).

What follows is an attempt to summarize the development of the major formal assessments and the theories that underpin them. For greater detail the reader is recommended to read Howard and Hatfield (1987), Messick (1980) and the Clinical Forum in *Aphasiology* (1990).

Philosophy and development of assessment procedures

Early testing, often carried out by physicians, was an attempt to define the problems underlying acquired language disorders, in order to increase understanding of brain pathology and normal brain function. Much of it was descriptive, based on observation, but none the less interesting for that. The quality of the data gathered was a function of the bias and methodology of the tester, and interpretation of results was often in the form of conclusions regarding what they revealed about neuropathology, such as localization of function (e.g. Broca, 1865).

The nineteenth century saw a growth of interest in neuropathology, and with it much informal testing, based on observation. In 1888, Reiger, professor of psychiatry, constructed an 'aphasia test battery' (Weisenberg and McBridge, 1935), but at that time such objective methods of examination were unfashionable. In 1926, Head produced an aphasia examination, apparently tested on normal subjects, and was at pains to point out that testing should be systematic, containing progressively more difficult tasks in order that impairment could be assessed accurately.

In 1935 Weisenburg and McBride produced a battery of tests that were to prove a landmark in aphasiology. They applied the framework that psychologists had developed to test intelligence, bringing the concept of standardization to the field of aphasia-testing. Nevertheless, as late as 1967, Benton pointed out that the rationale of standardized test procedures was slow to be adopted. He observed that different clinics developed different assessments, but not only were these not widely available, they also did not contain enough detail regarding standardization, procedures and interpretation of results to make them easily usable by others elsewhere.

Since that time, researchers and the authors of tests have increasingly used the psychological principles of test construction and standardization, with varying degrees of enthusiasm and success. A number of formal test batteries, for example, the Boston Diagnostic Aphasia Examination (Goodglass and Kaplan, 1972; 1983) and the Minnesota Test for the Differential Diagnosis of Aphasia (Schuell, 1965; 1973), have been developed which have attempted to address the criticisms of Benton, by providing systematically graded tasks, with detail about rationale, administration, scoring and interpretation, for example, in terms of classification of disorders. All, within their own theoretical frameworks, were intelligent attempts to solve a problem that revealed itself to be increasingly complex. Most were fallen on with enthusiasm by clinicians, in the hope of finding a definitive 'answer'. With hindsight, we can see many flaws in these tests, primarily springing from inappropriate aims, for example a mania for classification, inadequate understanding of the heterogeneous nature of aphasia, or a limited grasp of the many variables that operate in language processes.

Underlying theories of aphasia

As developments in aphasia-testing occurred, and not only physicians but also psychologists and others became interested, the differing theoretical frameworks within which they operated became obvious. Two main and opposing approaches were evident in the late 1800s and early 1900s, and are still evident now. Indeed, they form the basis of on-going discussion which continues up to the present day.

Neuroanatomical/localizationist approach

The first was a physically based approach, which held that different anatomical structures were responsible for particular language functions. These could, therefore, be selectively impaired by damage to discrete areas of brain. The thrust of study was to demonstrate where different language functions were located, in order to 'map' functions on to anatomical structures, and thus be able to predict localization of lesion according to surface language symptomatology. Thus, Broca (1865) and Wernicke (1874) mapped expressive and comprehension skills on to the third frontal convolution of the left hemisphere and the temporal convolution of the left hemisphere, respectively.

Localizationist theory has had continued support since that time, and has been developed by many researchers, for example, Geschwind (1965), to arrive at detailed descriptions of aphasia syndromes assumed to reflect distinct language disorders caused by damage to discrete areas of brain. Assessments generated from this approach, for example the Western Aphasia Battery (WAB) (Kertesz, 1982) and the Boston Diagnostic Aphasia Examination (BDAE) (Goodglass and Kaplan, 1972; 1983) have two basic characteristics. First, they use a 'modality' approach, comparing and contrasting performance in differing areas of language function, that is, expression, auditory comprehension, reading and writing. Second, they are syndrome-based: they seek to classify the patient into one of a number of mutually exclusive categories based on the co-occurrence or association of symptoms. The urge to classify patients is not exclusive to those proposing a localizationist approach, indeed it has driven much assessment, usually in order to be able to draw conclusions regarding group characteristics. The success with which this has been achieved has been greatly undermined by the realization that dysphasic patients do not form homogeneous groups (Howard and Hatfield, 1987). Nevertheless, localizationist theory continues to have a number of strong advocates (e.g. Goodglass, 1990; Kertesz, 1990) and the syndrome approach is usually, although not always, indicative of a localizationist rationale.

Unitary approach

The opposing approach viewed aphasia symptomatology as indicative of a single underlying disorder of language, manifested in different ways in different patients. It was first described explicitly by Hughlings-Jackson in 1878, but has continued to find support since then amongst a number of recognized authorities (e.g. Head, 1926) and to be developed, most notably by Schuell. The Minnesota Test for the Differential Diagnosis of Aphasia (MTDDA) (Schuell, 1965) remained an influential test for some time. While she too classified patients, in this case into five syndrome-like categories, Schuell did not attempt to explain their similarities and differences in specific anatomical terms, although she did believe that differences between diagnostic categories were true differences related to loci and extent of lesions (Schuell, Jenkins and Jimenez-Pabon, 1964). Her categories were primarily significant in terms of prognosis, and patients could evolve from one to another if or as they recovered. The rationale was the belief that aphasia symptomatology, however diverse, was an outward sign of one underlying deficit, which might vary in severity and be further complicated by additional sensory, motor or other impairment. The underlying deficit was assumed by Schuell to be one of auditory recall. She hypothesized that all language skills were fundamentally dependent on this ability, and that disturbance was due to impairment of auditory short-term memory. Thus, all Schuell's treatment was based on auditory stimulation. While this premise, the universality of auditory short-term memory impairment in aphasics, and the fundamental importance of short-term memory to all language skills, has been shown to be false, Schuell's work remains influential. She was a pioneer in the field of aphasia assessment and treatment, presenting a unified theory of language breakdown and developing this into a much-needed rationale for treatment. She also risked giving a prognosis based on classification. Although we now know her theory was erroneous, the 'stimulation' approach in its broadest form – facilitation of access to language skills by repeated stimulation – is still used and Schuell is held in much affection by researchers and clinicians.

Current approaches

Current theories of acquired language disorder include both traditional theories, and many remain strongly localizationist (e.g. Goodglass, 1990). However, recently emerging disciplines such as cognitive neuropsychology and the study of functional communication attempt to enlarge our understanding of language impairment and its functional effects, and show a move away from traditional theoretical frameworks. They reflect a rejection of the supremacy of neuroanatomy; indeed, for some, a negation of the drive to map brain function on to anatomical structures or sites (Mehler, Morton and Juscyzk, 1984). This has been replaced by attempts to study interaction and the contextual use of language (see Lesser and Milroy, 1987) and to elucidate levels of language-processing and break-down (e.g. Coltheart, 1984). Such moves away from traditional theory spring from a basic unhappiness with the medical model hitherto adopted of 'pathology – symptoms – syndrome classification'. This is, in part, because the work of speech and language therapists encompasses more than intervention within a 'medical management' framework (Eastwood, 1988) but more importantly, because the syndrome approach has served us so poorly in terms of helping us to understand acquired language problems, investigate levels of breakdown, elucidate the underlying nature of the problems, devise appropriate treatment plans, or monitor efficacy of inter-vention (Byng et al., 1990). It has blinded us to the differences between patients, hidden the variables so important in facilitating performance and covered up improvements that may have taken place as a result of therapy. Many authors (e.g. Howard and Hatfield, 1987) have pointed out the flaws in the syndrome approach. Study of patients reveals that features do not necessarily co-occur and many patients in a particular category do not show all of the characteristics of that category (Spreen and Risser, 1981). The search for a single defining feature for a given category has been fruitless, and one is forced to conclude that dysphasics are heterogeneous: they each have a cluster of problems and strengths that, in type, quality and quantity, are different from those of other patients. Howard and Hatfield (1987) admirably demonstrate the multiplicity of possibilities of impairment and conclude: 'any group of patients is bound to be heterogeneous: the mean score of any group is therefore meaningless' (p. 99). This understanding, if developed, leads to the worrying realization that a group result may apply to *none* of the individuals in that group.

In developing alternative approaches to the assessment of acquired language disorders, the cognitive neuropsychologists and those interested in functional communication have drawn on the methodology of psychology, neuropsychology and social psychology, including the need for normal data and careful recording of responses, and emphasize the need for a specific methodology appropriate to speech and language therapy. Much of the impetus for research originated in the field of psychology and the study of normal brain processes and interaction. This came to include pathological manifestations of breakdown when it was suggested that theories of normal processing and interaction could be tested by studying those in whom processes and behaviours had been impaired or changed.

Functional approach

At its broadest, this approach may be said to encompass the functional effects of impairment on communicative adequacy and social interaction, and includes the study of emotional factors and normal interaction. Nomenclature varies according to the researchers, for example 'communicative effectiveness' (Davis and Wilcox, 1986; Lomas *et al.*, 1989), 'functional communication' (Skinner *et al.*, 1984), 'pragmatics' (Lesser and Milroy, 1987), but 'functional' may apply to all, in that all seek to emphasize what the patient is still able to achieve despite impairment, albeit sometimes in a non-standard way. Equal emphasis is given to both linguistic skills and overall communicative ability, as in PACE (Promoting Aphasics Communicative Effectiveness) (Davis and Wilcox, 1986), and the effects of context, the listener role and the communicative goal are all considered. Assessment may be via controlled or constructed situations and role-play, as in Communicative Abilities in Daily Living (Holland, 1980), the Functional Communication Profile (Sarno, 1969), or the Communicative Effectiveness Index (Lomas *et al.*, 1989), or by observation and the use of questionnaires and check-lists, for example, the Edinburgh Functional Communication Profile (Skinner *et al.*, 1984). Recently there has been a small but notable push away from the medical or psychological science of testing and treatment towards what might be termed a 'psychotherapeutic' approach, based on careful observation, description, reflection and interpretation (Eastwood, 1988).

Cognitive neuropsychological approach

This approach applies the methodology of cognitive psychology, neuro-psychology and psycholinguistics to the study of normal and disordered cognitive processes. The ability of theories regarding function to account for normal processing can be assessed by testing impaired individuals, thus providing an additional means of evaluating their validity. This implies a reductionist rationale of language breakdown, that is, that when language breakdown occurs, its presentation is the function of a normal system operating minus certain units. In itself, this is not a revolutionary idea: much clinical neurology is based on the same tenet (Abbs, 1986).

Speech and language therapists have adopted this approach with enthusiasm, probably because of their training in the psychological sciences and because they recognize that it represents a rigorous framework within which to assess and treat patients. For a detailed description and demonstration of this rationale, see Byng *et al.* (1990) and Ellis and Young (1988).

Models developed using this approach provide more precise explanations of what is impaired and what is intact in individual patients. Such an approach has practical advantages for the clinician, for one 'can use such explanations to devise rational therapies, that is, rehabilitation programmes based upon theoretical analysis of the nature of the disorder to be treated' (Coltheart, 1984: 2).

Using the principles of cognitive neuropsychology, it is possible to arrive at a model of language-processing that can explain the symptomatology of patients in terms of 'modules' arranged in hierarchical order. Modules are commonly represented as boxes, and are named according to the operation assumed to take place there, usually the ability to store and retrieve specific information. Arrows from the boxes represent transmission of coded information. Storage, retrieval or transmission of information may all be affected in the dysphasic patient. Thus, one can arrive at a model of the recognition, comprehension and production of spoken and written words and non-words such as that proposed by Patterson and Shewell (1987). It should be noted that, as Byng *et al.* (1990) state, no model is 'a holy grail, inviolable and sacrosanct' (p. 77). The model shown in Figure 6.1 has been in use for some time, but just as important as the model itself is the fact that it provides a framework within which systematic assessment may take place, and from which 'rational therapy' may be generated. Furthermore, this framework is not incompatible with the functional approach: the two complement each other.

AIMS OF ASSESSMENT

The aims of assessment vary according to the tester's theoretical framework and reason for testing, and the form an assessment takes will depend on

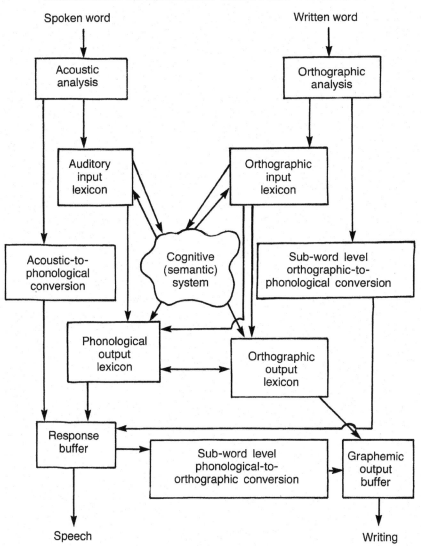

Figure 6.1 A model for the recognition, comprehension and production of single spoken and written words and non-words
Source: Patterson and Shewell, 1987.

107

its aims (Byng *et al.*, 1990). A therapist may test a patient for research purposes, to plan current and future services, to arrive at a differential diagnosis, to plan therapy or to monitor efficacy of intervention. He or she may be working in a community clinic, a district hospital, on a domiciliary basis, in a research department or as part of a diagnostic team in a regional specialist unit. Assessment may be one-off, on-going or repeated. The tools to achieve a variety of coexisting aims may differ, and it is this that can make selection of the appropriate assessment difficult.

Just as importantly, the span and depth of assessment will vary according to the patient's needs. These may be influenced by factors such as pathology, medical state, time post-onset, environment and emotional state (Chapey, 1981). These will determine the feasibility, appropriateness and scope of testing, and indicate needs, be they for support, information, compensation strategies, alternative methods of communication, elimination of complications and distractions or structured treatment.

Assessment may be constrained by time, resources, manpower and equipment (Byng *et al.*, 1990; Kertesz, 1990), all commodities that tend to be in short supply. Precisely because of this, it is important to remember that the therapist has an ethical and legal obligation to provide appropriate and relevant assessment, in order to fulfil his or her duty of care to the patient. There is little in favour of providing detailed assessment for one patient and nothing for another. Equally, as Spreen and Risser (1981) point out, 'brevity is no virtue if crucial information is not collected' (p. 119).

The most important lesson to be drawn from this is that every effort should be made to provide assessment that is as full and reliable as possible, and that the nature of the assessment carried out should be aim-driven, that is, chosen on the basis of the questions that need to be answered, and not on the basis of expediency. That ultimately all assessment should serve the patient also needs to be reiterated. This has as much to do with rapport, how the assessment is administered and results are interpreted and explained as it has with the particular tool chosen (David, 1990).

Controversies over aims

Unfortunately, there is little consensus regarding the aims of assessment among researchers or clinicians. Thus, the therapist is presented with a bewildering diversity of tests from which to choose.

In the past, standardized batteries were aimed at classification, for example into categories according to presentation and prognosis (e.g. MTDDA, Schuell, 1965; 1973) or syndromes assumed to determine localization of lesion (e.g. BDAE, Goodglass and Kaplan, 1972; 1983). Many researchers still believe this should be a primary aim of assessment (e.g. Goodglass, 1990), in part because such classifications are assumed to have significance in terms of selection for treatment, the type of treatment that is appropriate, or prognosis (Kertesz, 1990). While these issues are obviously vital, the recent demolition of the credibility of the syndrome approach means that we must seriously doubt the reliability of information from formal test batteries in answering such questions. David (1990: 104) points out that 'the only information to be derived from existing tools is a rather ad hoc measure of ... severity', and further remarks that 'all assessments are blunt instruments'.

Byng et al. (1990) argue strongly that the aim of assessment should be to elucidate the underlying nature of the impairment, and in this they have the support of many others (e.g. Weniger, 1990). Such information is a prerequisite to planning treatment (Byng et al., 1990; Chapey, 1981), and as such is stated as an aim of assessment by the majority of therapists (David, 1990).

Such a single aim may, nevertheless, be under-inclusive, for therapists have other reasons for assessing, such as screening, monitoring recovery, predicting outcome and establishing a database (David, 1990). All these goals may be better served by standardized rather than informal measures. David herself stresses the need to measure incidence, severity and recovery in order to implement and audit appropriate case-load management. She suggests that a more comprehensive framework of assessment should address the concepts of impairment, disability and handicap (Harris, Cox and Smith, 1971), where impairment is the defect in a mechanism, disability is the loss of a skill directly resulting from the impairment, and handicap is the limitation on normal activity caused by impairment. This emphasizes the importance of measuring the functional consequences of impairment: David suggests that cognitive neuropsychological tests assess impairment, standardized batteries assess disability and functional assessments gauge handicap.

Thus, we are left with a number of coexisting or even conflicting aims. Perhaps it is too much to expect one assessment to fulfil all these goals while restricting assessment time to manageable limits (Byng et al., 1990). Kertesz (1990) points out that a place exists for a variety of assessments serving different aims, and Weniger (1990) suggests that the skill lies in selection and administration. As long ago as 1878, Hughlings-Jackson recognized that 'the tendency to appear exact by ignoring the complexity of the factors is the old failing of our medical history'.

Suggested aims

Chapey (1981) highlights the breadth of aims such as differential diagnosis and selection of clients, and identifies certain goals which assessment should serve: aetiologic; linguistic, cognitive and communicative; intervention.

109

David (1990) points out that 'the process of testing is often more important than the product'. Bearing these points and previous discussions in mind, the following list of goals is suggested. They are not exhaustive, nor necessarily mutually exclusive.

1 differential diagnosis
2 selection for treatment
3 elucidation of impairment
4 planning of treatment
5 monitoring treatment efficacy
6 classification and prognosis
7 liaison with colleagues and family
8 planning and auditing the service

ASSESSMENT PROCEDURES

Aims must be defined explicitly in order to be fulfilled by the selection of relevant assessments. It is appropriate to choose tests that first address the patient's needs, and extrapolate information that serves other aims from the results. In this way the 'test until you and the patient drop' syndrome may be avoided. As Weniger (1990) has pointed out: 'Whatever the tool ... it remains as good or as poor as the skill of the hand using it' (p. 112).

Furthermore, David (1990) states that it is 'unlikely that a single test could meet all ... functions' (p. 104). Thus, selection, administration and interpretation remains firmly the responsibility of the therapist.

Characteristics of useful assessment

In the absence of a single definitive test, selection remains individual, dependent on aims and resources. Nevertheless, certain characteristics seem desirable in any testing procedure; these spring directly from the aims and current understanding of test construction. Chapey (1981) summarized some of these characteristics, and Enderby (1983) listed six criteria that dysarthria assessment should fulfil. These may be specified and expanded as follows:

1 Appropriate administration time   A screening test is necessarily short, while a test on which treatment will be based may be time-consuming.

2 Appropriate in order and scope   Logic in test order avoids unnecessary testing. Testing first the function that may affect ability on other tasks allows one to 'extract' this effect on later tasks. Thus, therapists commonly start with comprehension. Sequencing of tasks within a modality is relevant, for success in one task may indicate intactness of another skill.

110

Assessment should have sufficient breadth to screen all modalities. Depth will be determined by functional consequences of impairment and the patient's needs, and indicates a progression in the specificity of the skill being tested. In the case of a number of modalities being equally impaired, this may indicate the need to search for a single underlying problem, for example a central semantic deficit.

3 Number of stimuli   Sufficient to allow one to draw valid conclusions, at least ten.

4 Stimuli constancy   Employing the same items in different modalities and across time enables one to compare and contrast performance.

5 Size of scoring increments   Large enough to ensure reliability, yet small enough to detect change.

6 Control of variables   Attempts to control all relevant variables and, in particular, to control systematically the variable operating at the level being tested, while holding others constant. In practice this may be difficult without access to controlled word lists.

7 Normal data   From a group of similar age, background and so on, or even from the patient's spouse or sibling.

8 Task purity   Tasks uncontaminated by skills other than that being tested. Thus a test of the patient's knowledge of the phonology of a word should not require him or her to say it, for that is a different skill and may be selectively impaired, as in dyspraxia (see later).

9 Qualitative as well as quantitative data   How the patient approaches the task and the nature of the errors; such data may be incorporated into the scoring system, noted as observation, or gathered in a separate assessment.

10 Recording of data   Materials used, administration, scoring criteria and responses should all be made explicit.

11 Associated problems   Testing should seek to encompass but differentiate between and within language, visual, hearing, memory and other skills.

12 Information for planning future management   For example, suitability for treatment may be decided on criteria such as insight, communication need, motivation, support and access.

13 Data on strengths and weaknesses Strengths may be exploited to overcome deficits.

14 Functional consequences of impairment Comparing and contrasting impairment, disability and handicap, highlighting strategies the patient is already using, and identifying his or her needs.

15 Type, characteristics and severity of impairment Traditional terminology may be applied.

16 Family Their understanding of the difficulties, strategies for dealing with them, involvement and needs.

The acute phase

The misdiagnosis of communication disorders, even by experienced medical staff, is a strong indication of the dangers inherent in assessment and the use of labels without full understanding. Mercifully, this is not always the case; many physicians and neurologists are skilled at making a differential diagnosis. Nevertheless, because the aims in the acute phase do not end with differential diagnosis, it is essential that it is the therapist who assesses, to define such factors as type and characteristics of communication impairment, contribution of other deficits to the overall picture, severity of impairment, functional consequences and the patient's immediate communication needs.

Aims

These may be summarized as follows:

1   screening
2   differential diagnosis
3   monitoring fluctuations and stability
4   identifying immediate needs
5   planning future management
6   liaison with family and medical staff

Testing

In the acute stage, testing is made difficult by fluctuations in performance and the patient's medical state. Formal test batteries explicitly state that they cannot give reliable results until there is neurological stability. Thus, the therapist often has to use his or her own informal methods.

The Aphasia Screening Test (Whurr, 1974) provides an overview of communication abilities, and includes a pretest section for the identification of visual problems. It should be remembered that patients may fail later for reasons other than language deficits, for example, confusion, and that any error on a test with such a low ceiling indicates the need for further assessment. It should never be used as a basis for treatment, although it can give a broad label to the impairment. Although, strictly speaking, it should not be readministered at intervals of less than three months, it can be used repeatedly as a measure of stability. Learning effects are a positive indication of suitability for treatment, although it is often difficult to differentiate between learning effects and spontaneous recovery. This is equally true of informal assessments. These should span all modalities, and use the same tasks and materials in both input modalities and both output modalities in order that comparisons may be made. Materials should include objects, pictures and verbal material for the same reason. Stimuli should be chosen on the basis of familiarity, usefulness, word length, phonological complexity, frequency of occurrence/use and imageability. Objects and pictures should be easily recognizable.

Problems of vision and hearing may be assessed at a superficial level by observing the patient's reaction to environmental stimuli, and by noting patterns of performance in response to stimulus location or intensity. Perceptual abilities may be tested by matching tasks such as matching identical objects, pictures, environmental and speech sounds, and categorization tasks. Care should be taken, as poor performance may be due to a central semantic problem rather than peripheral sensory or cortical perceptual difficulty.

Memory is very difficult to assess accurately in the acute stage, but inferences may be made on the basis of responses to longer items, the content of output, ability to persevere without prompts and awareness of ward routine. Alertness, stamina and concentration should be measured, perhaps by timing the onset of deterioration in performance as tasks progress.

Markedly better comprehension than expression, especially in the presence of obvious motor problems, should alert the therapist to the possibility of dysarthria and orofacial or articulatory dyspraxia: facial or oral difficulties due to paralysis or motor-planning problems respectively. Evidence of paralysis, such as facial or oral asymmetry, changes in reflex behaviours, problems of eating or drinking or drooling indicate that dysarthria is present. Differences between conscious, volitional movement to command or imitation and those made reflexively or automatically, or evidence of struggle in lip or tongue placement are indicative of dyspraxia. (See later section.)

In-depth assessment

In this context in-depth assessment may be regarded as any assessment beyond screening or that designed to yield a broad differential diagnosis.

Differential diagnosis between communication disorders may require more in-depth testing. In addition, the therapist may wish to classify the 'type' of dysphasia. Nevertheless, the most obvious aim of in-depth assessment is to provide a basis for treatment (Byng *et al.*, 1990). It has been shown that formal test batteries yield little information for this purpose, and that the cognitive neuropsychological approach to testing is more appropriate. Moreover, the therapist may extrapolate information from such testing to fulfil other goals. For example, a broad label such as 'non-fluent' or 'fluent' may be applied on the basis of characteristics of the patient's spoken output using the Boston Diagnostic Aphasia Examination (BDAE) (Goodglass and Kaplan, 1972; 1983) as a guideline, for use with colleagues or in monitoring referrals and incidence of disorder. Nevertheless, the fact that efforts to classify patients meaningfully have proved fruitless and that many patients resist classification means that one is forced to question the validity of basing management decisions or prognosis on such categorization. The therapist may need to remain fluent in the vocabulary of traditional tests while educating others in the new theoretical framework and terminology, always choosing assessments relevant to the patient's functional needs.

Until now, cognitive neuropsychological tests have not been widely available. Usually, therapists have had to look for detail regarding stimuli, administration and scoring in the literature, or contact researchers direct. Nevertheless, more and more therapists have adopted this approach in their work, for reasons previously discussed. There is now available a comprehensive set of resource materials for use in cognitive neuropsychologically inspired testing. *Psycholinguistic Assessments of Language Processing in Aphasia (PALPA)* (Kay, Lesser and Coltheart, 1992) comprises a set of approximately sixty controlled tests, with guidelines regarding task selection. It can be used for differential diagnosis, elucidation of underlying difficulties, as a basis for planning treatment and to monitor efficacy. Although it is large and expensive, and its clinical usefulness has still to be demonstrated, it is a resource for which therapists have been crying out. Its use is advocated but, in addition, tasks and stimuli will be described in order that therapists may cull materials from elsewhere if *PALPA* is unavailable (e.g. from Kucera and Francis, 1967; Snodgrass and Vandervart, 1980). What follows is based on a cognitive neuropsychological model, and the model previously shown is reproduced with suggestions regarding specific tasks in Figure 6.2. It should be noted that for some of the tasks suggested (for example rhyme judgements, homophone judgements) no clear consensus exists about the processes needed to perform these tasks. Some of the tasks require more than one level of processing, or module. In addition, only processes represented by modules (that is, storage and retrieval) are addressed in Figure 6.2. Other tasks would be required to assess the transmission of information from one

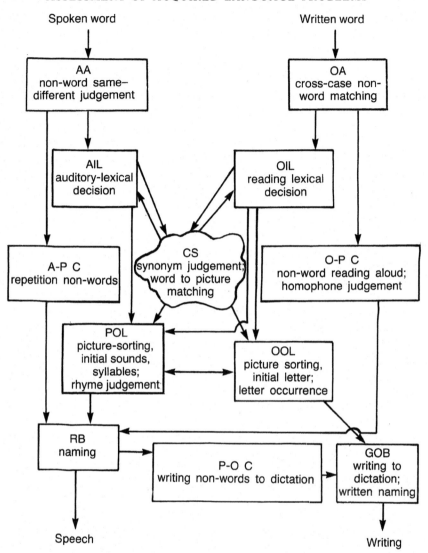

Figure 6.2 Single-word processing model with tasks appropriate for testing each level

Source: Patterson and Shewell, 1987.

module to another, represented in the model by arrows. Further reading is recommended on this method of assessment, and the appropriate tasks to accomplish this, such as Ellis and Young (1988). The importance of the patient's functional needs should always be remembered, and functional and qualitative data should also be collected.

Auditory comprehension

Franklin (1989) demonstrated that single-word auditory comprehension can show at least five different levels of impairment, using a set of three phoneme-discrimination tests, two lexical-decision tests, a semantic test and two repetition tests. It is worth noting that only some of the tests came from *PALPA*; others were tests devised by the author, or used stimuli from other sources (e.g. Coltheart, 1980).

Acoustic analysis may be tested using non-word pair same–different judgement tasks, in which the patient is presented with identical or non-identical pairs of non-words about which he has to make a judgement: 'same' or 'different'. It is useful to exclude high-frequency speech sounds as this population is likely to be from an age group known to have an increased incidence of presbycusis, that is, age-related high-frequency hearing loss. In addition, a word-to-word picture-matching task may be used in which the distractor (i.e. incorrect) pictures are phonologically related to the target.

The auditory-input lexicon may be tested using a lexical-decision task, in which the patient is presented with words and matched non-words, and has to indicate whether each word is 'real' or not, regardless of whether he knows its meaning.

Semantics may be assessed using a synonym-judgement task, where the patient hears pairs of words, half of which are synonymous. He or she indicates whether each pair is similar in meaning. Stimuli may include both high- and low-imageability words in order to detect an imageability effect, and the task should be administered in both auditory and reading modalities to discriminate between modality-specific impairment and a central verbal semantic problem. A word-to-picture matching task in which distractors are semantically related to the target may also be used in both auditory and reading modalities, but may show a different pattern of results due to the additional picture-processing involved (see later sections: 'semantics' and 'vision').

Repetition may be tested by ability to repeat non-words, and words controlled for imageability and frequency (Howard, 1987, in Coltheart *et al.*, 1987) to detect effects of these variables.

Care should be taken that all stimuli are delivered in the same tone of voice, at the same pace and with the same intonation in order that consistency is maintained and differences do not alert the patient to the

116

correct response. This is difficult in non-word same–different and lexical-decision tasks. Taping is one way of ensuring consistency. Careful modelling of the nature of the task and required response may be necessary, perhaps initially using non-verbal material to convey the concept. Inability to grasp the nature of the task indicates impairment at that level of cognitive processing.

In many cases, starting with semantic and repetition tasks is appropriate, as good performance indicates intactness of previous levels of processing. Impairment on auditory-synonym judgement indicates the need for testing of reading-synonym judgement. If this is OK, this implies that semantic processing is not the problem, and therefore previous levels of auditory processing such as auditory-input lexicon should be tested. If reading-synonym judgement is also impaired, this indicates a central verbal semantic deficit which needs to be investigated further. Reassessment performance and response to cueing will show if the problem is of access or loss from the store. Intact performance on all semantic tasks when auditory impairment is suspected indicates that sentence comprehension needs assessing.

Similarly, intact single-word repetition skills indicate that acoustic analysis is intact, and memory may be the problem. If single-word repetition is impaired, acoustic analysis should be assessed.

Reading comprehension

There are more materials available for the assessment of single-word reading comprehension. The Coltheart assessment (1980) may be used, and the same strategies adopted regarding rationale, choice and order of testing as for auditory input.

Speech output

Assessment of speech in the presence of naming difficulties should adopt the same rationale as previously outlined. The reader is also directed to Howard and Orchard-Lisle (1984).

Testing should commence with assessment of the more 'central' processes, taking into account the types of errors the patient makes. If naming errors are semantic, this indicates a semantic deficit, or a difficulty of access to the phonological form. Intact performance on verbal semantic tasks, as previously outlined, or sound errors in production indicate the latter is the case, and the phonological output lexicon should be tested. This should be done using tasks that do not require the patient to say anything, but reveal his or her knowledge of the sound form of words, for example, picture-sorting on the basis of initial sound, number of syllables or rhyme. Poor performance indicates impaired access to the store, or

117

reduction of items in storage. Consistency of errors across time and poor response to cueing indicate that loss has occurred. Relatively good performance on picture-sorting tasks compared with spoken output indicates that the problem may be motor in origin, that is dyspraxia (see later).

An overall measure of naming ability is useful, and may be gained from the Graded Naming Test (McKenna and Warrington, 1983) or the Boston Naming Test (Goodglass and Kaplan, 1983). Care should be taken as stimuli are poorly controlled in the latter, and both involve pictorial processing prior to a naming response. Response to cueing indicates level of impairment and optimal treatment technique. This can be measured by dividing the failed items into groups and retesting, applying different facilitation to each group. For further reading on facilitation, see Howard *et al.* (1985).

Writing

This can be assessed using the rationale outlined for speech output, and incorporating information from reading assessment. Both dictation and written picture-naming should be tested, using the same items across each condition. Keeping test stimuli constant across tests of speech and writing also allows direct comparisons to be made. Additional variables such as regularity and number of letters should also be controlled.

Semantics

Difficulties with verbal semantics indicate that non-verbal, that is, picture semantics should be assessed, for example, via picture sorting/categorization, or a picture-association task such as Pyramids and Palmtrees (Howard and Orchard-Lisle, 1984). Inability to match pictures or objects despite modelling indicates visual problems or intellectual difficulties.

Syntax

Syntax, both in input and output, has revealed itself to be an increasingly complex subject. An outline of some initial assessment strategies is given, but the reader is directed also to Byng (1988), and Howard (1985).

That syntax problems do not arise from a single central deficit has been demonstrated (Howard, 1985); therefore, it is necessary to compare syntax abilities across modalities. Subtests of *PALPA* are available, or this may be achieved using other tests such as the Test for the Reception of Grammar (TROG) (Bishop, 1983) and connected speech-output tasks. The TROG tests syntax comprehension by sentence-to-picture matching, with one syntactic and two lexical distractors, in addition to the target picture; that is, mistakes may be made on the basis of lexical (word) or syntax errors. It

118

was originally devised for testing children, and the 'blocks', or sets of four sentences involving a particular structure, do not conform to an intact adult syntactic framework; that is, particular 'adult' structures are scattered over a number of blocks. In addition, there are no adult norms, only a small set of nouns and verbs are used and chance performance on just the syntactic element (target and one distractor) is normally 50 per cent. Nevertheless, it is a useful starting point, and a good indicator of comprehension of connected speech. If problems are evident, the therapist should analyse the pattern of errors and devise further tests, perhaps on the basis of judgement tasks – the patient's ability to judge the 'legality' of certain clause, phrase, word or morphemic combinations.

Output may be measured using a sentence or story completion task (e.g. Goodglass *et al.*, 1970). This may be extended to include additional structures for testing. Asking the patient to retell a familiar story such as the Cinderella tale is a better way of eliciting connected speech than complex picture description, which often simply results in lists of nouns. The target is usually guessable as the story is familiar. Output stimulated in this way may then be analysed with attention to the presence and combination of elements, providing quantitative as well as qualitative measures.

Some patients show a difficulty 'mapping' semantics on to syntactic structures, and with the specific semantic properties of verbs. Further reading (e.g. Byng, 1988) is recommended.

Head injury

It is beyond the scope of this chapter to discuss the assessment of head-injured patients in depth, as their management constitutes a speciality in itself. This is unfortunate; although most speech and language therapists working with adults see head-injured patients, this usually occurs only occasionally and for specific periods dictated by the clinical environment, making it difficult to develop expertise or gain a breadth of experience from acute care to long-term placement.

Further reading can be found in Adamovitch, Henderson and Auerbach (1985), Hagen (1984), Holland (1982), and the *Speech Therapy in Practice. Special Supplements*: *Head Injury* (I–III) (1990).

Differences from the CVA population

That closed head-injury (CHI) patients are very different from the CVA population is well accepted (Adamovitch *et al.*, 1985). This is true of initial presentation, scope of impairment, recovery and long-term outcome. Communication difficulties tend to be mixed (Hagen, 1984), and language problems qualitatively different from those of dysphasia (Holland, 1982).

119

Problems are overlaid and linked with disorders of alertness, behaviour, affect, insight, drive, memory, cognitive organization and perception (Adamovitch *et al.*, 1985).

The acute phase

In the acute stage, management tends to be multidimensional. Timing of referral varies, but the therapist may be involved from the coma stage. During this time and subsequently, level of consciousness may be monitored using the Glasgow Coma Scale (Jennett *et al.*, 1981). Length of post-traumatic amnesia (PTA) and return of attention control may be measured using the guidelines suggested by Hagen (1984).

The acute stage lasts longer in head injury than in CVA (Adamovitch *et al.*, 1985). Assessment takes the form of informal monitoring of global functions such as motor skills, behaviour and language, using check-lists and guidelines (e.g. Hagen, 1984). Most patients are ventilated and fed non-orally initially, and much of the focus of initial management is on assessing and stimulating feeding abilities in conjunction with the physiotherapist, in preparation for the removal of the tracheostomy tube and the resumption of oral feeding.

Prognosis is difficult to judge, as length of coma and of PTA are not wholly reliable indicators (Adamovitch *et al.*, 1985). Wise clinicians refuse to give a prognosis for at least three months.

Types of communication problems

Hagen (1984) states that three groups ultimately emerge from the diffuse symptomatology of CHI: those with disorganized language secondary to cognitive disorganization, with or without specific language disorder; those with a predominant feature of a specific language disorder and coexisting minimal cognitive impairment; and those with memory impairments but without language dysfunction. Patients in all these groups may have motor deficits. Open head-injury patients tend to present more like CVA patients, after an initial period of unconsciousness and confusion.

In all groups, naming is the language function that appears most vulnerable (Holland, 1982).

Detailed language assessment

In-depth testing of language impairment in CHI is made difficult by behavioural and cognitive problems. Rating scales (e.g. Hagen, 1984) are often employed. Formal test batteries are of little use, for they do not distinguish between true language impairment, cognitive organizational problems and cognitive deficits that may depress performance. Moreover, task ceilings are often inappropriately low, skills such as naming are not assessed in enough depth and scoring does not reflect the uniqueness of responses. Standardization of such tests is on CVA populations, rendering scores for CHI patients meaningless. This is especially true of the localizationist tests, since CHI patients have multiple and diffuse lesions.

The cognitive neuropsychological approach may have more to offer, in terms of specificity, depth and selectivity of testing. Nevertheless, testing the majority of severely impaired subjects is likely to be very problematic.

Joint assessment with other disciplines is essential to define accurately the nature and functional consequences of impairment. Access to a clinical psychologist is a boon.

Open head-injury patients tend to present with impairment more akin to dysphasia, and may therefore be assessed using tests outlined previously.

Associated problems

Neurological patients with acquired language problems frequently present with associated deficits that are relevant in terms of differential diagnosis and management.

Vision

The ability to see and recognize is important functionally, and in relation to response to testing and treatment, as these tend to utilize visual materials. Visual recognition and understanding involve not only peripheral structures but also cognitive skills (Riddoch and Humphreys, 1987). Difficulties at one of the stages in visual processing may be suspected if performance on tasks using visual stimuli is depressed compared with that on purely verbal tasks.

Right homonymous hemianopia, loss of the right visual field, is common in dysphasics. Its presence is indicated by consistent failure to respond to visual stimuli in the right visual field. Referral to the ophthalmologist may be indicated.

Visual processing involves stages analogous with those of verbal processing. Further reading (e.g. Howard and Orchard-Lisle, 1984; Riddoch and Humphreys, 1987) is strongly recommended, but simple matching tasks, for example, of identical and non-identical objects and pictures, may be used to test visual analysis and recognition initially.

Hearing

As in the case of vision, hearing skills also involve peripheral structures and cognitive processing, and include the understanding of not only speech but other sounds.

Difficulties of hearing may be reported by the patient or may be evident from responses to the environment or language testing. Many CVA patients are in the age range where presbycusis may be present, thus a full history, ear examination and audiometry are indicated.

Differentiating between a pre-language auditory processing problem and a problem of acoustic speech analysis may be difficult. A pre-phonemic problem is indicated if acoustically identical sounds cannot be matched. This can be compared with performance on a non-word same–different task (see before) where two different voices are used for each syllable in the pairs. Intact performance on the former task but poor performance in the latter indicates the problem is one of acoustic analysis at a phonemic level; that is, a language problem.

The reader is referred to Franklin (1989) for further reading.

Memory

This is a vast subject in itself, to which cognitive neuropsychological investigation has also been applied (see Ellis and Young, 1988). While received wisdom used to hold that intact memory was necessary for language-processing to take place (e.g. Schuell, 1965), and many patients and families identify language deficits as a memory problem, we now know that memory is not integral to language-processing, although it is linked to it. Decoding is not sequential, as there is a high level of redundancy in the speech signal. Not all dysphasics show an impairment of auditory memory span, and many function perfectly well with a reduced memory span. Short-term memory may play a significant role when the patient has a comprehension deficit, as intact memory skills may allow retention of the signal while attempts are made to decode the missed element or dis-ambiguate complex structures.

Memory may be assessed using digit repetition or matching tasks (see Ellis and Young, 1988). Functional memory may be assessed using the Rivermead Behavioural Memory Test (Wilson, Cockburn and Baddeley, 1985).

Dementia

It is well recognized that dementia results in communication changes that differ qualitatively from aphasia. Nevertheless, dysphasia may co-exist with dementia or mimic it. Fuller discussion of dementia is provided in Chapter 9, and further reading (e.g. Gravell, 1988) is recommended.

Dysarthria

Indications of the presence of dysarthria, a speech impairment due to paralysis, in the acute stage, have already been discussed. When it is

122

suspected, more detailed testing may be indicated if it appears to be a major feature of the communication handicap.

Testing may be carried out informally using the Point-Place system (Rosenbek and LaPointe, 1980) or a standardized test such as the Frenchay Dysarthria Assessment (Enderby, 1983). Objective, or formal, measurement may be available; for example, the laryngograph, electro-palatography or nasal anemometry. Intelligibility may be rated using the system described by Yorkston and Beukelman (1981).

Dyspraxia

Controversy has raged over dyspraxia for some time, with conflict arising over whether it exists and, if so, what it is – an associated motor problem or part of a language disorder. Unfortunately, it is simply not possible to outline opposing viewpoints and evidence here, but the reader is directed to Buckingham (1981) and Miller (1986) for fuller discussion and explanation.

Having said that, most therapists work on the premise that it does exist. This necessitates differentiation between other disorders with which it may be confused, namely dysarthria and a pre-motor (phonological) speech impairment.

Dyspraxia may be defined as a difficulty initiating and sequencing voluntary movement, that is not caused by paralysis, sensory loss or a comprehension deficit. It appears to exist in many forms and can affect any purposeful movement, for example, of the limbs as well as facial and oral structures. This is reflected in the many labels applied to it (e.g. limb dyspraxia, dressing dyspraxia) which may overlap.

This discussion is centred on those dyspraxias that affect communication. These are chiefly orofacial dyspraxia and verbal or articulatory dyspraxia, but include limb and other dyspraxias which may affect gesture or writing. These tend to co-occur with non-fluent aphasia (Goodglass and Kaplan, 1983).

The chief feature of all dyspraxias appears to be the difference between performance of automatic or unconscious movement and that of volitional movement; for example, to command. Impairment of orofacial reflex activity and evidence of paralysis indicate the presence of dysarthria, while a difference between reflex and automatic movement and that carried out purposefully indicates dyspraxia. There may be a difference between movement to command or imitation within the dyspraxia, and it is important to exclude comprehension effects by modelling. Orofacial, or non-speech, and articulatory dyspraxia may exist in isolation.

Articulatory dyspraxia may be confused with a language problem, phonological output deficit. Guidelines for discriminating between the two have been outlind previously, and are further provided in Huskins'

Diagnostic Checklists (1986). In addition, repetition, reading and naming of the same stimuli may be used: if the patient finds all equally hard, the problem is post-lexical; that is, probably dyspraxia. Once identified, articulatory dyspraxia may be quantified and patterns isolated using the dimensional framework outlined by Trost and Canter (1974) or by using the assessment suggested by Wertz *et al.* (1984).

Assessment of limb and hand function, relevant in terms of gestural and writing ability, may be assessed using the Apraxia Battery for Adults (Dabul, 1979) or the supplementary tests of the BDAE (Goodglass and Kaplan, 1983).

SUMMARY

Assessment may have a variety of aims, and these aims dictate the selection of tests. Chief amongst aims is usually the elucidation of the underlying problems in order to plan treatment, and the cognitive neuropsychological approach appears most appropriate for this. Assessment should compare and contrast between and within language and other cognitive, sensory and motor skills. To do so meaningfully, it should be rigorous in its methodology in order that sound conclusions may be drawn.

REFERENCES

Abbs, J. (1986). 'The speech neuromotor process: implications for dysarthria assessment and treatment'. Paper presented at the *Third National Conference on Dysarthria*, Bristol.

Adamovitch, B., Henderson, J. and Auerbach, S. (1985). *Cognitive Rehabilitation of Closed Head-Injured Patients*. London: Taylor & Francis.

Benton, A. (1967). 'Problems of test construction in the field of aphasia'. *Cortex*, 3, 32–53.

Bishop, D. (1983). *Test for the Reception of Grammar*. University of Newcastle.

Broca, P. (1865). 'Remarques sur la siège de la faculté du langage articulé'. *Bulletin de la Société d'Anthropologie de Paris*, 6, 30–57.

Buckingham, H. (1981). 'Explanations for the concept of apraxia of speech'. In M. Sarno (ed.), *Acquired Aphasia*. London: Academic Press.

Byng, S. (1988). 'Sentence processing deficits: theory and therapy'. *Cognitive Neuropsychology*, 5, 629–76.

Byng, S., Kay, J., Edmundson, A. and Scott, C. (1990). 'Aphasia tests reconsidered'. *Aphasiology*, 4:1, 67–91.

Chapey, R. (ed.) (1981). *Language Intervention Strategies in Adult Aphasia*, Baltimore: Williams & Wilkins.

Clinical Forum (1990). *Aphasiology*, 4:1, 67–113.

Coltheart, M., Sartori, G. and Job, R. (1987) *The Cognitive Neuropsychology of Language*. London: Lawrence Erlbaum.

Coltheart, M. (1980). 'Analysing acquired disorders of reading'. Unpublished manuscript. Birkbeck College.

Coltheart, M. (1984). Editorial. *Cognitive Neuropsychology*, 1, 1–9.

Dabul, B. (1979). *Apraxia Battery for Adults*. Tigard, Oregon: CC Publications.

David, R. (1990). 'Aphasia assessment: the acid tests'. *Aphasiology*, 4, 103–7.

Davis, G. and Wilcox, M. (1986). 'Incorporating parameters of natural conversation in aphasia treatment'. In R. Chapey (ed.), *Language Intervention Strategies in Adult Aphasia* (2nd edn). London: Williams & Wilkins.

DHSS Field Research Division (1975). *Epidemiology of Head Injuries in England and Wales.* London: DHSS.

Eastwood, J. (1988). 'Qualitative research: an additional research methodology for speech pathology?' *British Journal of Disorders of Communication*, 23, 171–84.

Eisenson, J. (1973). *Adult Aphasia: Assessment and Treatment.* Englewood Cliffs, NJ: Prentice-Hall.

Ellis, A. and Young, A. (1988). *Human Cognitive Neuropsychology.* Hove: Erlbaum.

Enderby, P. (1983). *Frenchay Dysarthria Assessment.* San Diego, CA: College-Hill Press.

Enderby, P. and Philipp, R. (1986). 'Speech and language handicap: towards knowing the size of the problem'. *British Journal of Disorders of Communication*, 21, 151–65.

Franklin, S. (1989). 'Dissociations in auditory word comprehension: evidence from nine fluent aphasic patients'. *Aphasiology*, 3, 189–207.

Geschwind, N. (1965). 'Disconnexion syndromes in animals and man'. *Brain*, 88, 237–94, 585–644.

Goodglass, H. (1990). 'Commentary: cognitive psychology and clinical aphasiology'. *Aphasiology*, 4, 93–5.

Goodglass, H., Gleason, J., Bernholtz, N. and Hyde, M. (1970). 'Some linguistic structures in the speech of a Broca's aphasic'. *Cortex*, 8, 191–212.

Goodglass, H. and Kaplan, E. (1972, 1983). *Assessment of Aphasia and Related Disorders.* Philadelphia: Lea & Febiger.

Gravell, R. (1988). *Communication Problems in Elderly People.* London: Croom Helm.

Hagen, C. (1981). 'Language disorders secondary to closed head injury: diagnosis and treatment'. *Topics in Language Disorders*, September, 73–87.

Hagen, C. (1984). 'Language disorders in head trauma'. In A. Holland (ed.) *Language Disorders in Adults.* San Diego, CA: College-Hill Press.

Harris, A. I., Cox, E. and Smith, C. (1971). *Handicapped and Impaired in Great Britain*, Part 1. London: OPCS, Social Survey Division.

Head, H. (1926). *Aphasia and Kindred Disorders of Speech.* Cambridge: Cambridge University Press.

Holland, A. (1980). *Communicative Abilities in Daily Living.* Baltimore: University Park Press.

Holland, A. (1982). 'When is aphasia aphasia? The problem of closed head injury'. In R. Brookshire (ed.), *Clinical Aphasiology: Conference Proceedings.* Minneapolis, Minnesota: BRK Publishers.

Howard, D. (1985). 'Agrammatism'. In S. Newman and R. Epstein (eds), *Current Perspectives in Dysphasia.* Edinburgh: Churchill Livingstone.

Howard, D. (1987). 'Reading without letters?' In M. Coltheart, G. Sartori and R. Job (eds), *The Cognitive Neuropsychology of Language.* London: Erlbaum.

Howard, D. and Hatfield, F. (1987). *Aphasia Therapy: Historical and Contemporary Issues.* London: Erlbaum.

Howard, D. and Orchard-Lisle, V. (1984). 'On the origin of semantic errors in naming: evidence from a case of a global aphasic'. *Cognitive Neuropsychology*, 1, 163–90.

Howard, D., Patterson, K., Franklin, S., Orchard-Lisle, V. and Morton, J. (1985).

'Treatment of word retrieval deficits in aphasia: a comparison of two therapy methods'. *Brain*, 108, 49–80.

Hughlings-Jackson, J. (1878). 'On affectations of speech from disease of the brain'. *Brain*, 1, 304–30.

Huskins, S. (1986). *Working with Dyspraxics*. Bicester: Winslow Press.

Jennett, B., Snoak, J., Bond, M. and Brooks, N. (1981). 'Disability after severe head injury: observations in the use of the Glasgow Outcome Scale'. *Journal of Neurology, Neurosurgery and Psychiatry*, 44, 285–93.

Kay, J., Lesser, R. and Coltheart, M. (1992). *PALPA: Psycholinguistic Assessments of Language Processing in Aphasia*. Hove: Erlbaum.

Kertesz, A. (1982). *Western Aphasia Battery*. London: Harcourt, Brace & Jovanovich.

Kertesz, A. (1990). 'What should be the core of aphasia tests?' *Aphasiology*, 4: 1, 87–101.

Kucera, H. and Francis, W. (1967). *Computational Analysis of Present-day American English*. Providence: Brown University Press.

Lesser, R. and Milroy, L. (1987). 'Two frontiers in aphasia therapy'. *College of Speech Therapy*, 420, 1–3.

Lomas, J., Pickard, L., Bester, S., Elbard, H., Finlayson, A. and Zoghaib, C. (1989). 'The Communicative Effectiveness Index: development and psychometric evaluation of a functional communicative measure for adult aphasia'. *Journal of Speech and Hearing Disorders*, 54, 113–24.

McKenna, P. and Warrington, E. (1983). *Graded Naming Test*. Windsor: NFER-NELSON.

Mehler, J., Morton, J. and Juscyzk, P. (1984). 'On reducing language to biology'. *Cognitive Neuropsychology*, 1, 83–116.

Messick, S. (1980). 'The validity and ethics of assessment'. *American Psychologist*, 35, 1012–27.

Miller, N. (1986). *Dyspraxia and its Management*. London: Croom Helm.

Patterson, K. and Shewell, C. (1987). 'Speak and spell: dissociations and word-class effects'. In M. Coltheart, G. Sartori and R. Job (eds), *The Cognitive Neuropsychology of Language*. London: Erlbaum.

Riddoch, M. and Humphreys, G. (eds) (1987). *Visual Object Processing: a cognitive neuropsychological approach*. London: Erlbaum.

Rosenbek, J. and LaPointe, L. (1980). 'The dysarthrias: description, diagnosis and management'. In D. Johns (ed.), *Clinical Management of Neurogenic Communication Disorders*. Boston: Little Brown.

Sarno, M. (1969). *Functional Communication Profile*. Institute of Rehabilitation Medicine, New York University, New York.

Schuell, H. (1965, 1973). *Differential Diagnosis of Aphasia with the Minnesota Test*. Minneapolis: University of Minnesota.

Schuell, H., Jenkins, J. and Jimenez-Pabon, E. (1964). *Aphasia in Adults: Diagnosis, Prognosis and Treatment*. New York: Harper & Row.

Skinner, C., Wirz, S., Thompson, I. and Davidson, J. (1984). *Edinburgh Functional Communication Profile*. Buckingham: Winslow Press.

Snodgrass, J. and Vandervart, M. (1980). 'A standardized set of 260 pictures: norms for name agreement, image agreement, familiarity and visual complexity'. *Journal of Experimental Psychology: Human Learning and Memory*, 6, 174–215.

Speech Therapy in Practice. Special Supplements: Head Injury. (1990). Parts I, II and III, June, August and October.

Spreen, O. and Risser, A. (1981). 'Assessment of aphasia'. In M. Sarno (ed.)

Acquired Aphasia. New York: Academic Press.

Trost J. and Canter, G. (1974). 'Apraxia of speech in patients with Broca's Aphasia. A study of phonemic production accuracy and error patterns'. *Brain and Language*, 1, 63–79.

Weisenburg, T. and McBride, K. (1935). *Aphasia.* New York: Commonwealth Fund.

Weniger, D. (1990). 'Diagnostic tests as tools of assessment and models of information processing: a gap to bridge'. *Aphasiology*, 4: 1, 109–13.

Wernicke, C. (1874). *Der aphasische Symptomenkomplex: eine psychologische Studie auf anatomischer Basis.* Breslau: Cohn & Weigert. Translated by G. Eggert (1977), in *Wernicke's Works on Aphasia: A Sourcebook and Review.* The Hague: Monton.

Wertz, R., LaPointe, L. and Rosenbek, J. (1984). *Apraxia of Speech in Adults: the disorder and its management.* London: Grune & Stratton.

Whurr, R. (1974). *Aphasia Screening Test.* London: Cole & Whurr.

Wilson, B., Cockburn, J. and Baddeley, A. (1985). *Rivermead Behavioural Memory Test.* Fareham: Thames Valley Test Company.

Yorkston, K. and Beukelman, D. (1981). 'Communication efficiency of dysarthric speakers as measured by sentence intelligibility and speaking rate'. *Journal of Speech and Hearing Disorders*, 46, 296–301.

127

7

ASSESSMENT OF CHILDREN WITH SPECIAL NEEDS

Jannet A. Wright

Many children with special needs have communication problems. They may be referred to a speech and language therapist for the assessment and management of their difficulties either because a Statement of Need is proposed for such a child or because a specific communication assessment is required. If a statement is being prepared, the speech and language therapist will write a report, which will be included in the statement.

In this chapter the speech-and-language-therapy assessment of children with special needs will be discussed. Particular attention will be given to those with physical and sensory disabilities, and to those with specific language difficulties. Children with learning difficulties are the subject of the next chapter. The reader seeking detailed knowledge about the cause and manifestation of each of the disabilities is referred to other information sources. Speech and language therapists can also seek support and advice from specialist speech and language therapists in their health authority and from the advisors at the College of Speech and Language Therapists. It is hoped that this material will be relevant to both the generalist speech and language therapist and the student therapist who has to assess a child with special needs.

The chapter begins with a review of information about special needs. It covers issues that arise when a speech and language therapist is assessing any child who has a severe communication problem. The child with a communication difficulty may or may not have additional disabilities. The final part of the chapter looks at assessment procedures for children with physical and sensory disabilities, and those with specific language difficulties.

SPECIAL NEEDS

The school environment of children with special needs is in a state of change, following the introduction of the Education Reform Act (ERA) (1988). The ERA ushered in both the National Curriculum and local management of schools (LMS). The ERA has major implications for schools and support services, including speech and language therapy. The delivery of the curriculum, its content and the assessment of pupils at the four key stages at ages 7, 11, 14 and 16 years, have caused concern in both education and health services. The reporting of assessment results inside and outside the school has serious implications for all pupils, but particularly for a child with special needs. Support services that have provided specialist input for children with special needs, both in special and mainstream schools, have also been left in an uncertain position as they try to respond proactively to the issue of LMS (Lunt, 1990).

To understand some of the confusion in this area and the implications for children with special needs, it is helpful to look briefly at the Warnock Report (DES, 1978) and the 1981 Education Act (DES, 1981). Both these documents led to a greatly increased awareness among all professionals working in health, education and social services about those children with special needs.

Before the Warnock Report (DES, 1978), children who were identified as having difficulty in learning and so seen as being different from their peer group, were described using specific-categories labels. In 1921, the Education Act only recognized four categories – blind, deaf, defective and epileptic. But by 1945, there was an increase in the number of categories that were recommended for use when 'labelling' children; this suggests that professionals were more skilful in making a differential diagnosis. The Handicapped Pupils and School Heath Service Regulations (DES, 1945) defined eleven categories – blind, partially sighted, deaf, partially deaf, delicate, diabetic, educationally subnormal, epileptic, maladjusted, physically handicapped and speech-defective. A vast number of children identified and labelled under these categories received their education in special schools, away from the mainstream schools. However, there was a group of children with very severe learning difficulties that were still the responsibility of the health service until the 1970s. The Education (Handicapped Children) Act (DES, 1970) brought all handicapped children within the framework of special education. From 1970 onwards no child was to be thought of as ineducable.

The 1978 Warnock Report

The Committee of Inquiry into the Education of Handicapped Children and Young People was established in 1974, when the Rt Hon Margaret Thatcher MP was Secretary of State for Education and Science. This was the first Committee of Inquiry set up by a British government in order to review educational provision for all handicapped children.

A significant recommendation by the committee was that children should no longer be seen as two distinct groups, handicapped and non-handicapped; special education should be seen as a continuum of educational provision. Children should not be labelled according to their handicaps, but should be considered according to their need. This marked the introduction of the term Special Educational Need (SEN). It was hoped that this change in terminology would encourage people to describe a child's strengths and weaknesses and not resort to a label that implied a uniformity among all children who were given a specific label. This change in the conceptual framework of how children with difficulties were viewed led to a move away from the use of a 'within child' model of assessment and intervention in education circles. This concept was already familiar to speech and language therapists, as they had been utilizing this approach with their clients for some time.

The Warnock Report recommended the following terminology when describing a child's difficulties:

- physical disabilities, sensory disabilities
- learning difficulties – mild, moderate or severe
- specific learning difficulties
- emotional or behavioural problems

Many of the recommendations from this report were incorporated into the 1981 Act.

The 1981 Education (Handicapped Children) Act

When this Act was implemented in 1983, the concept of special educational needs was adopted. The rights of the individual were stressed; for example, there was increased parent power and SENs were seen to occur across a continuum of difficulty. The 1981 Education Act highlighted the need for professionals in health and education to come together to plan and deliver an effective and efficient service for children with Special Educational Needs in mainstream primary schools (Goacher et al. 1988).

The 1981 Act gave local education authorities the task of identifying children with special needs and 'recording' them. This could begin before two years of age with parental consent, between two and five years at the parents' request and between five and sixteen years while the child was at school.

The Warnock Report recommended five stages of assessment (paragraph 4.35). The first three were to take place in school. During stage three, professionals may be brought in by the headteacher or school doctor. At stages four and five a multiprofessional assessment is required (paragraph 4.48). Such an assessment may lead to a Statement of Special Needs being prepared. In the statement the special educational provision required by the child will be stated. The local education authority (LEA) must submit a draft copy of the statement to the child's parents; they then have fifteen days in which to make a response to the statement and to ask for an interview with an LEA officer. Such a statement should be reviewed annually. As practitioners know, the preparation of such statements has often taken longer than initially envisaged and some LEAs have accumulated a backlog of statements.

Speech and language therapists contributing to such a statement should now be reassured by the recommendations of paragraph 42, Circular 22/89, which replaced Circular 1/83. In Circular 22/89 it is stated that advice about all therapy services provided by the district health authority (DHA) should be passed 'in full' to the LEA and attached as Appendix G. This should ensure that all headteachers and class teachers will have full details of the child's needs from the speech and language therapist's viewpoint and the way in which provision for these needs will be made.

Provision

Planning of services for children and young people should be based on the assumption that about 1 in 6 children at any time and up to 1 in 5 children at some time during their school career will require some form of special educational provision.

(Warnock Report, paragraph 3.17)

This recommendation from the Warnock Report meant that a much larger number or wider group of children would be seen as having SENs than had previously been catered for, although the numbers of children being recorded would vary, depending on LEA policy. In some authorities children with special needs have always been educated in ordinary schools, and in these cases the LEA may decide to continue this practice and not produce a statement. In other authorities a statement was seen as a way of securing the personnel and equipment to support a child with special needs in mainstream or special schools. The Warnock Report supported the view that children who may previously have been educated in special schools could remain in mainstream schools if their needs could be appropriately met.

There remains a need for LEAs and governors to take steps to satisfy parents of children without statements that appropriate educational provision will be available in schools to meet their particular needs. Schools should publish information for parents indicating their special support provision for children with SEN, but with no statements.

(Paragraph 16, Circular 22/89)

Influence on speech and language therapy practice

As the majority of children seen by speech and language therapists do not have a statement, paragraph 16 from Circular 22/89 is particularly relevant to speech-and-language-therapy services. The child may be referred by a teacher, parent or doctor, in fact anyone concerned about the development of the child's speech and language. In some cases the speech-and-language-therapy service may only be involved for a short time. However, for children with a communication problem and an additional primary or secondary difficulty such as a hearing loss or physical disability, speech and language therapy may be a necessary support throughout their school life. This in itself raises issues of prolonged intervention and the effectiveness of the speech and language therapist as the sole provider of speech and language therapy.

> How much sense is there in operating a speech therapy service on an individual treatment basis to all pupils who have delayed speech and language development? Instead, a training/advisory role vis-à-vis teachers and parents may be a more profitable alternative for such services.
>
> (Dessent, 1987, p. 103)

Dessent writes from an educator's perspective, but, since the 1981 Education Act, new posts have been created for speech and language therapists to work in mainstream schools or to support statemented children in the mainstream. This changing approach to children with special needs has brought many innovations in the delivery of speech-and-language-therapy services. However, for school-age children with communication problems, the recent High Court rulings have failed to clarify whether speech and language therapy is an educational or non-educational provision. This situation is re-stated in the Circular 22/89:

> In the case of speech therapy provision LEAs should be aware that the High Court case of R. v Lancashire County Council ex parte CM (March 1989) ruled that speech therapy provision could be considered as either educational or non-educational provision.
>
> (Paragraph 63)

The 1988 Education Reform Act

The publication of the National Curriculum will mean that, at least in theory, speech and language therapists will be aware of the requirements of the curriculum. This may make it easier to plan therapy programmes that are more relevant to the child's classroom activities. At the same time, the prominence given to oracy in the English curriculum (DES – Kingman Report, 1988; NCC – National Oracy Project, 1987) will have an influence on the way teachers think about language and communication. Teachers may wish to make more referrals to speech and language therapy or ask for greater speech-and-language-therapy support in school. Alongside this, there are fears that with LMS (Local Management of Schools) speech-and-language-therapy services may not reach the children with communication problems who require them. Local speech-and-language-therapy services will have to be publicized in order to enable headteachers to make an informed choice about the type of help to buy in for children with communication problems.

SPEECH-AND-LANGUAGE-THERAPY ASSESSMENT OF CHILDREN WITH SPECIAL NEEDS

Children with special needs require a multidisciplinary assessment. In some areas this assessment will be carried out by a multidisciplinary team who are all based in the same place, for example, a regional child development centre. In other areas, the child, being assessed by several different professionals, has to travel to different centres to be seen and any inter-disciplinary discussion between professionals will occur on the telephone. Whatever the local arrangements, certain general points apply to any speech-and-language-therapy assessment of a child with special needs. In the following section these general assessment issues will be outlined. Many points in this section are applicable to any child referred for a speech-and-language-therapy assessment, not only one seen to have special needs.

In carrying out a speech-and-language-therapy assessment the aims are:

- to identify any difficulty with communication
- to measure the degree of that difficulty and the individual's strengths and weaknesses
- to plan the goals of an intervention strategy
- to plan procedures for intervention and negotiate with other professionals as well as the family
- to evaluate progress

These aims make the assessment of a child with communication problems sound very straightforward. In fact, the variability of the behaviour and performance of many children with special needs makes the task complex and particularly demanding. The points below, which cover the structural aspects of an assessment, as opposed to the content, are applicable to all children with special needs.

- assessment venue
- number of assessment sessions
- length of assessment session
- people present during the assessment
- material
- communication medium
- parental anxiety
- previous speech-and-language-therapy contact

Assessment venue

A child referred for assessment, who is thought to have or known to have special needs, should be seen in as many different settings as possible. If the child attends a nursery or school, it is imperative that some of the assessment takes place in that setting. This enables the therapist to observe the child's communication environment, how the child uses language in the classroom and the 'coping' strategies used by the child. At least one assessment session will need to take place in a quiet room, with furniture of an appropriate height. There needs to be enough light and it should be as quiet as possible to ensure that the child will perform as well as possible. The interaction of the data collected in all settings will influence the goals of therapy and the method used to reach these goals.

Number of times each child is seen

It is important to ensure that the adults requesting an assessment for a particular child realize that more than one appointment is required. However long a single session takes, it is rarely sufficient. Speech and language therapists may find themselves under pressure from other professionals who may feel that this slows down the statementing procedure, but a report based on one meeting is inappropriate. Thus, the time taken will vary from client to client; for example, a child with physical problems that affect the oral musculature will need to be seen when eating and drinking; this in itself will dictate the time of day that the session takes place and the length of the session.

Length of each assessment session

The expectation that a child's concentration span will increase with chronological age is challenged by this client group. Several different activities will need to be offered in each assessment session in order to maintain a child's attention and establish an accurate picture of the child's skills. One needs to record which material holds the attention most successfully, the longest period of concentration, and the average length of time the child can spend on any task. Both motivation and fatigue, especially with the physically disabled child, influence the length of the assessment sessions.

People present during the assessment

When relatives or teachers are present during assessment sessions, the therapist has a chance to observe family and educational interaction patterns. This ensures that parents also have some idea of the therapist's

134

views prior to receiving a copy of the official report. When assessing children from a linguistic or cultural background that differs from that of the therapist, the presence of other family members and an interpreter is crucial.

The ideal situation is one in which one worker can assess the child while another worker watches with the parents. This provides an opportunity to explain to the parents what is happening and to collect their immediate thoughts about their child's performance.

In spite of the problems a teacher may have being released from the classroom, every effort should be made to involve the teacher in the assessment. If there is a designated special-needs teacher in the school it may be possible for this teacher to cover for the child's class teacher. Alternatively, the special-needs teacher could sit in on the speech-and-language-therapy assessment and act as a mediator between therapist and class teacher. Similarly, if an assessment can take place jointly with another relevant professional, such as the physiotherapist, occupational therapist, teacher of the visually impaired or hearing impaired, then the final report and recommendations for therapy from the speech and language therapist will have greater relevance to the needs of the child.

Material used

When assessing a child with SENs the same care will be taken to select appropriate material for the child's chronological age, interests and cultural background, as when assessing any child being seen by the speech and language therapist. The therapist needs to choose material that is relevant to the child's experience so that errors on tests are not due to lack of familiarity with the material. This is particularly true when using tests which have been designed in America. Larger objects and pictures may need to be used as they are easier to pick up, or to see if a child has visual or physical difficulties. They may need to be spread out if eye-pointing or fisting is used as a response mode. The consistency and specificity of the child's mode of response will influence the material chosen. Some children with specific language impairment find certain pictures are too abstract or difficult to understand and respond to. The book by Musselwhite (1986) offers useful strategies and ideas for material to use in assessments, particularly when considering non-verbal/pre-verbal communication.

Therapists need to be aware of the volume level of their voice, their rate of speech and the position in which they sit in relation to the child as well as the level of light in the room. Therapists are more likely to concentrate on non-verbal aspects of communication when assessing children with special needs, either because the children take longer to develop spoken language than their peers, or because they are unlikely to develop verbal skills due to the severity of their disability.

Communication medium

For many children with special needs, an alternative or augmentative system may be utilized to initiate communication, to support verbal interaction or as a main tool to facilitate learning and communicating. The therapist will need to be aware which communication medium the child uses; it could be a sign or symbol system. The therapist also needs to be aware of the generalized description 'they use x at school', because this may mean one or two signs are used in class or it may mean that they are used in specific teaching sessions when signs or symbols are taught but not much more. At any assessment procedure, for a hearing-impaired child who uses British Sign Language (BSL), an interpreter whose first language is BSL will need to be present.

The therapist, whilst observing the child in a school or home setting, needs to note the type of language input the child receives.

Parental anxiety

As with any other speech-and-language-therapy assessment, relatives of a child being seen by the therapist may be anxious. With a child with special needs who may or may not be statemented, this anxiety can be even greater. This tension and expectation cannot be underestimated, especially in situations in which a communication problem has become the only difficulty that the parents are willing to acknowledge and accept.

Prior contact with speech and language therapy

Speech and language therapists are well advised to acquaint themselves with the child's prior contact with other such therapists. It is this previous contact that will influence the family's and school's expectation of what speech and language therapy can offer. At the initial meeting, the therapist needs to explain his or her aims and establish what the parents and teachers understand of the therapist's role, especially if the child is being statemented.

INDIVIDUAL ASSESSMENT

A therapist seeing a child with special needs for a speech and language assessment should try to collate previous reports, to build up a background picture of the child prior to face-to-face contact. The reports may come from the following sources: medical, neurological, audiological, ophthalmological, social, psychological, educational and linguistic.

The child's communication competence and performance needs to be established and a baseline measure of his or her receptive and expressive language skills obtained. This will involve an assessment of:

- the child's communication with adults and peer group, both verbal and non-verbal
- the comprehension and expression of language, including phonology, syntax, semantics, pragmatics, fluency, voice

The methods used will include those already mentioned elsewhere in this book which fall under the broad headings of:

- interviews and reports
- observations – descriptive. For example, a diary is kept; time- or event-sampling is used. Manner and style of interaction are noted as well as verbal and non-verbal aspects. The child's attention and concentration is recorded, as well as the responses made to own name, noise outside the room, favourite toys, games. The child's relationship with adults and peers. Child's fine and gross motor skills
- language samples which may be displayed using a profile format
- non-standardized procedures developed by individual therapists.

(Plus an interaction of all these methods.)

Standardized assessment material is referred to in this chapter, although tests which are norm-referenced are not always appropriate for the child with special needs. An assessment report that includes details of the child's strengths and weaknesses in the communication field will be more valuable in planning an intervention programme than one that only gives test scores. If modified test material is presented to children with special needs, they can indicate their knowledge or level of understanding without the standardized scores being recorded.

Bilingual clients

A child whose first language is not English is not necessarily someone with special needs in terms of the 1981 Act:

> a child is not taken as having a learning difficulty solely because the language (or form of the language) in which he is or will be taught is different from the language (or form of the language) which has at any time been spoken in his home.

(p. 18)

However, bilingual children may have a sensory, physical or specific impairment. They may also have a communication problem. In this situation they will need to be assessed in their mother tongue. Any therapist who sees children who have special needs, who are also bilingual, is referred to the work of Miller (1984) and Duncan (1989).

137

PHYSICAL DISABILITIES

Children who have a physical disability may include those with cerebral palsy, spina bifida and muscular dystrophy. The variability of the type and severity of the motor problem is matched by the variation in the neurological origin of the problem. The child may be at risk of some sensory impairment, and so the sections in this chapter relating to these areas of difficulty are also relevant to some children with physical problems. The child may have such difficulty with control of the oral musculature that dribbling, poor sensation of touch and lack of awareness of muscle and joint movement will add to his or her problems when trying to eat, drink and produce intelligible speech. The child may have dysarthria and dyspraxia.

When assessing a child who has physical problems, the speech and language therapist must have a copy of the medical report. This report should indicate whether the child's condition is stable or degenerative. This information is crucial when planning therapy and the prognosis. Because of the child's physical difficulties, the therapist will need to liaise with both the physiotherapist and the occupational therapist. This will help to establish the appropriate positioning to achieve the maximum performance during a speech-and-language-therapy assessment and future intervention (Hacker and Porter, 1987). Particular attention will need to be given to the assessment of hand–eye co-ordination because this will influence material used in further assessments. The information from all these sources, together with the reports from the neurologists, will help the therapist to decide where to focus attention during the sessions, whether on the non-verbal aspects of communication or on the verbal aspects. Factors such as the child's ability to co-ordinate respiration and phonation, to produce intelligible speech, and his or her cognitive abilities, will be taken into account when the family, school and therapist consider whether to encourage the child to use an alternative or augmentative communication system (Shane, 1987).

Non-verbal communication

Assessment in the area of non-verbal communication can be considered for both the child who is unaided and will not be using a communication aid, and for someone who will use an aid. An alternative or augmentative system can be selected from a range of sign and symbol systems and technical communication aids (Kiernan, 1987; Shane, 1987; Udwin, 1987). The therapist needs to be aware of the advantages and disadvantages of each system and of the Communication Aids Centres (Allen *et al.*, 1989) which offer assessments, information and an opportunity to view a range of aids, switches and computer programmes. The choice of technical aid as well as the appropriate switch to use the aid will be influenced by the child's physical ability, cognitive and linguistic skills.

In the initial stages of gathering information the Pragmatic Profile of Early Communication Skills (Dewart and Summers, 1988) offers the therapist a valuable way of interviewing parents to establish how their child uses the language he or she has to express needs, feelings and emotions. This profile is a useful way of recording information both for children with verbal skills as well as those who have little or no verbal language. The Pre-Verbal Communication Schedule (Kiernan and Reid, 1987), although designed for use with clients who have severe learning difficulties, is a useful tool when assessing very physically handicapped children.

When devising material to use in a session the point that Bishop (1988) makes about the fact that the direction of gaze to establish the shared reference is likely to be well developed in these children and may be seen as one of the child's strengths, is useful to remember. Also, many of the strategies suggested by Musselwhite (1986) offer possible ways of assessing non-verbal skills. The book edited by Coupe and Goldbart (1988) offers valuable ideas and material when assessing the severely impaired child.

Tests such as the Boehm Test of Basic Concepts can be used to assess concept development, as the material can be responded to by eye-pointing or fisting.

Children with physical disabilities require a detailed assessment of their feeding by a speech and language therapist (Evans Morris, 1982; Evans Morris and Klein, 1987; McCarthy, 1984). This provides an opportunity to evaluate the oral structure and function, co-ordination of respiration and phonation and non-speech movements.

Verbal communication

In situations where family and relatives report that they understand everything the child says, ask them to interpret several of the child's utterances and give examples of the child's utterances. This can help them to establish the value of other means of communication. An assessment of the child's articulation (Milloy and Morgan Barry, 1990) and his or her phonological system (Grunwell, 1985) enable the therapist to make a diagnosis of dysarthria or dyspraxia.

One of the results of a motor impairment is the limitations it places on children's ability to explore their environment and learn. Assessment of receptive vocabulary using the British Picture Vocabulary Scale (BPVS) (Dunn et al., 1982) often reveals large and unexpected areas where vocabulary is not known because the child has had a limited life experience. The BPVS lends itself to adaptation so that eye-pointing can be an appropriate response. Two tests for assessing verbal comprehension, the Test of Reception of Grammar (TROG) (Bishop, 1977) and the Test for Auditory Comprehension (TACL-R) (Carrow-Woolfolk, 1985), are presented in such a way that a child could respond by eye-pointing.

SENSORY DISABILITIES – AUDITORY

As a result of the introduction, by the College of Speech and Language Therapists, of the Advanced Certificate of Study for those working with the hearing-impaired, many more speech and language therapists have specialist knowledge about the assessment and management of clients with hearing difficulties. Therapists asked to assess any client who may have or who has had a hearing loss diagnosed should seek out such specialists. The child who has been diagnosed as deaf or partially hearing presents the speech and language therapist with a different challenge from the one referred where a hearing loss is suspected but has not been confirmed. It is the latter case which is more likely if the child has additional special needs. Where a hearing loss has been diagnosed, the therapist will also need to liaise with the teacher of the deaf.

In the case of a child with a suspected but unconfirmed hearing loss, much of a therapist's assessment and initial management may be aimed at preparing the child to respond appropriately to audiological assessments. Such investigations may be lengthy, and at each appointment only one response may definitely be established at one frequency. The use of objective, but 'invasive' measures of hearing, for example, electrocochleography, may be used but their availability will depend on geographical location and local waiting lists. Thus, it is often necessary for the therapist to work with a child in the absence of a definite diagnosis. The reader searching for a description of hearing assessments and conditions is referred to McCormick (1988) and Webster and Wood (1989).

Therapists assessing the communication abilities of a hearing-impaired child need to pay particular attention to the noise levels in and outside the therapy room. They also need to be aware of the volume of their own voice. Soft furnishings in the room will help to reduce reverberation. The therapist's make-up, jewellery, even perfume, may influence the child's ability to concentrate on and respond to the therapist's verbal and non-verbal communication.

The therapist assessing a child with a possible hearing loss needs to have an awareness of the history and politics of educational approaches to deaf children. The advice and information that the parents of this child have already received will have been influenced by the opinions and beliefs of the local medical and educational staff.

If a child, to be seen by the speech and language therapist, has had a hearing loss diagnosed, the therapist needs to find out what amplification has been recommended. When the therapist sees the child for assessment, it will be necessary to check that the child's hearing aid is working. If the therapist is not sure how to do this, he or she should seek help from specialist therapists, a teacher of the deaf or hearing-aid centre.

Non-verbal communication

A child who uses a communication medium other than speech needs to be assessed by someone who uses sign or symbol system. The child will be disadvantaged if he or she uses British Sign Language (BSL) to communicate and the speech and language therapist is not familiar with this system; an interpreter will need to be involved in the assessment procedure.

If the child does not use a recognized system, then the Pragmatic Profile of Early Communication Skills (Dewart and Summers, 1988) is a structured way of interviewing the parents about how their child communicates. Observation of the child with parents and peers will also provide information about turn-taking, shared attention and joint reference (Bruner, 1975; Halliday, 1975; McTear 1985).

Verbal communication

When using standardized tests to assess comprehension, the therapist needs to be aware of errors, which are in fact due to the child's inability to hear the sounds which signal, for example, plurality or possession. This would be the case in tests such as TROG (Bishop, 1977) and TACL-R (Carrow-Woolfolk, 1985).

Samples of the child's output can be analysed using any of the currently available procedures such as the Language Assessment, Remediation and Screening Procedure (LARSP) (Crystal *et al.*, 1976; Williams and Dennis, 1979; Bamford and Bench, 1979), Bristol Language Development Scales (Gutfreund, 1989) and Bloom and Lahey (1978). These, together with reference to texts on language acquisition in the hearing-impaired (Gregory and Mogford, 1981; Wood *et al.*, 1986), will help the therapist to plan an appropriate intervention scheme.

Investigation of the child's articulation (Milloy and Morgan Barry, 1990) and phonological system (Grunwell, 1985) will be necessary, as well as detailed recordings and analysis of intonation and voice quality.

SENSORY DISABILITIES – VISUAL

Therapists asked to see the visually disabled child for assessment are referred to such authors as Fraiberg (1977), Mills (1983) and Fitt and Mason (1986) for information on visual handicap and the implications in development. They will also need to confirm that they have copies of the ophthalmologist's report, and understand the implications of these findings for learning.

The child with a visual disability may be someone who has problems with the field of vision or the focus of vision. Focusing difficulties may be helped by glasses or other aids. Problems in the field of vision can be

141

divided into problems with peripheral vision and problems within the field of vision, where a fragmented or fuzzy image is seen by the child (Fitt and Mason, 1986; Dunlea, 1989). Some children have problems with both the field and the focus of their vision. A child born without eyes, who has no concept of light as the sighted person knows it, presents a different challenge to a speech and language therapist.

The child with a visual deficit appears to develop language in different ways from sighted peers (Andersen, Dunlea and Kekelis, 1984; McConachie, 1990). These variations appear to be related to cognitive development, in which lack of visual information alters the experiences and activities that the blind child is able to experience.

Non-verbal communication

The Pragmatic Profile of Early Communication Skills (Dewart and Summers, 1988) offers a useful way of gathering information from care-givers. Its focus on the use of language and thus social skills makes it an ideal starting point for assessing children with visual problems. It is particularly important for therapists to seek details from the parents about the child's associated physical movements when engaged in communi-cation. Much of the blind child's apparent 'bizarre' behaviour may arise from a response to their visual difficulties, for example, the child who rocks back and forth. This activity may help the child to gain some visual stimu-lation from the environment.

The young blind baby will not be able to engage in the non-verbal communication games and routines that rely on seeing the other person's face. Rather, he or she relies on touch and tone of voice. The therapist needs to seek information about and observe the way in which parents help their child to learn language. When drawing the child's attention to something, do they help the child to use their other senses by saying 'listen, it's a —' or 'feel this, it's a —'? How specific are both parents and teachers in giving instructions to the child; for example, by saying 'put the book on the table' rather than 'put it over there'?

Children's listening skills will need careful assessment as they can be an important aid to future learning. The recognition of environmental sounds is important for safety and mobility. In the classroom their schoolwork may be presented on audiotape. When looking at these areas in the younger child there are useful suggestions of materials and activities in Barbara Riddick's book (1982).

Verbal communication

A child with a visual disability is likely to have delayed or incomplete concept development, due to his or her restricted visual experiences. This has implications for the growth of the child's vocabulary and classroom learning. The child's vocabulary will be shaped by visual experiences and so will differ from that of sighted peers, especially in the early stages of development (Landau and Gleitman, 1985; Dunlea, 1989). The child may also use a considerable amount of echolalia as he or she learns to talk.

The Reynell-Zinkin Scales for Young Visually Handicapped Children (1979) has among its five subscales one on response to sound and verbal comprehension and one assessing expressive language. The scales can be used with both blind and partially sighted children up to the age of five years.

A language sample can be collected from a visually impaired child's articulation (LARSP, Crystal *et al.*, 1976 and Bloom and Lahey, 1978). When transcribing and analysing the sample, the therapist needs to be aware of some of the anomalies that can arise from the language of a child who does not have the same visual information as his or her peers; for example, a blind six-year-old child may talk about the trees holding up the sky. This is an understandable comment and not one which indicates a semantic-pragmatic problem.

SPECIFIC LANGUAGE DISORDERS

The identification and management of children with specific developmental language disorders is a complex task. The history of the terminology and evolution of clinical subtypes is well reviewed by Bishop and Rosenbloom (1987) and Byers Brown and Edwards (1989). These children have been labelled in a variety of ways: 'aphasic', 'dysphasic', 'developmentally dysphasic', 'language disordered' (Wyke, 1978). They are children who have undergone a thorough investigation in all areas of their development but the origin of their difficulty remains an area for speculation and continued research. Consequently, the term 'specific language disorder' means that all the possibilities that could have contributed to the condition have been excluded.

The child with a specific language disorder is a complex clinical and educational entity, who is often able to perform within the average range on non-verbal assessments. These children have great difficulty in acquiring language without structured teaching, either in language units and special language schools or with considerable support in mainstream schools.

Another group of children described as 'acquired childhood aphasics' are skilled language-users who lose these abilities due to neurological damage following, for example, a road-traffic accident. These children have marked language problems and difficulties with schoolwork.

Children who have Landau-Kleffner syndrome (Bishop, 1985) are small in numbers; they appear to lose their developing language skills when very

143

young. This loss may be associated with seizures. They have very severe comprehension problems and may develop written language in advance of their spoken language. These children need specialist teaching and speech-and-language-therapy support throughout their school life.

Children with a specific language problem can have problems at every linguistic level. They find it difficult to deal with abstract material, they are 'concrete' in their thinking and operate in the 'here and now' (Beveridge and Conti-Ramsden, 1987). They can understand slapstick humour because of the visual presentation but do not understand a sarcastic comment.

Non-verbal communication

The very young child needs a detailed assessment of its symbolic skills and concept formation using, for example, the Symbolic Play Test (Lowe and Costello, 1976) and/or the methods described in *Helping Language Development* (Cooper, Moodley and Reynell, 1974). The Boehm Test of Basic Concepts (Boehm, 1986) will provide additional information.

The Pragmatic Profile of Early Communication Skills (Dewart and Summers, 1988) offers a way to collect data about the child's use of language and the early stages of communication. Ideas from the work of Halliday (1975) will support this type of assessment.

Verbal communication

These children need a full assessment of their auditory sequencing and discriminatory abilities. The Auditory Discrimination and Attention Test (Morgan Barry, 1988) offers a structured way of beginning this investigation.

The young child's verbal comprehension can be assessed using the Reynell Developmental Language Scales (Reynell, 1977). This test emphasizes the conceptual base of comprehension. The Test of Reception of Grammar (TROG) (Bishop, 1977) and the Test for Auditory Comprehension (TACL-R) (Carrow-Woolfolk, 1985) focus on the comprehension of syntax. The Token Test for Children (DiSimoni, 1978) is useful for assessing comprehension in the older child. Assessment of the child's receptive vocabulary can be done using the British Picture Vocabulary Scale (BPVS) (Dunn *et al.*, 1982).

The LARSP (Crystal *et al.*, 1976), the Bloom and Lahey approach (1978) and the Bristol Language Development Scales (Gutfreund, 1989) offer alternative ways of analysing language samples. Evaluation of both articulatory and phonological skills is necessary for most of these children.

The Edinburgh Articulation Test (Anthony *et al.*, 1971) and the Phonological Assessment of Child Speech (Grunwell, 1985) may be used as well as material devised by the individual therapist.

CONCLUSION

Children with special needs require detailed investigation. The assessment procedure is a continuous process with material being adapted to suit the individual child. In this chapter some general issues have been outlined; these apply to any assessment situation. Specific disability areas have been dealt with under separate headings, but these are only introductory sections. Further reading, research and practice are required in order to become a skilled assessor of children with sensory, physical and specific language impairment.

When assessing a child with special needs the members of a multi-professional team need to keep in mind the purpose of the assessment and how the results or information gained will be used. If all the professionals, as well as the child's family, are aware of the individual's strengths and weaknesses following an assessment, then the child's communication development should be enhanced.

ACKNOWLEDGEMENTS

I would like to thank my colleagues Myra Kersner, Michael Jackson, Magdalene Moorey and Sandy Winyard for the helpful comments on this chapter.

REFERENCES

Allen, J., Cockrill, H., Davies, E., Fuller, P., Jollife, N., Larcher, J., Nelms, G. and Winyard, S. (1989). *Augmentative Communication: more than just words.* Oxfordshire: ACE Centre.

Andersen, E. S., Dunlea, A. and Kekelis, L.S. (1984). 'Blind children's language: resolving some differences'. *Journal of Child Language,* 11, 645–64.

Anthony, A., Bogle, D., Ingram, T. T. S. and McIsaac, M. W. (1971). *The Edinburgh Articulation Test.* Edinburgh: Churchill Livingstone.

Bamford, J. M. and Bench, J. (1979). 'A grammatical analysis of the speech of partially-hearing children'. In D. Crystal (ed.), *Working with LARSP.* London: Edward Arnold.

Beveridge, M. and Conti-Ramsden, G. (1987). *Children with Language Disabilities.* Milton Keynes: Open University Press.

Bishop, D. V. M. (1977). *Test of Reception of Grammar (TROG).* Manchester: University of Manchester.

Bishop, D. V. M. (1985). 'Age of onset and outcome in "Acquired Aphasia with Convulsive Disorder" (Landau Kleffner Syndrome)'. *Developmental Medicine and Child Neurology,* 27, 705–12.

Bishop, D. (1988). 'Language development in children with abnormal structure or function of the speech apparatus'. In D. Bishop, and K. Mogford (eds), *Language Development in Exceptional Circumstances.* Edinburgh/London: Churchill Livingstone.

Bishop, D. and Rosenbloom, L. (1987). 'Childhood language disorders: classifi-

145

cation and overview'. In W. Yule and M. Rutter (eds), *Language Development and Disorders*. London: Mac Keith Press.

Bloom, L. and Lahey, M. (1978). *Language Development and Language Disorders*. Chichester: Wiley.

Boehm, A. (1986). *Boehm Test of Basic Concepts*. Revised edn. New York: Harcourt Brace Jovanovich.

Bruner, J. (1975). 'The ontogenesis of speech acts'. *Journal of Child Language*, 2, 1–19.

Byers Brown, B. and Edwards, M. (1989). *Developmental Disorders of Language*. London: Whurr.

Carrow-Woolfolk, E. (1985). *Test for Auditory Comprehension of Language*. Windsor: NFER-NELSON.

Cooper, J. M., Moodley, M. and Reynell, J. (1974). *Helping Language Development*. London: Edward Arnold.

Coupe, J. and Goldbart, J. (eds) (1988). *Communication Before Speech*. London: Croom Helm.

Crystal, D., Fletcher, P. and Garman, M. (1976). *Language Assessment, Remediation and Screening Procedure*. London: Edward Arnold.

DES (1921). *The Education Act*. London: HMSO.

DES (1945). *The Handicapped Pupils and School Health Service Regulations*. London: HMSO.

DES (1970). *Education (Handicapped Children) Act*. London: HMSO.

DES (1978). *Special Educational Needs: report of the Committee of Inquiry into the education of handicapped children and young people* (the Warnock Report). London: HMSO.

DES (1981). *Education Act*. London: HMSO.

DES (1983). *Assessment and Statements of Special Educational Need*, Circular 1/83. London: HMSO.

DES (1988). *Report of the (Kingman) Committee of Inquiry into the Teaching of English Language*. London: HMSO

DES (1988). *The Education Reform Act*. London: HMSO.

DES (1989). *Assessment and Statements of SEN: procedures within the education, health and social services*, Circular 22/89. London: HMSO.

Dessent, T. (1987). *Making the Ordinary School Special*. London: Falmer Press.

Dewart, H. and Summers, S. (1988). *Pragmatic Profile of Early Communication Skills*. Windsor: NFER-NELSON.

DiSimoni, F. (1978). *The Token Test for Children*. Hingham: Teaching Resources.

Duncan, D. M. (ed.) (1989). *Working with Bilingual Language Disability*. London: Chapman and Hall.

Dunlea, A. (1989). *Vision and the Emergence of Meaning: blind and sighted children's early language*. Cambridge: Cambridge University Press.

Dunn, L., Dunn, L., Whetton, C. and Pantile, D. (1982). *British Picture Vocabulary Scale*. Windsor: NFER-NELSON.

Evans Morris, S. (1982). *The Pre-Speech Assessment Scale*. Clifton, N.J.: Preston.

Evans Morris, S. and Klein, M.D. (1987). *Pre-Feeding Skills*. Tucson, AZ: Therapy Skills Builders.

Fitt, R. A. and Mason, H. (1986). *Sensory Handicaps in Children*. Stratford-upon-Avon: National Council for Special Education.

Fraiberg, S. (1977). *Insights from the Blind*. Human Horizon series. London: Souvenir Press.

Goacher, B., Evans, J., Welton, J. and Wedell, K. (1988). *Policy and Provision for Special Educational Needs*. London: Cassell.

Gregory, S. and Mogford, K. (1981). 'Early language development in deaf children'. In B. Woll, J. Kyle and M. Deuchar (eds), *Perspectives on British Sign Language and Deafness.* London: Croom Helm.

Grunwell, P. (1985). *The Phonological Assessment of Child Speech (PACS).* Windsor: NFER-NELSON.

Gutfreund, M. (1989). *Bristol Language Development Scales.* Windsor: NFER-NELSON.

Hacker, B. J. and Porter, P. B. (1987). 'Use of standardized tests with the physically handicapped'. In L. King-Thomas and B. J. Hacker (eds), *A Therapist's Guide to Paediatric Assessment.* Boston: Little Brown.

Halliday, M. (1975). *Learning How to Mean: explorations in the development of language.* London: Edward Arnold.

Kiernan, C. C. (1987). 'Non-vocal communication systems: a critical survey'. In W. Yule and M. Rutter (eds), *Language Development and Disorders.* London: Mac Keith Press.

Kiernan, C. C. and Reid, B. D. (1987). *Pre-Verbal Communication Schedule.* Windsor: NFER-NELSON.

Landau, B. and Gleitman, L. R. (1985). *Language and Experience: evidence from the blind child.* Harvard: Harvard University Press.

Lowe, M. and Costello A. J. (1976). *The Symbolic Play Test.* Windsor: NFER-NELSON.

Lunt, I. (1990). 'Local management of schools and education services'. In H. Daniels and J. Ware (eds), *The National Curriculum and Special Educational Needs.* London: Kogan Page.

McCarthy, G. T. (ed.) (1984). *The Physically Handicapped Child: an inter-disciplinary approach to management.* London: Faber & Faber.

McConachie, H. (1990). 'Early language development and severe visual impairment'. *Child: Care, Health and Development,* 16, 55–61.

McCormick, B. (1988). *Paediatric Audiology 0–5 Years.* London: Taylor & Francis.

McTear, M. (1985). *Children's Conversations.* Oxford: Basil Blackwell.

Miller, N. (ed.) (1984). *Bilingualism and Language Disability – assessment and remediation.* London: Croom Helm.

Milloy, N. and Morgan Barry, R. (1990). 'Developmental neurological disorders'. In P. Grunwell, (ed.), *Developmental Speech Disorders.* Edinburgh: Churchill Livingstone.

Mills, A. E. (1983) (ed.) *Language Acquisition in the Blind Child.* London: Croom Helm.

Morgan Barry, R. (1988). *The Auditory Discrimination and Attention Test.* Windsor: NFER-NELSON.

Musselwhite, C. R. (1986). *Adaptive Play for Special Needs Children.* London: Taylor & Francis.

NCC (National Curriculum Council) (1987). *National Oracy Project. Planning Brief.* York: NCC.

Reynell, J. (1977). *Reynell Developmental Language Scales* (revised). Windsor: NFER-NELSON.

Reynell, J. and Zinkin, P. (1979). *Scales for Young Visually Handicapped Children.* Windsor: NFER-NELSON.

Riddick, B. (1982). *Toys and Play for the Handicapped Child.* London: Croom Helm.

Shane, H. C. (1987). 'Trends in communication aid technology for the severely speech-impaired'. In W. Yule and M. Rutter (eds), *Language Development and Disorders.* London: Mac Keith Press.

Udwin, O. (1987). 'Analysis of the experimental adequacy of alternative and augmentative communication training studies'. *Child Language Teaching and Therapy*, 3: 1, 18–39.

Webster, A. and Wood, D. (1989). *Children with Hearing Difficulties: Special Needs in Ordinary Schools.* London: Cassell.

Williams, J. E. and Dennis, D. B. (1979). 'A partially-hearing unit'. In D. Crystal (ed.), *Working with LARSP.* London: Edward Arnold.

Wood, D. J., Wood, H. A., Griffiths, A. J. and Howarth, C. I. (1986). *Teaching and Talking with Deaf Children.* Chichester: Wiley.

Wyke, M. A. (1978). *Developmental Dysphasia.* London: Academic Press.

8

ASSESSMENT OF MENTALLY HANDICAPPED INDIVIDUALS

Julie Dockrell and Clare Henry

a single isolated test score is of little or no value. For a score to have meaning and to be of social or scientific utility some sort of frame of reference is needed.

(Gardner, 1962: 7)

Assessment of the 'mentally handicapped' has posed a problem for practitioners for much of the past century. As our understanding of the issues surrounding mental handicap has become more sophisticated so the terminology used to identify this diverse set of problems has expanded (Fryers, 1984). The terms *feeble-minded* and *mentally deficient* are no longer in common usage. Yet there is no agreement among professionals about which term should be used despite the WHO's attempt to establish a consensus (Heron and Myers, 1983).[1]

In this chapter we have opted for the term 'learning difficulties' to describe the problems experienced by these individuals. There are two reasons for the choice of the term *learning*. In the first instance this prevents confusion with mental illness. More importantly it describes the characteristic limitation with which we are dealing, that is learning, without discriminating among such functions as memory, attention span, language or spatial abilities. Our choice of the term *difficulties* focuses attention on the nature of the disorder without specifying a priori whether patterns of development are characterized *only* by delay or *only* by differences (see section on the nature of the population). Moreover, this term is preferred by those who experience such problems (King's Fund Centre, 1980).

Our focus is on the assessment of children and young people who would traditionally have been called 'mentally handicapped'. In the subsequent sections we will (1) discuss the function of assessments in this population,

[1] In terms of the WHO proposed usage, 'intellectually disabled' is most often the expression of choice.

(2) outline the general problems that are experienced by individuals who have learning difficulties and the ways in which these problems should guide assessment and (3) provide details of assessment techniques.

WHY ASSESS?

Assessment is a process by which information is collected for a specific purpose. Assessment fulfils two main functions: differential diagnosis; and a basis for intervention and evaluation. Assessment and intervention should be linked, though this has tended not to be the case (Ysseldyke, 1987). Few of the existing assessment procedures have been designed to lead directly to remediation (Muller, Munro and Code, 1981). In this chapter we consider assessment to be an activity the objective of which is to elicit accurate and reliable information about a particular individual's competence. It will involve either one or a combination of the following: formal tools (through the use of standardized norm-referenced criteria); informal tools (through the use of developmental profiles or check-lists); exploratory tools (through the use of observational procedures or teaching experiments).

The existence of a learning difficulty is commonly taken to imply depressed performance on cognitive tests. However, assessment *cannot* be equated with a test result, rather it is a process that allows one to construct a profile of a particular individual's strengths and weaknesses (see Mittler, 1976). The exact procedures will be determined by the aim of a particular assessment. Appropriate testing may well form an integral part of the assessment. Assessment should be hypothesis-driven. That is, the assessment is begun with the aim of testing out ideas and, as it proceeds, further hypotheses will need to be considered. For example, it is commonplace to begin an assessment by searching for gross differences in expected behaviour patterns. As the process continues, specific and possibly explanatory mechanisms are considered.

Identification of learning difficulties often occurs prior to school entry but the need for assessments and interventions can continue to the older years. The questions addressed by the speech and language therapist will differ at various times in the life-cycle and in relation to the particular services being provided. The common thread of learning difficulty does not lead to a common package of assessment tools.

During the preschool and school years the speech and language therapist's role in differential diagnosis will be important. Specifically, contributions to the statement of special educational needs will serve to highlight specific speech, language and communication requirements. In such cases there will be a need to provide objective results from the assessment. During adolescence and adulthood different foci will be important. There may be a need to re-establish an individual in the community following an extended period in an institution. Alternatively, supporting an individual in his or her attempts to cope with the demands of daily life may guide assessment. Such goals will require a detailed analysis of the context and the development of situation-specific monitoring of skills. In generating a framework for assessment a constant tension should exist between the appropriate and informative. However, there is often poorly controlled use of naturalistic measures and the reliable, replicable but often inappropriate use of standardized measures.

Hypotheses need to be limited by an understanding of the factors that influence individual performance. Thus, it is necessary to consider what effect the individual's learning difficulties will have on processes which are required for successful performance on a particular task but which are not, in theory, being assessed. When we consider the domain of speech and language it will not be sufficient to highlight a delay for a child with learning difficulties but to consider that delay within the context of the child's overall level of performance.

What one does during the process of assessment and what one hopes to achieve by the assessment must be guided by a knowledge of the particular problem(s) experienced by individuals who have learning difficulties. How homogeneous is the target group? Are there similar patterns of development and difficulties or is there a range of developmental patterns? It will be argued that it is inappropriate to assume that all children with learning difficulties exhibit similar types of cognitive and language deficits with the extent of the problem being the single explanatory variable. Given this, the assessment process can never follow one simple pattern.

THE NATURE OF THE POPULATION

Mental handicap is operationally defined as sub-average intellectual functioning (i.e. IQ < 70), existing concurrently with deficits in adaptive behaviour and manifested in the developmental period (APA, 1980). The emphasis on the developmental period has focused our chapter.

It has been estimated that at least 2.5 per cent of children have learning difficulties (IQ < 70) and half of these show a severe language deficiency, articulation disorder or a combination of the two (Enderby and Davies, 1989; Rutter, Tizard and Whitmore, 1970). However, there is a significant difference between the levels of observed and predicted incidence of severe learning difficulties (Fryers, 1984). People with learning difficulties constitute the largest disabled population with communication disorders (Ingram, 1972). While there is a general consensus about which individuals are experiencing severe learning difficulties, the situation with respect to milder problems is not always clear-cut (Gillham, 1986).

A distinction is frequently drawn among those individuals whose difficulties are of organic origin and those whose difficulties are of unknown aetiology. For those individuals experiencing *severe* learning difficulties (roughly IQ < 50) aetiological implications can be identified in 85–90 per cent of the cases (Fryers, 1984). In contrast, for those individuals experiencing *mild* learning difficulties aetiological implications are less clear. At least 75 per cent of all those identified as having learning difficulties have no evidence of organic brain dysfunction (Balla and Zigler, 1982).

In fact, Zigler (1969) posits that there are two groups of people experiencing learning difficulties – definite organic pathology (25 per cent of learning difficulties) and cultural-familial factors[2] (75 per cent of learning difficulties). Moreover, he argues that the cognitive difficulties of the cultural-familial group can be explained in terms of a developmental-delay hypothesis, i.e. slower rate of development with a lower ceiling. However, the status of the developmental-delay position is still unclear for this group (Weiss, Weisz and Bromfield, 1986). Zigler's theory does not address the organically 'retarded'. There is evidence that patterns of difficulties vary across and to a lesser extent within this group (Burack, Hodapp and Zigler, 1990). For example, Down's syndrome children show initial high IQ scores due to early motor competencies. This initial developmental trajectory slows down and reflects the fact that linguistic items cause these children most problems.

There are two immediate implications for assessment:

1   learning difficulties arise from a wide range of interacting biological and social determinants
2   the ways in which learning difficulties manifest themselves will vary

Researchers have attempted to clarify the types of difficulties experienced by examining the ways in which individuals process information (Weiss, Weisz and Bromfield, 1986). Persistent problems have been identified in a number of different cognitive areas. In general, there are difficulties in identifying and maintaining attention to the relevant stimulus dimensions (Owens, 1989). These problems have direct implications for assessing learning difficulties and language skills in particular (Kahmi and Masterson, 1989). At the most basic level it must be established that the individual with learning difficulties is in fact focusing on the relevant task dimensions.

In addition, there has been extensive work on memory (Campione, Brown and Ferrara, 1984) which demonstrates that individuals with learning difficulties fail to employ strategies that help in learning new

---

[2]Persons who have no evidence of organic brain dysfunction are referred to by the American Association on Mental Deficiency as suffering from retardation due to psychosocial disadvantage. The older and more widely used term is cultural-familial which reflects the combination of environmental and genetic factors.

material. Individuals can be taught to employ strategies and are most likely to generalize a new strategy if they understand the reasons for its use. However, while differences in memory performance can be reduced, they are not eliminated and there is some indication that the speed at which information is retrieved from memory is a limiting factor (Kail, 1990). The majority of these studies have taken place with individuals experiencing mild learning difficulties; the evidence that exists indicates that generalizing to individuals with severe learning difficulties may be inappropriate (Broman *et al.*, 1987). None the less these problems highlight the complexities of assessment and the need to be clear about which skills are being tapped.

Standardized intelligence tests cannot begin to sort out the influence of various information-processing factors on performance. Nor can they offer direct predictions of what sorts of language competencies or difficulties might exist. The relation between cognition and language is unclear. For an individual to use symbols to communicate, that individual must possess a certain level of cognitive functioning (Owens, 1989) but there is only a moderate relation between language and intelligence (Clarke and Clarke, 1974).

Examination of the development of language and language-related skills in association with learning difficulties has further highlighted the need for careful examination of both the individual and the various components of the linguistic system. As we have stated, Down's syndrome children have specific difficulties with language. In addition, their linguistic impairments are most evident in grammatical, as opposed to social or pragmatic, aspects of language (Beeghly and Cicchetti, 1987). However, no straightforward conclusions can be drawn (Rondal, 1987). Once again the assessment procedure must be focused on the individual with the awareness that unexpected patterns of development may occur. For example, language development can still occur after puberty in some individuals (Rondal, 1987). Recent studies have indicated a high incidence of speech problems in children with learning difficulties. In particular, the severity of the learning difficulty and the high level of hearing problems in this population increase the incidence of speech problems.

A number of researchers have reported that children with learning difficulties have specific problems in acquiring general communication skills, particularly imitation behaviours. There are also indications that parents may use functionally different language towards the child and are less likely to follow the child's initiative. This latter point highlights the need to consider environmental mediators and the communicative potential in the environment when planning an assessment.

Some individuals will not acquire language or develop functional speech. In such cases the aim of developing communication skills to a level adequate to meet communicative needs will be dominant. It is inaccurate to

153

assume that the individual with severe learning difficulties has nothing to communicate. There are a range of systems that can be used in such circumstances, for example, Makaton and Blisssymbolics.

TOOLS FOR ASSESSMENT

At the very least the issues outlined above indicate that a detailed analysis of the individual's strengths and weaknesses needs to be considered. As Fryers (1984) states, 'Taxonomies are for groups, categories serve the needs of professionals; individual clients require thorough multidisciplinary assessment of their individual situation, constantly updated' (p. 17).

There are two more implications from the data. First, the extent to which the tests are appropriately standardized on the population must be considered. When a standardized test is administered to a person not comparable to the standardizing population, there is no assurance the test is measuring the same constructs. This is of central import for norm-referenced tools.

Second, the additional demands that any standardized or non-standardized measures place on the individual must be considered. For example, a child may fail to learn vocabulary items not because of the language component *per se* but because of memory problems. Language and communication skills cannot be seen in isolation from the individual's overall functioning.

Since by definition learning difficulties require norm-referenced assessment, i.e. IQ, and criterion-referenced performance, that is, adaptive behaviour, we have used this framework to discuss tools for assessment. Our main emphasis is on tools that are related to language and communication skills. However, it is important that the professional views the child with learning difficulties within a broader frame of competencies. Even a slight impairment in a single area can cause otherwise typically functioning areas to readjust.

NORM-REFERENCED ASSESSMENTS

Norm-referenced tests provide information about where an individual lies on a particular ability or attainment in comparison with peers of the same age. The basic principle of norm-referenced tests is to define a continuum of performance from lowest to highest and the measure assigned to a particular member of the group locates their position on that continuum, for example, rank or standardized score. By definition, individuals with learning difficulties are performing significantly below their peers on tests of general intelligence. These tests present us with the product of the learning difficulty rather than elucidating the processes that are involved. We have already shown that there are differences among subgroups and

154

within particular types of tasks and it is erroneous to assume that the profile of skills presented by the individual with learning difficulties will be the same across all tasks. The assessor can assume that the individual with learning difficulties is likely to experience language and communication problems but this must be verified. These tests are often used in differential diagnosis of communication problems for children with learning difficulties but have rarely been adequately standardized on this population. They are of little practical relevance for children with severe learning difficulties.

During the 1960s there was a marked increase in the number of standardized language tests, for example, Reynell and the ITPA (Illinois Test of Psycholingistic Abilities) and tests of skills thought to be necessary for language competence, such as play. The latter types of assessments can be particularly problematic. For example, there are two ways in which play can be used – as a skill or as a medium. As a skill it is extremely problematic. The relationship between symbolic play and language development is unclear. The presence of symbolic play signals the presence of representational capacities; absence of play does not equal the absence of representations. However, play can be an excellent medium for intervention (McConkey, 1984).

Children with severe learning difficulties have frequently been overlooked when designing more formal assessment procedures. The basic cognitive skills required to respond to the task are often not evident. Thus, more basic skills such as self-help and rudimentary communication skills must be assessed for such individuals. On the whole, these are more appropriately assessed through the use of criterion-referenced tests. However, developmental scales for the use of teachers, parents and residential-care staff have been developed (Sheridan, 1973; Bellman and Cash, 1987; Jeffree and McConkey, 1974). Such scales provide a rough estimate of the stages and sequences of normal development. However, as Mittler (1976) notes, 'they are no substitute for more detailed observation but they do provide a useful starting point and framework'.

Norm-referenced tests thus serve as flags to the difficulties of individuals relative to their peers on specific skills. They are not aimed at intervention since the scores do not provide details of what a child knows or does not know. Some of these tests have a value in identifying the existence of a problem as a first-line method following referral, or they may be useful for screening a larger population. However, they often offer objectivity at the expense of relevance. Their use has particular limitations with those experiencing learning difficulties since the reference group is often not appropriate. For example, adults with learning difficulties frequently have restricted vocabularies and syntax. The use of tests standardized on children, albeit functioning at the same linguistic level, is both invalid and inappropriate in such cases. Some of these tests provide statistical procedures for establishing the discrepancy among subscales that serve to highlight where a child has a particular problem but they are not geared to pinpointing what each individual can and cannot do.

CRITERION-REFERENCED ASSESSMENTS

Criterion-referenced tests are concerned with some previously specified criterion of performance. Such tests help identify whether an individual does or does not possess some particular skill or competence. These tests are not built to discriminate in the same way that norm-referenced tests do. However, the task of identifying what needs to be measured in a criterion-referenced test is not simple. Each test must serve to distinguish between those individuals who have and those who have not achieved sufficient mastery of a particular skill, and mastery should be a valid and reliable predictor of the next developmental step. The steps should reflect a developmental progression and be specified in a clear and objective fashion. This is more easily attained for highly structured areas, such as self-help skills and less easily achieved for complex skills, such as pragmatics. Thus, the quality of a criterion-referenced test depends on the extent to which item content reflects the domain from which the items were derived. The detailed nature of these tests allows more specific and appropriate treatment decisions to be made for children with the whole range of learning difficulties.

Both the Derbyshire Language Scheme (Masidlover and Knowles, 1982) and the Nuffield dyspraxia programme (Connery *et al.*, 1985) are criterion-referenced tests that look specifically at the language system. The Derbyshire was designed for children with moderate learning difficulties and is closely linked to treatment. This scheme uses the principle of information-carrying words in the stimulus sentence to ascertain the level of the child's understanding. It follows normal developmental stages in detail, allowing progress to be charted. Expressive language development is described in terms of the number of words used and their function within the sentence. The scheme focuses the attention of all those involved on the need to modify their language not only in the sentence length but more importantly the number of information-carrying words. The Derbyshire includes teaching material directly related to the assessment data. The Nuffield Centre dyspraxia programme assesses oral-motor skills and sound-sequencing abilities of speech in isolation, single words with differing phonotactic structures and sentences using picture material and imitation. The assessment is closely linked to the treatment material provided. The programme has been successfully used with children with mild learning difficulties (Connery, personal communication).

Many of these tools require the active involvement of the individual's carer or teacher. It is important to acknowledge and use this information both to identify accurately present performance and to promote the

156

acquisition of new skills. The needs of parents and carers must also be acknowledged (Dockrell, 1989).

The Wessex-revised Portage check-list (White and East, 1983) extends the original Portage and is organized in small steps. A baseline is identified and interventions are planned that are task-specific and geared towards the child accomplishing a further task on the check-list. Instruction is generally carried out by the carer. Tasks are set so that the child will succeed and careful monitoring is an essential prerequisite of the procedure. This is an ideal way of providing a detailed profile of an individual's strengths and needs and is directly linked to intervention. The lack of items at the lower end of the check-list suitable for children with severe learning difficulties has been addressed with the EDY Project (Education of the Developmentally Young, see McBrien and Foxen, 1981).

The Pre-verbal communication schedule (PVCS) (Kiernan and Reid, 1987) is designed as an assessment of the communication skills of individuals with *severe* learning difficulties. It aims to assess existing nonverbal and verbal skills as a basis for planning treatment programmes, particularly the use of signs and symbols. Kiernan and Reid outline how at the early developmental levels, communication and language skills can be separated, and that certain communication skills develop before language. The schedule focuses on communication skills and aims to assess function rather than contrived behaviours.

The relationship between motor skills used in feeding and the speech process is still debated but should be evaluated in children with learning difficulties experiencing feeding problems. *Prefeeding Skills* (Evans Morris and Dunn-Klein, 1987) provides check-lists for prefeeding skills, a parent questionnaire, feeding assessments and a self-feeding check-list. The authors feel that normal development of feeding and speech skills are related. The process is based on establishing and testing hypotheses based on observation and evaluation throughout all interactions.

Criterion-referenced tests aim to identify the exact level and content of development. An effective and valid test would have to reflect an empirically supported developmental, hierarchical sequence of steps. Present understanding of both language and cognition prevents such a clear-cut analysis. Too great an emphasis on such hierarchies will lead to stultifying and unhelpful recommendations.

OBSERVATIONAL PROCEDURES AND TEACHING EXPERIMENTS

Norm-referenced tests and artificially elicited behaviours for criterion-referenced tests pose specific problems for this client group. Both occur in contrived situations and neither allows for the flexibility that may be required in the assessment process. Most importantly, such tools do not identify the factors which may be maintaining performance at a particular level. Nor do they attempt to identify the impact of a particular level of performance. For example, limited communication skills can increase the likelihood of challenging behaviours in both children and adults. Recent work with adults who have learning difficulties has shown that their breakdowns of communication are related as much to deficits in pragmatic skills and a restrictive communication environment as to syntax or speech problems (Leudar, 1989).

Observational procedures and teaching experiments play an important role in obtaining more useful and relevant data and developing a detailed functional analysis. A number of factors need to be considered in the development of these techniques:

- sampling of performance at the highest level possible
- sampling of behaviour in a range of different situations
- items of a variety of levels of difficulty
- fixed-response items to minimize examiner bias
- decisions about the amount of reinforcement/feedback used during the assessment
- practice items to eliminate difficulties with understanding the task
- consider the effectiveness of the assessment, its accuracy, and useful-ness as a guide for treatment
- recording how responses are elicited and the responses themselves so the assessment can be repeated to monitor change

Teaching experiments focus on the individual child and the interplay of information-processing skills. Using learning as an assessment technique, one can use a test–teach–test model as a means of gauging an individual's ability to retain the content of the material and to transfer the principles learned to new tasks. Moreover, they permit an analysis of the quality of responses and the pattern of errors made. Criterion-referenced tests can serve as an indicator of where to pitch initial teaching. This approach forces the clinician to be precise about the task components and can make the assessment both relevant and meaningful. This form of behavioural analysis is particularly appropriate for individuals with severe learning difficulties. However, the process is highly subjective and is limited by our under-standing of the learning process.

Observational procedures allow detailed assessment of an individual *in situ* and have the benefits of relevance and objectivity if carried out appropriately. There are a number of measures in addition to time- and event-sampling that can aid our understanding of the individual's skills, for example LARSP (Crystal, Garman and Fletcher, 1981).

Assessment of language use is of central importance for individuals with learning difficulties. Recent research into pragmatics emphasizes the communication purpose and goal of any interaction in terms of the

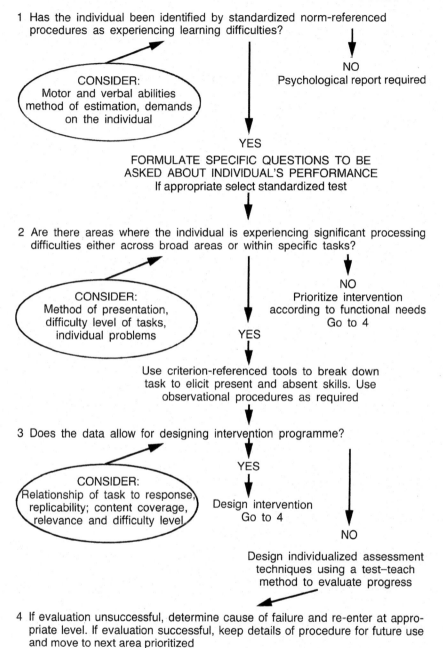

1 Has the individual been identified by standardized norm-referenced procedures as experiencing learning difficulties?

CONSIDER:
Motor and verbal abilities
method of estimation, demands
on the individual

NO
Psychological report required

YES

FORMULATE SPECIFIC QUESTIONS TO BE
ASKED ABOUT INDIVIDUAL'S PERFORMANCE
If appropriate select standardized test

2 Are there areas where the individual is experiencing significant processing difficulties either across broad areas or within specific tasks?

CONSIDER:
Method of presentation,
difficulty level of tasks,
individual problems

NO
Prioritize intervention
according to functional needs
Go to 4

YES

Use criterion-referenced tools to break down
task to elicit present and absent skills. Use
observational procedures as required

3 Does the data allow for designing intervention programme?

CONSIDER:
Relationship of task to response,
replicability; content coverage,
relevance and difficulty level

YES

Design intervention
Go to 4

NO

Design individualized assessment
techniques using a test–teach
method to evaluate progress

4 If evaluation unsuccessful, determine cause of failure and re-enter at appropriate level. If evaluation successful, keep details of procedure for future use and move to next area prioritized

Figure 8.1 Critical path of questions to be addressed when framing an assessment

speaker's intention and the communication needs of the listener for successful communication to occur. The pragmatics check-list (Dewart and Summers, 1988) can be used for direct observation of behaviour or as a questionnaire designed to elicit information from carers and other professionals about the child's development of language use. More specifically, joint action routines that are thought to be important in early infant communication can be tapped using a combination of structured observation and communication tasks (Coggins, Olswang and Guthrie, 1987).

SUMMARY

Speech-and-language-therapy assessments aim to address four basic questions:

1   is intervention warranted?
2   is the communication problem related to other difficulties in the multiply handicapped individual?
3   what are the priority areas for intervention within the presenting communication problem?
4   how can changes in communication behaviour be monitored and evaluated during the intervention?

Assessment and treatment can be seen as a cyclical activity. The selection of appropriate assessment materials depends on knowledge of the individual's problem and observation of behaviours so as to develop and test hypotheses which lead to treatment planning. This may involve direction and demonstration to the carer and exchange of information with other agencies. Reassessment during intervention and evaluation of change will restart the cycle.

As we have discussed earlier in this chapter there are three different forms of assessment. Work with clients experiencing learning difficulties will require judicious use of each form of assessment. Figure 8.1 provides a critical path of questions to be addressed when framing an assessment.

REFERENCES

American Psychiatric Association (1980). *Diagnostic and Statistical Manual of Mental Disorders* (3rd edn). Washington, DC: APA.

Balla, D. and Zigler, E. (1982). *Mental Retardation. The developmental-difference controversy*. Hillsdale, NJ: Erlbaum.

Beeghly, M. and Cicchetti, D. (1987). 'An organizational approach to symbolic development in children with Down's syndrome'. In D. Cicchetti and M. Beeghly (eds), *Symbolic Development in Atypical Children. New directions for child development*. San Francisco: Jossey Bass.

Bellman, M. and Cash, J. (1987). *The Schedule of Growing Skills in Practice*. Windsor: NFER-NELSON.

Broman, S., Nichols, P., Shaughnessy, P. and Kennedy, W. (1987). *Retardation in Young Children*. Hillsdale, NJ: Erlbaum.

Burack, J. A., Hodapp, R. M. and Zigler, E. (1990). 'Towards a more precise understanding of mental retardation'. *Journal of Child Psychology and Psychiatry*, 31: 471–5.

Campione, J. C., Brown, A. L. and Ferrara, R. A. (1984). 'Mental retardation and intelligence'. In R. J. Sternberg (ed.), *Handbook of Human Intelligence*. New York: Cambridge University Press.

Clarke, A. M. and Clarke, A. D. B. (1974). *Mental Deficiency: the changing outlook* (3rd edn). London: Methuen.

Coggins, T., Olswang, L. and Guthrie, J. (1987). 'Assessing communicative intents in young children'. *Journal of Speech and Hearing Disorders*, 52, 44–9.

Connery, V., Henry, C., Hammond, C., Williams, P. and Riley, J. (1985). *Nuffield Centre Dyspraxia Programme*. London: Nuffield Hearing and Speech Centre.

Crystal, D., Garman, M. and Fletcher, P. (1981). *Language Assessment, Remediation and Screening Procedure*. University of Reading.

Dewart, H. and Summers, S. (1988). *Pragmatics Profile of Early Communication Skills*. Windsor: NFER-NELSON.

Dockrell, J. E. (1989). 'Meeting the needs of the parents of children with speech and language difficulties'. *Child Language Teaching and Therapy*, 5, 146–56.

Enderby, A. and Davies, P. (1989). 'Communication disorders: planning a service to meet the needs'. *British Journal of Communication Disorders*, 24: 3, 301–32.

Evans Morris, S. and Dunn-Klein, M. (1987). *Prefeeding Skills*. Buckingham: Winslow Press.

Fryers, T. (1984). *The Epidemiology of Severe Intellectual Impairment: the dynamics and prevalence*. London: Academic Press.

Gardner, E. G. (1962). 'Normative standardized scores'. *Journal of Educational and Psychological Measurement*, 22: 1, 7–14.

Gillham, B. (1986). *Handicapping Conditions in Children*. London: Croom Helm.

Heron, A. and Myers, M. (1983). *Intellectual Impairment: battle against handicaps*. New York: Academic Press.

Ingram, T. T. S. (1972). 'Classification of speech and language disorders in young children'. In M. Rutter and J. A. M. Martin (eds), *The Child with Delayed Speech*. Clinics in developmental medicine, no. 43. London: SIMP.

Jeffree, D. M. and McConkey, R. (1974). *Child Development Charts*. Parental Involvement Project, Hester Adrian Research Unit, University of Manchester.

Kahmi, A. and Masterson, J. (1989). 'Language and cognition in mentally handicapped people: last rites for the difference-delay controversy'. In M. Beveridge, G. Conti-Ramsden and I. Leudar (eds), *Language and Communication in Mentally Handicapped People*. London: Chapman and Hall.

Kail, R. (1990). *The Development of Memory in Children* (3rd edn). New York: Freeman.

Kiernan, C. and Reid, B. (1987). *Pre-verbal Communication Schedule*. Windsor: NFER-NELSON.

King's Fund Centre (1980). *An Ordinary Life: comprehensive locally based residential services for mentally handicapped people* (project paper 24). London: King Edward's Hospital Fund for London.

Leudar, I. (1989). 'Communicative environments for mentally handicapped people'. In M. Beveridge, G. Conti-Ramsden and I. Leudar (eds), *Language and Communication in Mentally Handicapped People*. London: Chapman and Hall.

McBrien, J. and Foxen, T. (1981). *Training Staff in Behavioural Methods*. Manchester: Manchester University Press.

161

McConkey, R. (1984). 'The assessment of representational play: a springboard for language remediation'. In D. J. Muller (ed.), *Remediating Children's Language*. London: Croom Helm.

Masidlover, M. and Knowles, W. (1982). *The Derbyshire Language Scheme*. Ripley: Derbyshire County Council, Educational Psychology Service.

Mittler, P. (1976). 'Assessment for language learning'. In P. Berry (ed.), *Language and Communication in the Mentally Handicapped*. London: Edward Arnold.

Muller, D., Munro, S. M. and Code, C. (1981). *Language Assessment for Remediation*. London: Croom Helm.

Owens, R. (1989). 'Cognition and language in the mentally retarded population'. In M. Beveridge, G. Conti-Ramsden and I. Leudar (eds), *Language and Communication in Mentally Handicapped People*. London: Chapman and Hall.

Rondal, J. (1987). 'Language development and mental retardation'. In W. Yule and M. Rutter (eds), *Language Development and Disorders*. Oxford: MacKeith Press.

Rutter, M., Tizard, J. and Whitmore, K. (1970). *Education, Health and Behaviour*. London: Longman.

Sheridan, M. D. (1973). *Children's Developmental Progress from Birth to Five Years*. Windsor: NFER-NELSON.

Weiss, B., Weisz, J. and Bromfield, R. (1986). 'Performance of retarded and non retarded persons on information processing tasks: further tests of the similar structure hypothesis'. *Psychological Bulletin*, 100: 157–75.

White, M. and East, K. (1983). *The Wessex Revised Portage Language Checklist*. Windsor: NFER-NELSON.

Ysseldyke, J. E. (1987). 'Do tests help in teaching?' *Journal of Child Psychiatry and Psychology*, 28: 1, 21–4.

Zigler, E. (1969). 'Developmental versus difference theories of mental retardation and the problem of motivation'. *American Journal of Mental Deficiency*, 73, 536–56.

9

ASSESSING THE OLDER COMMUNICATION-IMPAIRED PERSON

Linda Armstrong

Speech and language therapy for old people is a relatively new concept for the profession, one for which clinicians may, until recently, have been ill-equipped and one that remains underexplored and undervalued in some areas. It is already a cliché to state that the number of people surviving into senescence is snowballing and will continue to do so into the twenty-first century. Nevertheless, this demographic shift is real, and speech and language therapists will have to rise to its challenge with appropriate and valid assessment procedures, therapy methods and materials.

From the outset, the position of the 'geriatric' patient should be defined. 'Geriatric' does not provide a superordinate type for a group of communication disorders, nor does it describe a specific type of communication disorder. It says that the person is over some arbitrary age (usually 65 years), considered to be old enough to warrant specialist physician care, is able to qualify for retirement from full-time employment and for the state old-age pension. Therefore, there are no speech-and-language-therapy assessments for 'geriatrics', but there are assessments used to assess communication problems in old people.

While working with older patients, speech and language therapists will primarily use formal and informal tests designed for administration to adults with communication problems following neurological damage and surgical intervention. The skill in assessing older patients lies in the therapist's knowledge of the effects of normal ageing on communication and the more general effects of ageing that will affect testing. The focus of this chapter will be on these aspects. But first, the process of assessing the old person with communication problems will be discussed.

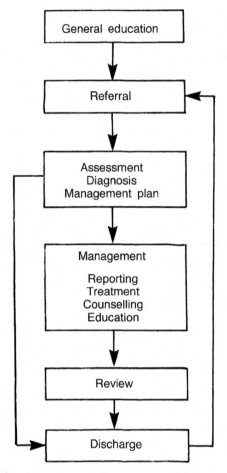

Figure 9.1 A model of speech-and-language-therapy care for elderly people

ASSESSMENT

Assessment can be seen within the context of a speech-and-language-therapy model of care for elderly people – see Figure 9.1. From this model, it can be seen that assessment is initially a precursor to diagnosis and the establishment of a management plan. Assessment, however, enters the therapeutic process at various other stages of the patient's speech-and-language-therapy management.

The clinician must decide whether to use informal or formal assessment procedures. There are arguments for both, and the decision should be made in the patient's best interest. Informal assessment is indicated when

164

the patient is not neurologically stable, when he or she is not able to co-operate in formalized procedures (perhaps because of sensory deficits) or when appropriate formal tests are not available. On the other hand, formal assessment should be carried out whenever possible, so that a recognized baseline measurement is available should the patient be transferred to another therapist, and from which to compare the patient's performance both to available test norms and to performance following a contract of therapy.

Initial assessment tells the clinician whether the patient has a communication disorder, how severe that disorder is, its type and whether treatment is indicated. A one-off formal assessment may not give the clinician enough information to make such firm decisions, but should at least give indicators to other assessment procedures.

When the clinician has administered the battery of tests and decided on a diagnosis, then the patient may be offered treatment based on assessment findings. Once a contract of therapy has been worked through, then the patient will be reviewed, to evaluate whether intervention has been successful and goals have been reached. Evaluation of the success of treatment is becoming increasingly necessary, and clinicians should use assessments that are fine-grained enough to show even small improvements. Review will consist of reassessment of the patient to compare pre- and post-therapy performance. Particularly with geriatric patients, goals may have to be adjusted to take into account other factors, such as general health and environmental influences. The much-acclaimed, but rarely achieved, multidisciplinary team approach to the management of the elderly should be nurtured where possible to ensure the best and the most conservative treatment of the older patient. Each discipline will make its own contribution to the assessment, but each should be willing to act jointly to implement management decisions.

After review, the patient may be discharged or may receive more therapy. Eventually, the review process will lead to the decision to discharge, at which time it is useful to carry out a final assessment – from which to provide a final report to the referring source and to hold for future reference, should the patient be re-referred.

In some areas, patients attending geriatric or psychogeriatric day hospitals are routinely screened on admission. This system has obvious merits in the early identification of problems, but has to be seen within the constraints of limited resources. Screening assessment may consist of a locally developed informal battery or some permutation of formal tests, according to the length and intensity of the screening desired.

Assessment, then, is a continual part of the therapeutic process and is involved in diagnosis, treatment-planning, review, evaluation and as the basis for counselling patients and their carers.

Common causes of communication breakdown in older patients are

Box 9.1

Common causes of communication breakdown in old age

Disorder	Cause
Aphasia	stroke
	tumour
	head injury
Dysarthria	stroke
	degenerative neurological disease
	(e.g. Parkinson's Disease)
Dyspraxia	stroke
Language of dementia	Alzheimer's Disease
	multi-infarct dementia
	Pick's Disease
Dysphonia	Carcinoma of larynx
Presbycusis	normal ageing
Cataract, poor vision	as above
Withdrawal	institutionalization
	depression
	social isolation
	bereavement

given in Box 9.1. This shows the range of disorders that may be encountered by clinicians working with older patients.

Older patients present unique problems for assessment, in terms of the effects of linguistic ageing and of the normal ageing process. These will be briefly outlined below, before some resulting practical considerations for testing are described.

AGEING

It is generally recognized that language abilities change with age. These changes are not always negative in nature; for example, passive vocabulary increases throughout life. Most changes do, however, reflect negative trends, such as slower responses, poorer scores and greater variability in performance.

Confrontation picture-naming is probably the most researched area. Whilst this is an artificial task, especially for older people, it does lend itself to easy analysis and is used to describe the degree and type of word-finding difficulty (WFD) experienced by the testee. It is almost universally agreed

166

that there is a relationship between ageing and naming difficulty, so that with increasing age more WFDs are experienced.

There has been comparatively little published research carried out to describe language comprehension in old age. Results, notably by Cohen (1979) and Maxim (1982), indicate that older people do have difficulty in understanding complex constructions, although this may not interfere with daily functioning.

Discourse in old age has been considered by Ulatowska *et al.* (1985), who found that 'statistically significant age related decrements emerged for a variety of complex discourse measures' (p. 133), and by Obler (1980) who describes four studies of verbal and written discourse.

Several studies describe communication function in old age via aphasia-test performance. Walker (1982), for example, found that even 'apparently well-preserved volunteers' (pp. 16–17) made errors on the Minnesota Test for the Differential Diagnosis of Aphasia (Schuell, 1965).

Age effects on communication skills are subtle and reflect intelligence, education, life history, motivation, sensory integration, mental status and vigour. It is worth reiterating the fact that ageing *per se* does not reduce a person's communication level below the 'functional' barrier, although laryngeal changes may cause some normal older people to be misclassified as mildly dysarthric (Amerman and Parnell, 1990). Davis (1984: 80) states 'some changes in language function in normal ageing may be considered to

---

Box 9.2

Normal ageing effects

Physical effects
Skin, nails, hair, bones, muscles, joints, hearing, vision, smell, teeth, constipation, prostate glands/urinary infections, incontinence, lungs – chronic bronchitis, pneumonia, heart failure, high blood pressure, atheroma, diabetes, anaemia, cancer, hypothermia, accidents

Psychological effects
Intellect, personality, lack of creativity and flexibility, slowed responses, memory loss, introversion

Losses
Status, income, health, company, independence, accommodation, life

Basic needs
– physical – nutrition, warmth, shelter, comfort, cleanliness
– psychological – respect, security, self-determination

Professional attitudes (negative)
Defeatism, domination, insularity

---

represent a *decline* of function, while pathological changes such as in dementia may be thought of as *deficits* of function'.

For more detailed descriptions of communication in old age, see Bayles and Kaszniak (1987), Davis (1984), Gravell (1988), Sandson, Obler and Albert (1987) and the College of Speech Therapists' 1982 monograph (Edwards).

The ageing process affects communication ability directly (for example, by reducing access to semantic memory) and indirectly (for example, by reducing opportunity to communicate), so it is important in testing to be aware of potential ageing influences and those ageing effects that are evident in the patient. Pitt (1982) devotes a chapter to normal ageing. Box 9.2 summarizes his description of the effects of the ageing process, all of which may indirectly affect a patient's performance in assessment.

TESTING CONSIDERATIONS

Formal assessments have standardized procedures and often standard instructions, for example, the Minnesota Test for the Differential Diagnosis of Aphasia (MTDDA) (Schuell, 1965) gives scripted instructions. It may be necessary to forgo rigid administration for the benefit of the information that can be gleaned by allowing the older patient the best opportunity for responding representatively, by repeating the instructions that were not heard, by enlarging picture and word stimuli and by allowing the patient the time required to respond. This, of course, means that the assessment will not be carried out as intended and therefore the patient's performance cannot be compared accurately with available norms. The clinician must weigh up which approach is more appropriate for him or her to use. The length of aphasia batteries may also call into doubt their validity with geriatric patients. Sullivan (1990) asks the very pertinent question – 'Have you ever completed a whole Boston with any one of your patients?'

Few of the routinely used formal assessments have readily available norms for older people, especially for older British people. Therefore, care is required not to over-interpret errors as evidence of pathology. Wherever possible, prior examination of the test should include investigation of its validity with older subjects (in terms of clarity of materials, length and standardization). Individual differences in terms of education, sex, previous occupation and level of intelligence will bear on competence and potential performance probably more in older people than in younger groups of patients, as will cultural factors. Most aphasia batteries are American in origin, with the exception of Whurr's (1974) Aphasia Screening Test and, more recently, the Frenchay Aphasia Screening Test (Enderby *et al.*, 1987).

None of the speech-and-language-therapy assessments currently available

168

was developed specifically for elderly people. (The Edinburgh Functional Communication Profile (Skinner *et al.*, 1984) was designed specifically for older patients for whom formal assessment was not appropriate, but is not strictly an assessment.) Formal tests used with older people are most often those developed for use with adult neurologically impaired patients (dysarthric, dysphasic and dyspraxic). The classification of older aphasic people may prove less clear-cut than for younger patients. They may not 'fit' the syndromes described by the Boston Diagnostic Aphasia Examination and MTDDA because of ageing changes in the cerebrum.

Many non-linguistic factors potentially influence performance by an older patient on formal speech and language assessments. The therapist should at least be aware of these and any obvious non-linguistic problems contributing to test failure must be noted. Vision and hearing problems are the most obvious examples here – both some degree of deafness and vision loss can be expected in old age. If normally worn, spectacles and hearing aids should be available, but rarely worn hearing aids or spectacles can hinder rather than help assessment.

Patients should not feel that they are 'back at school' after an absence of fifty years or more, so the purpose and relevance of testing must be explained to the patient and to the relative or carer if this is appropriate. As with all types of patient, rapport must be established and maintained, especially when a patient is being assessed using tasks which seem to have no relation to daily functioning. Some tasks used in aphasia batteries could be easily construed as insulting to an elderly man or woman, whereas tasks used in motor-speech assessments have more immediate pertinence to the presenting difficulty.

Fatigue, poor concentration and perseveration may accompany communication problems following cerebral insult and may be exacerbated by poor health, confusion or memory problems in old age. Fatigue will cause the patient to perform below his or her optimum. Alertness to the onset of fatigue will prevent the therapist from continuing testing where discontinuation is indicated. Poor concentration can be the result of fatigue or can be a more generalized symptom of brain injury. Perseveration is another sequela of brain injury that can interfere with testing and may require testing to be suspended or carried out over several sessions to minimize its effect.

Pacing is very important to allow the patient optimum time for response and to identify the onset of fatigue or loss of concentration. Insistence on finishing a test may have long-term repercussions in the loss of rapport and motivation and in causing anxiety and depression at perceived failure. In effect, the pace of assessment should be the patient's pace and not that dictated by the clock. It is better to assess over two or more sessions than to insist on completing an assessment that will not reflect the patient's abilities. However, variability of performance from day to day or week to week may give unexpected assessment outcomes.

The possible detrimental effects of prescribed drugs should not be underestimated. Therapists should know which drugs a patient has been prescribed and find out, if possible, if they are being taken as instructed. Poor compliance is recognized as a problem in the elderly population, where tablets may remain in medicine cabinets, be taken infrequently or at incorrect intervals. Polypharmacy interactions (the effects of taking two or more drugs prescribed at different times or by different doctors), can cause the old person to underperform or become confused. Some drugs have specific side-effects that can depress communication ability, for example, dry mouth, drowsiness, oral thrush. Felstein (1985) and Gawel (1981) provide more detailed descriptions of drug effects on old people.

It would seem that the geriatric patient cannot be formally assessed! Certainly such assessment is not straightforward and should not be entered into without prior planning or without good reason. However, it is possible to achieve a valid assessment if aspects of ageing and testing described above are respected by the therapist.

Box 9.3

Tests used in geriatric assessment

Aphasia
Minnesota Test for the Differential Diagnosis of Aphasia (Schuell), shortened or very shortened versions
Boston Diagnostic Aphasia Examination (Boston or BDAE)
Western Aphasia Battery (Western)
Aphasia Screening Test (Whurr)
Test for Reception of Grammar (TROG)
(Revised) Token Test
Boston Naming Test (BNT)
Frenchay Aphasia Screening Test (FAST)

Motor speech
Frenchay Dysarthria Assessment
Dysarthria Profile

Functional communication
(Revised Edinburgh Functional Communication Profile)
Communication Abilities in Daily Living (Holland)

Others
Informal assessment
Mental Status Evaluation (various)
Clifton Assessment Procedures for the Elderly (CAPE)
Arizona Battery for Communication Disorders of Dementia
Set Test

TESTS COMMONLY USED

Most of the formal assessments used with geriatric patients are those used to assess speech and language in adults with acquired neurological damage. In addition to the use of those formal tests listed in Box 9.3, informal assessment of speech and language is the mode most often used. Clinicians may also find that tests developed by other disciplines give additional information. For example, an evaluation of mental status may be indicated. There are many of these used, for example, the Mini-Mental State Examination of Folstein *et al.* (1975) and Hodkinson's 1972 Abbreviated Mental Test Score. Care must be taken in using these to assess memory and orientation with patients who have language comprehension or expression difficulties, so that linguistic difficulty is not analysed as cognitive loss. More general assessments may be used to give an overall picture of functioning. The Clifton Assessment Procedures for the Elderly (Pattie and Gilleard, 1979) includes a behavioural check-list among its subtests, which could prove useful in differential diagnosis.

TESTING DEVELOPMENTS

Increasingly, researchers are providing test norms for older subjects, for example. Nicholas *et al.* (1985) and LaBarge *et al.* (1986) assessed older subjects on the Boston Naming Test (Kaplan *et al.*, 1983) – with different outcomes. This will improve test validity and encourage more clinicians to use formal procedures with their older patients. It is hoped that with recognition of demographic changes, tests may be developed specifically to take into account the effects of the ageing process. 'Functional communication' became fashionable in the 1980s, and its tenets should be strongly upheld while assessing older people so that treatment will have direct relevance to that person's daily communicative functioning.

Therapists are already involved in making the differential diagnosis of aphasia/language of dementia and in assessing the language skills of demented people. This will increase in the future and so appropriate tools will have to be developed to ensure valid assessment. The research literature is replete with studies using aphasia batteries to describe the language of dementia. Whilst nomenclature is a subject in itself, it is appropriate to note here that the labelling of the language of dementia as aphasia is felt to be very unhelpful, given the different underlying pathology, progressions and different therapeutic approaches required. Knowledge gained by studies such as Stevens (1985) and Thompson (1986) will aid in the development of batteries designed to assess and describe language in dementia of different types.

At present, therapists asked to diagnose a patient as aphasic or with the language of dementia have no appropriate tool devised specifically for this

171

task. They use observation, intuition and unsuitable assessments to make a differential diagnosis. Bayles and her colleagues have worked for many years on the Arizona Battery of Communication, which they describe in Chapter 7 of their 1987 book. This is a lengthy procedure that includes tests of language comprehension and expression along with tests of memory and orientation. Modalities other than speech and writing are explored (drawing and pantomime). The published research version (Bayles and Tomoeda, 1990) is slightly modified and consists of fourteen subtests which assess linguistic comprehension, linguistic expression, mental status, verbal learning and memory, and visuo-spatial function. Its aim is to identify and quantify linguistic communications deficits in Alzheimer's Disease. Work continues in other centres endeavouring to construct a differential test. Stevens (1989), for example, considered different types of visual presentation of naming materials and resultant types of errors made by demented and aphasic patients.

CONCLUSION

Many of the formal assessments used by therapists may not be appropriate for use with older people without some modification, for example, by improving picture clarity, increasing print size, allowing more response time. These modifications may not allow maintenance of stringently given instructions for administration but will give the therapist much more useful information concerning that person's level of communication ability.

Many therapists may continue (with justification) to prefer not to use formal assessments with their older patients until normative data for elderly British people are provided for tests already in use or until more suitable and valid assessments especially designed for elderly people are available.

Above all, therapists must remember that elderly people represent a heterogeneous population and *not* a homogeneous one and that assessment decisions must be based on the needs of the individual older person rather than on the therapist's expectations of the patient dictated by that individual's chronological age.

REFERENCES

Amerman, J. D. and Parnell, M. M. (1990). 'Auditory impressions of the speech of normal elderly adults'. *British Journal of Disorders of Communication*, 25, 35–43.

Bayles, K. A. and Kaszniak, A. W. (1987). *Communication and Cognition in Normal Ageing and Dementia*. London: Taylor & Francis.

Bayles, K. A. and Tomoeda, C. K. (1990). *Arizona Battery for Communication Disorders of Dementia*. Tucson, AZ: Canyonlands Publishing.

Cohen, G. (1979). 'Language comprehension in old age.' *Cognitive Psychology*, 11, 412–29.

Davis, G. A. (1984). 'Effects of ageing on normal language'. In A. Holland (ed.), *Language Disorders in Adults.* San Diego, CA: College-Hill Press.

Edwards, M. (1982). *Communication Changes in Elderly People.* London: College of Speech Therapists' Monograph.

Enderby, P., Wood, V. and Wade, D. (1987). *Frenchay Aphasia Screening Test.* Windsor: NFER-NELSON.

Felstein, I. (1985). 'When drugs are also a problem for the old'. *Therapy Weekly,* 24 October, p. 7.

Folstein, M. F., Folstein, S. E. and McHugh, P. R. (1975). '"Mini-mental state" – a practical method for grading the cognitive state of patients for the clinician'. *Journal of Psychiatric Research,* 12, 189–98.

Gawel, M. J. (1981). 'The effect of various drugs on speech'. *British Journal of Disorders of Communication,* 16, 51–7.

Gravell, R. (1988). *Communication Problems in Elderly People.* London: Croom Helm.

Hodkinson, H. M. (1972). 'An evaluation of a mental test score for assessment of mental impairment in the elderly'. *Age and Ageing,* 1, 233–8.

Kaplan, E., Goodglass, H. and Weintraub, S. (1983). *The Boston Naming Test.* Beckenham: Lea & Febiger.

LaBarge, E., Edwards, D. and Knesevich, J. W. (1986). 'Performance of the normal elderly on the Boston Naming Test'. *Brain and Language,* 27, 380–4.

Maxim, J. (1982). 'Language change with increasing age'. In M. Edwards (ed.), *Communication Changes in Elderly People.* London: College of Speech Therapists' Monograph.

Nicholas, M., Obler, L., Albert, M. and Goodglass, H. (1985). 'Lexical retrieval in healthy ageing'. *Cortex,* 21, 595–606.

Obler, L. K. (1980). 'Narrative discourse style in the elderly'. In L. K. Obler and M. L. Albert (eds), *Language and Communication in the Elderly: clinical, therapeutic and experimental issues.* Lexington, MA: D. C. Heath.

Pattie, A. H. and Gilleard, C. J. (1979). *Clifton Assessment Procedures for the Elderly (CAPE).* Sevenoaks: Hodder & Stoughton Educational.

Pitt, B. (1982). *Psychogeriatrics: an introduction to the psychiatry of old age* (2nd edn). Edinburgh: Churchill Livingstone.

Sandson, J., Obler, L. K. and Albert, M. L. (1987). 'Language changes in healthy ageing and dementia'. In S. Rosenberg (ed.), *Advances in Applied Psycholinguistics,* vol. 1. Cambridge: Cambridge University Press.

Schuell, H. (1965). *Minnesota Test for the Differential Diagnosis of Aphasia.* Minneapolis: University of Minnesota Press.

Skinner, C., Wirz, M., Thompson, I. and Davidson, J. (1984). *The Edinburgh Functional Communication Profile.* Bicester, Oxon: Winslow Press.

Stevens, S. (1985). 'The language of dementia in the elderly: a pilot study'. *British Journal of Disorders of Communication,* 20, 181–90.

Stevens, S. (1989) 'Differential naming difficulties in elderly dysphasic people and subjects with senile dementia of Alzheimer type'. *British Journal of Disorders of Communication,* 24, 77–92.

Sullivan, C. (1990). 'Putting our patients to the test'. *Therapy Weekly,* 22 March, 4.

Thompson, I. M. (1986). *Language Pathology in ATD and Associated Disorders.* Ph.D. thesis. University of Edinburgh.

Ulatowska, H. K., Cannito, M. P., Hayashi, M. M. and Fleming, S. G. (1985). 'Language abilities in the elderly'. In H. K. Ulatowska (ed.), *The Ageing Brain: communication in the elderly.* London: Taylor & Francis.

Walker, S. A. (1982). 'Communication as a changing function of age'. In

M. Edwards (ed.), *Communication Changes in Elderly People.* London: College of Speech Therapists' Monograph.
Whurr, R. (1974). *An Aphasia Screening Test.* London: Whurr.

FURTHER READING

Beasley, D. S. and Davis, G. A. (eds) (1984). *Ageing: Communication Processes and Disorders.* New York: Grune & Stratton.

de Beauvoir, S. (1970). *La Vieillesse.* Paris: Editions Gallimard.

Bryan, K. L., Maxim, J. and Thompson, I. (1993). *Language and the Elderly.* London: Whurr.

Eisenberg, S. (1985). 'Communication with elderly patients: the effects of illness and medication on mentation, memory, and communication'. In H. K. Ulatowska (ed.), *The Ageing Brain: Communication in the Elderly.* London: Taylor & Francis.

Gordon, L. (1986). 'A comparative study of confrontation naming skills in normal elderly and demented elderly people'. Available from author.

Hull, R. H. and Griffin, K. M. (1989). *Communication Disorders in Ageing.* Newbury Park, CA: Sage Publications.

Oyer, H. J. and Oyer, E. J. (eds) (1976). *Ageing and Communication.* Baltimore: University Park Press.

Schow, R. L., Christensen, J. M., Hutchinson, J. M. and Nerbonne, M. A. (1978). *Communication Disorders of the Aged: a guide for health professionals.* Baltimore: University Park Press.

Wells, N. and Freer, C. (eds) (1988). *The Ageing Population.* Basingstoke: Macmillan.

Williamson, H. and Chopinn, J. M. (1980). 'Adverse reactions to prescribed drugs in the elderly: a multicentre investigation'. *Age and Ageing,* 9, 73–80.

Woods, R. T. and Britton, P. G. (1985). *Clinical Psychology with the Elderly.* London: Croom Helm.

10

ASSESSMENTS OF PSYCHIATRY

Jenny France

It has become increasingly apparent that speech and language therapy has an essential role to play in mental health, as it is recognized that changes in communication are among the earliest signs of the onset of mental illness (France, 1985). As illness develops into chronicity, in many cases, social isolation that accompanies the developing illness further exacerbates the patient's communication problems.

It is known that no one profession has all the skills necessary for assessment, treatment and rehabilitation of mentally ill people (Hume and Pullen, 1986), just as no one treatment has been found to be fully effective in all cases. The multidisciplinary team has a role to play in individual assessments and treatment as each profession contributes areas of expertise and with the resulting skill mix provides a comprehensive service; within this the speech and language therapist's specialist role is that of communication.

Over the last decade, speech and language therapy in psychiatry has become established in many settings: closed institutions, conventional psychiatric hospitals, homes for the elderly, day centres, patients' own homes when appropriate and in forensic, child and adolescent units and hospitals, and so assessments used will vary as they need to be appropriate to each client/patient group.

GENERAL PSYCHIATRIC ASSESSMENTS

As part of the psychiatric diagnosis, a full medical and social history is necessary, together with investigations into the possibility of physical illness and organic brain disease, drug and alcohol abuse. Other forms of mental disorder should be identified or eliminated as, for instance, a patient diagnosed as schizophrenic might also be suffering from depression.

Most diagnostic assessments will be carried out by psychiatrists and clinical psychologists who are trained to administer them and skilled in interpreting the results. Such assessments will involve psychomotor, personality, neuropsychological and behavioural testing. Speech and language therapists can also be trained to use some of these assessments but even when they are completed by others it is vital to understand the results of these assessments. In stressing the importance of the interview as an essential part of assessment, Roberts (1984) states that through the patient's communication information is provided on the integrity of language functioning, the effective state, the coherence of thought processes, motor activity, memory and attention.

Therapy will depend on whether a behavioural or psychodynamic approach is adopted and so psychometric, behavioural, cognitive and projective assessments may be used for many psychiatric disorders. Investigations into the suitability for dynamic psychotherapy may be aided by results of projective tests such as the Rorschach Inkblot Test (Rorschach, 1942), which is a standard set of ten inkblots that serve as a stimulus for associations. As the thinking and associational patterns of the patient are highlighted, the ambiguity of the stimulus provides relatively few areas for what may be conventional or standard responses. Thematic Apperception Tests (TAT) (Murray, 1943) use pictures to provoke story-telling, the results of which may reflect the life experiences, thoughts and feelings of the story-teller (Muir *et al.*, 1991).

The Minnesota Multiphasic Personality Inventory (MMPI) (Hathaway and McKinley, 1970) measures traits such as depression, hysteria, psychopathic deviation, paranoia, schizophrenia, hypomania and social introversion. The inventory has 550 statements about attitudes, emotional reactions, physical and psychological symptoms and past experiences to which the subject answers 'true', 'false' or 'cannot say'. This test was designed to identify people with serious personality disorders but is generally widely used in psychiatry.

Memory tests are used to identify the occurrence of everyday memory problems and attempt to qualify the frequency and severity of such problems. Two such assessments are the Rivermead Behavioural Memory Test (Wilson *et al.*, 1985) and the National Hospital Memory Battery (Warrington, 1985). Speech and language therapists will assess memory in the context of how it affects the language breakdown and establish which pathway (visual, auditory, kinaesthetic) is most intact and therefore can be used in retraining.

Intelligence testing, also undertaken by clinical psychologists, will need to precede any other formal assessments and one of the most helpful intelligence tests is the Wechsler Adult Intelligence Scale (Wechsler, 1981), which gives qualitative and quantitative information via verbal subtests.

SPEECH-AND-LANGUAGE-THERAPY ASSESSMENTS IN PSYCHIATRY

Such assessments in psychiatry may add information assisting psychiatric diagnosis, highlight specific communication problems, and provide diagnosis of any speech pathology as well as assist in differential diagnosis between, for example, dementia and dysphasia, dementia and depression, schizophrenia and dysphasia, paranoia and hearing impairment, language disorder and intellectual impairment; they may also evaluate ongoing treatment and programme planning.

At this stage in the developing speech-and-language-therapy services in psychiatry there are no standardized formal assessments available for speech, language and communication problems in those suffering from mental illness, but many of the tests used by speech and language therapists in other therapeutic settings can be adapted to help fulfil the overall assessment needs. It has been found that a holistic approach to assessment and treatment is essential and should take into account not only the patients' present communication and speech behaviours but also their physical and emotional well-being as well as social and environmental factors.

A particular contribution of the speech and language therapist to the assessment process is explored through the interview, which is central to the implications for the processes of planning, implementation and evaluation (Griffiths, 1991).

In order to obtain a full communication assessment, a patient will need to be assessed and observed in as many different settings as possible. It is known that styles of communication changes occur when with different people and in different environmental settings, for example, on the ward, in a work area, in a social setting or a formal psychiatric interview.

Video and audio recordings are possibly the most popular means of assessing patients. Recording of clinical interviews is important for ongoing assessment and can also provide the therapist with samples of speech, language and communication behaviour that can be further analysed. The tapes and or transcripts can also be used for comparison of pre-/post-intervention levels of functioning. Furthermore, the recordings can demonstrate to members of the clinical team descriptions of communication, voice, language and articulation disorders and are useful when diagnosis of speech problems is confused by symptoms of mental illness.

Computers are becoming increasingly popular as a means of assessing the abilities and deficits of those suffering from mental illness. They are also being successfully used therapeutically to help develop communication skills.

The Edinburgh Functional Communication Profile (Skinner *et al.*, 1984) and the Functional Communication Profile (Sarno, 1963) are widely used and look at a range of behaviours including those vital areas of gesture, body cues and visual cues.

Check-lists and rating scales can provide a valuable source of information if suitably devised. The speech and language therapist or key worker can then record observations on various aspects of communicative behaviour. The speech and language therapist may also wish to devise check-lists to record receptive or expressive skills, attention levels, memory or any other skill related to communication which can be measured objectively but informally. A speech and language therapist may be asked to devise a language and communication section of a broader-based check-list to be used by the whole clinical team (Muir et al., 1991).

During the course of assessing a patient it is advisable to check on whether he or she owns or has owned spectacles, a hearing aid or dentures. However vigilant the carers are, these devices make an enormous difference to the patient's general communication and well-being.

A pure-tone audiometric assessment is a helpful addition to psychiatric assessments although results of formal audiological testing with patients experiencing paranoid feelings may be unreliable. Therefore, it may be necessary to use informal assessments and observation of the patient's hearing ability. If all else fails, closed-circuit audiometry may prove successful, and if this fails then stimulus-response testing or EEG may be necessary.

The Frenchay Dysarthria Assessment (Enderby, 1988) and the Dysarthria Profile (Robertson, 1982) are used for patients with symptoms of dysarthria caused either by side-effects of drug therapy or by organic involvement.

In the assessment of voice, the Victoria Infirmary Voice Questionnaire (Lockhart and Martin, 1987) is widely used. The Vocal Profiles Analysis Scheme (VPAS) (Laver et al., 1981) provides a comprehensive procedure for describing speaker characteristics of all speakers; results may be used to help assess patients as well as provide information for the clinical team presenting a unique contribution based on a speech and language therapist's special training, skills and expertise.

Language assessments to provide information on receptive and expressive language skills in mentally ill patients may include the Aphasia Screening Test (Whurr, 1974); the Minnesota Test of Differential Diagnosis of Aphasia (Schuell, 1965), and its shortened version (Schuell, 1973), the Boston Diagnostic Aphasic Examination (Goodglass and Kaplan, 1983) are formal wide-ranging language assessments which give a clear breakdown of abilities in certain areas. The Boston Naming Test (Kaplan et al., 1983) and the Graded Naming Test (McKenna and Warrington, 1983) are also regularly used. Several verbal fluency tests are used; Miller's Verbal Fluency Test (1984) makes an allowance for the effect of IQ level and assesses the verbal-fluency function as a measure of verbal intelligence and in relation to different types of cerebral pathology.

Testing reading skills establishes a patient's abilities and helps to devise therapy programmes involving many life skills. The National Adult Reading Test (Nelson, 1982) and the Neale Analysis of Reading Ability

178

(revised 1988) are weighted to elicit word meanings via the direct graphemic-semantic route rather than the graphemic-phonemic route (Muir *et al.*, 1991).

Occasionally in all forms of mental illness there may be some doubt as to whether the patient is dementing. In these cases the Dementia Checklist (Stevens, 1985) looks at general language signs in mild dementia, moderate dementia and severe dementia and will help rule out the possibility of dysphasia.

Assessments that assist care staff working in rehabilitation settings, many of which are devised for elderly people, will include cognitive and evaluation skills and prove valuable in assessing the level of dependency of long-stay patients. Examples are the Clifton Assessment Procedure for the Elderly (Pattie and Gilleard, 1979), the Rehabilitation Evaluation (Hall and Baker, 1983), the National Unit for Psychiatric Research and Development Questionnaires (Clifford, 1987) and the Social Behaviour Assessment Schedule (Platt, Hirsch and Weyman, 1983).

EVALUATION FOR SETTING UP A SPEECH-AND-LANGUAGE-THERAPY SERVICE IN PSYCHIATRY

For the purpose of setting up a speech-and-language-therapy service in psychiatry, assessments might include some of the formal tests already mentioned. The screening process will need to encompass a communication profile that assesses the patient's ability to initiate conversation, non-verbal communication such as eye contact, facial expression and gestures, and vocal quality, clarity, rate and amount of speech. Assessment batteries might therefore be drawn up to give a general insight into the patient's problems and to test motor speech skills, expressive language skills, receptive skills and auditory memory.

Many speech and language therapists have found that standardized tests are not always successful here due to their inflexible nature and length; they might therefore need to be adapted where appropriate. Patients should be reassessed using the same battery of tests and it is considered beneficial if two speech and language therapists work together to compile these assessments (Cross, 1987).

MENTAL DISORDERS, COMMUNICATION PROBLEMS AND FURTHER ASSESSMENTS

Neurotic disorders

Neurotic disorders is a global term used to cover minor psychiatric conditions such as anxiety, depression, and obsessional and phobic neuroses. The severity of the neurotic symptoms will determine treatment needs based on how long they have been present and whether the cause of the stress is likely to persist; also the patient's personality needs to be taken into account (France, 1991a). Behavioural assessments are most likely to be used for these disorders. An Interview Assessment Behavioural Check-list (France and Robson, 1986) can be used and might include the patient's description of the presenting problem(s) and other problem areas, antecedents, background, consequences and incompatible behaviour, development of the problem, previous coping attempts, expectations of outcome and effects of outcome; both internal (cognitive) and external factors should be considered.

Every aspect of speech, language and communication problems can be associated with neurotic disorders. Anxiety may produce social problems such as avoidance of communication situations and social reticence. Bodily tension can affect breathing and so create voice and resonance disorders, and language and speech fluency can be affected as a result of the patient's reticence by reducing the patient's social contacts and with rituals such as continuous checking, repeating and interruptions in conversation. As many of the speech disorders are associated with social problems, social- and communication-skills programmes are the usual choice of treatment.

Many professions are involved in social-skills assessment, including speech and language therapists. Each profession is likely to have its own bias towards assessment and will add a varied dimension to this complex area. Social-skills rating scales are a popular means of recording skills deficits; examples of these can be found in the *Social Skills Training Manual* (Wilkinson and Canter, 1982). A speech and language therapist's assessments are likely to include most of the communicative aspects of social interaction. What may be required from social-skills assessments is verbal, vocal and non-verbal behaviours. Speech and language therapists working in psychiatry also see the need for social-skills assessments to include information demonstrating the patient's insight into social and communicative behaviours, both his or her own and those of others. Check-lists can be devised to record deficits by looking at certain aspects of social interactions and specific skills; this may include eye contact, posture, facial expression, gesture, and listening skills, as the ability to initiate and maintain appropriate social contact and response needs to be rated (Muir *et al.*, 1991).

Psychotic disorders

The psychoses are considered to be the major mental illnesses and include organic psychoses, drug psychoses, the major affective (mood) disorders, schizophrenia and paranoid states. These illnesses include features such as incoherent speech, bizarre and idiosyncratic beliefs and purposeless or unpredictable or violent behaviour with apparent absence of concern for one's own safety and comfort (Roth and Kroll, 1986). Communication and speech disturbances can be divided into three possible areas for consideration: first, the communication and speech pathology evident prior to the onset of the illness and possibly maintained and exacerbated by the psychosis; second, communication and language disruption/disorder caused predominantly by the psychosis; and finally, additional problems resulting from drug and physical treatments and organic conditions (France, 1991b). Changes in speech behaviour can have a profound influence on some or all aspects of communication, both verbal and non-verbal, where mutism is one extreme and the overproductive, excitable speech of the manic patient is the other. Voice demonstrates changes in pitch, volume and quality, and vocalization can be influenced by bizarre behaviour. Dysarthrias may result from antipsychotic medication and other organic factors.

Assessments are hindered as patients do not usually believe that they are ill and so psychological tests can be used to indicate, confirm or rule out a diagnosis of schizophrenia, for example, and this diagnosis is supported if tests reflect unusual or bizarre perceptual and conceptual processes. Assessments that might be used are the Rorschach Inkblot Test (1942) and Thematic Apperception Tests (TAT) (Murray, 1943). As previously mentioned, these tests are used to examine thought processes. The Grid Test of Schizophrenic Thought Disorder (GTSTD) (Bannister and Fransella, 1966; 1967) is a diagnostic instrument designed to test whether a patient is thought-disordered or not. Psychometric assessments may add little to the diagnosis but quantitative assessments of specific abnormalities of behaviour are useful for planning and evaluating social relationships (Gelder et al., 1986).

There are no formalized tests that are likely to help differentiate schizophrenic language from aphasic disorder (as yet) and so it is more helpful to look closely at the language abnormalities present in these disorders. It has been found that formal aphasia assessments do not reliably record schizophrenic language problems but they will of course confirm or deny the presence of dysphasia. It is known that both psychiatrists and neurologists have difficulty differentiating schizophrenic from dysphasic speech, whereas a speech and language therapist's assessment is known to be more reliable (Muir et al., 1991).

Depression

Depression comes under the heading of the affective disorders, which are so called because the main feature is an abnormality of mood (France, 1991c). It includes a wide range from mild to severe states (severe depression or psychotic depression includes features such as delusions and hallucinations and is accompanied by feelings of worthlessness and guilt). It is characterized by depressed mood, pessimistic thinking, lack of enjoyment, reduced energy, and slowness. Psychiatrists have noted that depressed patients have difficulty communicating within their social environment and it is therefore important for speech and language therapists to take into account the overall communication problems as well as those of speech and language. These patients are usually reluctant to talk and share their problems; they experience feelings of low self-esteem and will avoid social intercourse if possible. The non-verbal aspects of communication will display dejection, slow and restricted body movements, and minimal eye contact and facial expressions. The tempo of speech is affected, it is usually slow, hesitant, lacking in variation of intonation and is often accompanied by poor vocal quality. Language tends to be limited to convey the minimum of information, responses are short and little speech is initiated. Kupfer *et al.* (1987) suggest that there are four methods of detecting depression, by observing the patient's body movement, facial expression, quality of voice and finally the tempo or pacing of speech.

The Beck Depression Inventory (BDI) (Beck *et al.*, 1979) can be used for measuring depression and might usefully be part of the speech and language therapist's initial assessment prior to treatment, as well as being used on occasions during the course of treatment. Many speech and language therapists are now trained to use personal-construct psychotherapy and so will be familiar with personal-construct repertory grids. These are a further useful means of assessing the patient's present state, monitoring progress and, in particular, identifying objectives and determining where change is needed (Fransella and Bannister, 1977).

A reliable method of discriminating dementia from depression is to use verbal fluency tests. Depressed patients show relatively normal verbal fluency (Kronfol *et al.*, 1978) whilst demented patients show poorer function (Miller and Hague, 1975). The Test for the Reception of Grammar (TROG) (Bishop, 1983) shows a difference in performance levels between demented and depressed patients: demented patients have difficulty in many areas of cognitive functioning including receptive-language skills, but depressed patients can usually manage the TROG with no obvious problems.

Personality disorders

In abnormal personality unusual behaviour occurs even in the absence of stressful events and, at times, these abnormalities of behaviour may be so great that it is difficult to decide whether they are due to personality or neurotic illness (Gelder *et al.*, 1986). Extreme cases of abnormal behaviour are obvious as, for example, in cases of violence and repeated behaviour of harming others and showing no remorse. It is not possible to judge the personality of these patients in the same way as judging other forms of mental illness: those with personality disorder seldom complain of any difficulties and so the diagnosis can rarely be made just by listening to the patient; reliable accounts of the person's behaviour will need to be obtained from other informants such as relatives, partners or employers and from social workers and public officers (Hibbert, 1988).

There are no communication problems associated specifically with personality disorder. A poor educational and social history may give rise to poor literary, numeracy and language skills, and this may limit vocabulary and create non-verbal abnormalities such as seeking excessive body distance between people, and a reluctance to be touched, accompanied by antisocial behaviour in some cases. Speech problems may be more to do with lack of experience through restricted exposure to the usual variety of speech situations. In some cases these difficulties are accompanied by speech pathology, such as a stutter, voice disorders and continuing articulatory disorders inherited from childhood complicated by a general impoverished language pattern. The patient's preoccupation with his or her own position and problems might well reduce his or her listening skills which may, as a result, become overselective and handicapping (France, 1991d).

Personality and intellectual-functioning assessments may well be used to give a lead towards detecting abnormal traits in personality. The Sixteen Personality Factor (Trait) Questionnaire (16PF) (Cattell and Ebel, 1968) is a hundred-question yes/no test, and by plotting the scores a personality profile results. The Eysenck Personality Inventory (EPI) (Eysenck and Eysenck, 1963) gives a useful assessment; as does, more recently, the Eysenck Personality Questionnaire (EPQ) (Eysenck and Eysenck, 1975) which also contains items for measuring psychoticism and has a lie scale.

The Fullerton Language Test for Adolescents (Thorum, 1986) is a varied language-assessment instrument that distinguishes normal from abnormal language-impaired adolescents and can assist in determining the deficiencies in linguistic-processing skills and language usage of the adolescent. The Sentence Completion Assessment (Coleman, 1970) explores the development of interpersonal relationships in adolescents and gives more information about attitudes, feelings and use of language.

CONCLUSION

Many speech and language therapists have designed, developed and used their own assessments and these include those concentrating in particular on the whole communication process. This chapter by no means gives a comprehensive list of assessments currently being used by speech and language therapists in psychiatric settings; the aim is to give a guide as to the types of tests used, to stress the value of some of the less formal assessments, and to urge the continuing development of research projects into this most important area. As speech and language therapy in psychiatry continues to develop, the need for research is paramount, particularly towards developing standardized assessments in all aspects of the service.

REFERENCES

Bannister, D. and Fransella, F. (1966). 'A grid test of schizophrenic thought disorder'. *British Journal of Social Clinical Psychology*, 5, 95–102.

Bannister, D. and Fransella, F. (1967). 'A grid test of schizophrenic thought disorder. A standard clinical test'. Barnstaple: Psychological Test Publications.

Beck, A. T., Shaw, A. J., Rush, B. F. and Emery, G. (1979). *Cognitive Therapy of Depression*. Chichester: John Wiley.

Bishop, D. (1983). *Test for the Reception of Grammar*. Manchester: University of Manchester.

Cattell, R. B. and Ebel, H. W. (revised 1968). *Sixteen Personality Factor Questionnaire*. Windsor: NFER-NELSON.

Clifford, P. I. (1987). 'The National Unit for Psychiatric Research and Development questionnaire'. Available from Lewisham Hospital, London SE13 6LH.

Coleman, J. C. (1970). 'The study of adolescent development using a sentence completion method'. *The British Journal of Educational Psychology*, 40, Part I, 27–34.

Cross, J. (1987). 'An evaluation of the effectiveness of speech therapy with mentally ill clients'. Speech Therapy Dept, Shirehall, Abbey Foregate, Shrewsbury.

Enderby, P. (1988). *The Frenchay Dysarthria Assessment*. Windsor: NFER-NELSON.

Eysenck, H. J. and Eysenck, S. B. G. (1963). *Eysenck Personality Inventory*. Windsor: NFER-NELSON.

Eysenck, H. J. and Eysenck, S. B. G. (1975) *Manual of the Eysenck Personality Questionnaire (junior and adult)*. London: Hodder & Stoughton.

France, J. (1985). 'Broadmoor: venture into the unknown'. *Speech Therapy in Practice*, 1: 2, 4–5.

France, J. (1991a). 'Neurotic disorders'. In R. Gravell and J. France (eds), *Speech and Communication Problems in Psychiatry*. London: Chapman and Hall.

France, J. (1991b). 'Psychotic disorders'. In R. Gravell and J. France, (eds), *Speech and Communication Problems in Psychiatry*. London: Chapman and Hall.

France, J. (1991c). 'Depression'. In R. Gravell and J. France (eds), *Speech and Communication Problems in Psychiatry*. London: Chapman and Hall.

France, J. (1991d). 'Personality disorders'. In R. Gravell and J. France (eds), *Speech and Communication Problems in Psychiatry*. London: Chapman and Hall.

France, R. and Robson, M. (1986). *Behaviour Therapy in Primary Care*. London: Croom Helm.

Fransella, F. and Bannister, D. (1977). *A Manual for Repertory Grid Technique*. London: Academic Press.

Gelder, M., Gath, D. and Mayou, R. (1986). *Oxford Textbook of Psychiatry*. Oxford: Oxford Medical Publishers.

Goodglass, H. and Kaplan, E. (1983). *The Boston Diagnostic Aphasic Examination*. Beckenham: Lea & Febiger.

Griffiths, H. (1991). 'The psychiatry of old age'. In R. Gravell and J. France (eds), *Speech and Communication Problems in Psychiatry*. London: Chapman and Hall.

Hall, J. and Baker, R. (1983). *Rehabilitation Evaluation.* Aberdeen: Vine Publishing.

Hathaway, S. and McKinley, J. (1970) *Minnesota Multiphasic Personality Inventory.* Windsor: NFER-NELSON.

Hibbert, G. A. (1988). 'The personality disorders'. In N. Rose (ed.), *Essential Psychiatry.* Oxford: Blackwell Scientific Publications.

Hillier, S. (1982). 'Vocal profile analysis protocol' in the Vocal Profiles of Speech Disorders Research Project. University of Edinburgh.

Hume, C . and Pullen, I. (1986). *Rehabilitation in Psychiatry.* Edinburgh: Churchill Livingstone.

Kaplan, E., Goodglass, H. and Weintraub, S. (1983). *The Boston Naming Test.* Beckenham: Lea & Febiger.

Kronfol, Z., Hamsher, K., Digre, K. and Wazir, R. (1978). 'Depression and hemispheric functions: changes associated with unilateral ECT'. *British Journal of Psychiatry*, 132, 560–7.

Kupfer, J., Maser, J. D., Blehar, M. C. and Miller, R. (1987). 'Behaviour assessments in depression'. In J. D. Maser (ed.), *Depression and Expressive Behaviour.* London: Erlbaum.

Laver, J., Wirz, S., MacKenzie, J. and Hillier, S. (1981). 'A perceptual protocol for the analysis of vocal profiles'. Edinburgh University Linguistics Department. *Work in Progress*, 14.

Lockhart, M. and Martin, S. (1987). The Victoria Infirmary Voice Questionnaire. In S. Martin (ed.), *Working with Dysphasics.* Bicester, Oxon: Winslow Press.

McKenna, P. and Warrington, E. K. (1983). *Graded Naming Test.* Windsor: NFER-NELSON.

Miller, E. (1984). 'Function of a verbal fluency assessment as a measure of verbal intelligence and in relation to different types of cerebral pathology'. *British Journal of Clinical Psychology*, 23, 53–7.

Miller, E. and Hague, F. (1975). 'Some characteristics of verbal behaviour in pre-senile dementia'. *Psychological Medicine*, 5, 255–9.

Muir, N., Tanner, P. and France, J. (1991). 'Management and treatment techniques: a practical approach'. In R. Gravell and J. France (eds), *Speech and Communication Problems in Psychiatry.* London: Chapman and Hall.

Murray, H. A. (1943). *Thematic Apperception Test (TAT).* Boston: Harvard University Press.

Neale, D. (1988). *Analysis of Reading Ability* (revised). Windsor: NFER-NELSON.

Nelson, H. E. (1982). *The National Adult Reading Test.* Windsor: NFER-NELSON.

Pattie, A. H. and Gilleard, C. J. (1979). *The Clifton Assessment Procedure for the Elderly.* Windsor: NFER-NELSON.

Platt, S., Hirsch, S. and Weyman, A. (1983). *The Social Behaviour Assessment Schedule.* Windsor: NFER-NELSON.

Roberts, I. K. A. (1984). *Differential Diagnosis in Neuropsychiatry.* Chichester: Wiley Medical.

Robertson, S. J. (1982). *Dysarthria Profile.* Bicester, Oxon: Winslow Press.

Rorschach, H. (1942). *Rorschach Inkblot Test Psychodiagnostics.* Berne, Switzerland: Hans Huber.

Roth, M. and Kroll, J. (1986). *The Reality of Mental Illness.* Cambridge: Cambridge University Press.

Sarno, M. T. (1963). *The Functional Communication Profile.* New York: University Medical Centre.

Schuell, H. (1965). *The Minnesota Test of Differential Diagnosis of Aphasia.* Minnesota: University of Minnesota Press.

Schuell, H. (1973). *The Shortened Schuell Test.* Minnesota: University of Minnesota Press.

Skinner, C., Wirz, M., Thompson, I. and Davidson, J. (1984). *The Edinburgh Functional Communication Profile.* Bicester, Oxon: Winslow Press.

Stevens, S. J. (1985). *Dementia Checklist.* Hammersmith Hospital, W12.

Thorum, A. R. (1986). *The Fullerton Language Test for Adolescents.* Palo Alto, CA: Consulting Psychologists Press Inc.

Warrington, E. K. (1985). *Recognition Memory Test.* Windsor: NFER-NELSON.

Wechsler, D. (1981). *The Wechsler Adult Intelligence Scale.* Sidcup, Kent: Psychological Corporation.

Whurr, R. (1974). *An Aphasia Screening Test.* London: Whurr.

Wilkinson, J. and Canter, S. (1982). *Social Skills Training Manual.* Chichester: John Wiley.

Wilson, B., Cockburn, J. and Baddeley, A. (1985). *The Rivermead Behavioural Memory Test.* Reading: Thames Valley Test Company.

TEST REVIEWS

As was mentioned in the preface, we did not set out to produce exhaustive review sections for these volumes. This would have defeated the object of producing reasonably short, readable introductions to a particular area. There are a number of regularly produced, encyclopaedic reference volumes in which the interested reader can find factual information about the full spectrum of assessments published around the world.

We canvassed the views of many academics and working professionals to compile a restricted list of tests for review. Some are widely used; others are less well known but throw an interesting light on the assessment of the elderly.

Reviewers were asked to write to a format, giving basic information on the test's purpose, age, components, availability and technical properties. Finally, they were asked to evaluate whether – in their view – the test did what it claimed to do. Some of these opinions may be controversial, but we hope they will contribute to the on-going discussions between test-users, authors and publishers.

Any choice such as this risks dissatisfying certain readers. Given the present interest in assessment, and the increase in test-development activities, we may produce new editions of this book in the future. If you have any suggestions for titles to be included in this review section, please let us know.

APHASIA SCREENING TEST (AST)

Test author   Renata Whurr

Purpose   This is a short aphasia battery of receptive and expressive function.

Subject population   Adults with moderate to severe acquired-language disorder

Administration time   Approximately 30 minutes

Structure and administration   This short aphasia battery comprises 20 tests of receptive function and 30 tests of expressive function. Each subtest contains five items that are scored on a pass/fail system, rendering a profile of performance across auditory and reading comprehension, speech production, oral language and writing. As the test relies heavily on visual material, four pre-assessment subtests are designed to screen for marked visual perceptual deficits. Two calculation subtests are also included for their common association with language impairment.

Within each modality, subtests typically follow an order of increasing difficulty as defined by the author's clinical experience. At the simplest level, therefore, the provision of basic visual-matching tasks and repetition of automatic sequences make the test well suited to the severely impaired patient. It does not, however, take account of these patients' use and comprehension of gesture or of any more functional communication in relation to social context and environment.

Technical details

Standardization   Despite its popularity as the most commonly used aphasia battery among UK clinicians (Beele, Davies and Muller, 1984), the AST is not theoretically robust, being based largely on the author's exceptional clinical experience and intuitions. Individual patient data are not provided for the 106 aphasic patients to whom the test was administered, with the exception of age, occupation and medical diagnosis of 14 sample cases. Similarly, data on the performance of non-aphasic adults are not provided.

Reliability   There are no details of inter-tester or test–retest reliability.

Validity   Data obtained from 106 patients on the fifty subtests were subjected to a factor-analysis study. This isolated three major factors: tasks requiring oral expression, visual-input matching and selection to auditory command, and two minor factors: tasks requiring copying and simple written output and those requiring more complex written output. The author does not comment on these results, nor does she attempt to define any theoretical standpoint on aphasia, though her analysis supports the hypothesis of aphasia as a multidimensional disorder.

Evaluation   The AST claims to screen impairments at a phonological, syntactic and semantic level, and samples performance at the single letter or sound, word and sentence level. However, given the limited number of items in each subtest and the choice of distractor items which vary in their visual, phonological, syntactic or semantic relatedness to the target, the degree to which these variables can be seen to influence good or poor performance is not evident. Thus, Patient A, who has a severe auditory-comprehension deficit due to poor auditory discrimination of sounds or word forms may perform relatively well when selecting to command from the phonologically distinct items of spoon, comb, toothbrush, envelopes and pen. Patient B, however, whose underlying deficit is more semantically based, may show functionally superior understanding in conversation whilst scoring poorly on the same subtest due to the close semantic relationship between certain pairs of words.

Similarly, success or failure on various other subtests should be interpreted with care. Poor repetition of words and sentences in subtests B3 and B4 of the speech-output section may indeed reflect a motor-speech or dyspraxic-type problem. Equally, though, this may be the result of a difficulty in speech perception at an auditory-input stage and/or of impaired language-processing for output.

In the years since the AST was published, cognitive neuropsychological approaches to the assessment and remediation of acquired language disorders have added a new dimension to speech and language therapists' understanding of aphasia (see, for example, Byng, Kay, Edmundson and Scott, 1990). Although, as a screening test, the AST does not claim to be exhaustive, its lack of attention to influential psycholinguistic variables such as phonological or semantic relatedness of items, together with some of the assumptions it makes about underlying processing deficits, means that its assistance in the planning of therapeutic strategies, as claimed, is not possible without further, more specific, language assessment and clinical observation.

Similarly, the small, uncontrolled number of items in each subtest means that retesting on the AST to measure improvement as advocated in the manual is unlikely to reflect change due to any specific intervention strategy, although a revised language profile may give a gross estimate of change due to spontaneous recovery or other non-linguistic factors.

Although many clinicians prefer to use their own short, informal assessments in the early days post-onset, an advantage of the AST over other aphasia tests is that it can be administered from one week post-onset. Visual materials are large, clear and unambiguous – presented in a constant two items above, two below and one centred layout in a foolscap-size display book. The test also uses five everyday objects, sixteen clear line drawings and a writing booklet to record all written responses, making the whole package easily portable for use on the ward or in the home environment.

The AST has recently been adapted for use with Punjabi speakers (Mumby, 1988). Potentially useful diagnostic indicators of acquired language disorders in dementing versus dysphasic patients as revealed by

189

performance on certain AST subtests has also been addressed in the literature (Stevens, 1985).

In addition to the pass/fail record form, a clear profile of patient performance across the fifty subtests can be graphically recorded on the Assessment Record Form, and this profile grid is duplicated on the Summary Record Form with space for the clinicians' summary and interpretation of results. Cut-off scores are given for identification of mild, moderate, moderately severe, severe and very severe deficits in both receptive and expressive functions. As a gross indication of language function, these details can be useful when patient management is transferred from one clinician to another, or as the basis for report-writing to other professionals.

Country of origin   UK

Publisher   Whurr Publications, London; Thomas Slatner and Co., Jersey City, NJ

References

Beele, K. A., Davies, E. and Muller, D. (1984). 'Therapists' views on the clinical usefulness of four aphasic tests'. *British Journal of Disorders of Communication*, 19, 169–78.

Byng, S., Kay, J., Edmundson, A. and Scott, C. (1990). 'Aphasia tests reconsidered'. *Aphasiology*, 4, 67–92.

Mumby, K. (1988). 'An adaptation of the Aphasia Screening Test for use with Punjabi speakers'. *British Journal of Disorders of Communication*, 23, 267–92.

Stevens, S. (1985). 'The language of dementia in the elderly: a pilot study'. *British Journal of Disorders of Communication*, 20, 181–90.

Carol Pound, Jenny Sheridan and Judith Williams

ASSESSMENT AND THERAPY PROGRAMME FOR DYSFLUENT CHILDREN

Test author   Lena Rustin

Purpose   This programme aims to simplify and objectify the challenging process of assessing the dysfluent child and to provide speech and language therapists and psychologists with a comprehensive therapy and monitoring programme which can be used with groups or individuals for group or weekly therapy. It actively involves parents in the process of assessment and therapy, and incorporates homework and follow-up activities which encourage the child to use the fluency developed during the programme in the course of their everyday life.

Subject population   Children aged 2½–11 years

Administration time   Untimed (a continuous assessment and treatment system)

Materials   The programme uses a manual and task sheet, an audio cassette, assessment booklets, and separate workbooks for children and parents.

Structure and administration   The parental interview is used by the clinician to obtain detailed information from both parents regarding the child, the dysfluency and the dynamics of the family. The extensive questioning process enables the clinician to build up a detailed and complete picture of the child and family as well as pertinent factors which may be contributing to or maintaining the dysfluency.

The child assessment consists of quantitative and qualitative analysis of the dysfluency in a variety of speaking tasks. This is followed by an interview format which helps the therapist understand the problem from the children's point of view. This covers a description of the stuttering, the strategies they have developed to help themselves, their relationships with family and peers, hobbies, interests, school achievement and their problem-solving abilities. The therapist notes their social skills including posture, eye contact, state of tension, avoidance and any speech and language problems. To close the interview the therapist and child experiment with various speech-modification tasks to establish the least intrusive method of obtaining fluency. The findings of the parent interview and child assessment are summarized by the clinician and related to the parents.

Evaluation   This procedure is detailed and comprehensive but requires more time than other assessments. The interview format enables the therapist to start building a sound relationship with the family which will facilitate the therapy process. It also helps in the vital understanding of the nature of the dysfluency, the family life-style and the perceived needs of the child. This information will form the basis of a management programme. A high level of concentration and the ability to process a considerable amount of information are required from the therapist in order to specify the type of treatment which would be appropriate for a particular child or adolescent.

Country of origin   UK

Publisher   NFER-NELSON, Windsor

E. Kelman

THE AUDITORY DISCRIMINATION AND ATTENTION TEST

Test author Rosemarie Morgan-Barry

Purpose This test is designed to assess one of the most important auditory skills, a child's ability to discriminate between sounds. It is intended to have a diagnostic function by indicating whether or not perceptual problems are a contributing factor to the child's speech-production difficulties.

Subject population Children aged between 3 and 12 years

Administration time 20 minutes

Materials An easel containing the manual and 18 coloured test plates, packs of counters and record forms.

Structure and administration This is a traditional auditory-discrimination and attention test that assesses the child's ability to discriminate between 17 minimal pairs; that is, words that are minimally distinguished by a single phoneme. The minimal feature contrasts are voiced/voiceless, place of articulation, manner of articulation, and constituents of consonant clusters. The 17 pairs of words are presented pictorially on laminated flip-over plates. The child is first asked to name the pictures to ensure that he or she uses the correct word. If not, the examiner teaches the child the name. The child's pronunciation is recorded in phonetic transcription; a practice which could provide useful corroborative data if the child's perceptual response is incorrect. The child is then required to respond to the examiner's production of one or other of the minimal pairs by placing a counter in a hole under one or other of the pictures. After a practice item administered three times, each of the 17 items is presented; for children between 3 and 5 there are three repetitions of each word in the pair; for 5–11-year-olds there are six repetitions. Examiners are instructed to be sensitive to the child's attention level and physical-manipulation skills in administering the test.

Scoring and interpretation Tables of standard scores are provided for children divided into three age groups; preschool (3–4), primary (5–6) and junior (7–11). These are divided into six-month age groups and provide an indication of the developmental status of the child's performance.

Technical details

Standardization A total of 300 children were tested to standardize the test.

Reliability Informal repeat tests established that there is a reasonable expectation of inter-tester reliability.

Validity The validity of the test was evaluated by testing children with known hearing impairments and a second group with attention-control difficulties. A low level of hearing loss was found not to correlate with discrimination ability. High level of correlation between attention-control difficulties and discrimination and attention problems was found. Within the items of the test certain pairs are significantly more difficult than others; specifically, sum/sun; fan/van; mouth/mouse. A correlation study with another older traditional test – Auditory Discrimination Test (Wepman, 1973) – was carried out on a small population of thirteen children (Cracknell, 1987). A poor correlation was found. This may be due to the fact that although the tests purport to assess the same skills, the methodology is very different.

Evaluation As Morgan-Barry points out, her test is essentially a speech-identification task. As such it is a welcome addition to the clinician's battery of procedures. It is simple to administer and interpret, uses familiar materials and can be used with a wide range of children with speech and language problems.

Country of origin UK

Publisher NFER-NELSON, Windsor (1988)

References

Cracknell, S. (1987). 'A theoretical comparison of two tests of auditory discrimination'. Unpublished dissertation. National Hospitals' College of Speech Sciences, University College, London.

Wepman, J. (1973). *The Auditory Discrimination Test.* Chicago: Language Research Association.

Pam Grunwell

BOSTON DIAGNOSTIC APHASIA EXAMINATION (BDAE)

Test authors   H. Goodglass and E. Kaplan

Purpose   Aims to diagnose the presence and type of aphasia, to infer localization of cerebral damage, to measure initial performance, to detect change over time and to assess deficits and abilities as a guide to therapy.

Subject population   People with acquired aphasia

Administration time   At least an hour and a half; more, depending on severity of communication problem

Materials   Manual, 16 test cards and record booklets. IBM-compatible database* for recording and storing data and for aiding diagnosis.

Structure and administration   Consists of 27 subtests in five sections – conversation and expository speech, auditory comprehension, oral expression, understanding written language and writing. Also supplementary language and non-language tasks, e.g. for apraxia. Instructions are given in the manual and in the record booklet. Some tests are timed.

Scoring and interpretation   Mostly plus/minus with some graded scoring for response latency and quality of response. Certain aphasic behaviours are noted but not scored, e.g. paraphasias. Scores are analysed into a severity-rating scale, a rating-scale profile of speech characteristics and are transformed into z-scores/percentiles. The pattern of scores can be compared with syndrome patterns given by the authors.

Technical details

Standardization   Carried out for each test using 50–195 aphasic subjects. Score ranges, means and standard deviations are given. Borod, Goodglass and Kaplan (1980) provide normative data based on 147 males from 25–85 years. Age and education were found to influence scoring. Normal cut-off scores are given.

Reliability   34 aphasics of varying degrees of severity were used in the reliability study. Results indicate good internal consistency. Variability may

---

*Computerized Boston available from Far Communications Ltd, 5 Harcourt Estate, Kibworth, Leicestershire LE8 0NE (tel: 0533 796166).

be found in test–retest performance in people who have not yet stabilized. Inter-tester agreement has been found to be good.

Validity Good face validity, as seen in its widespread clinical and research use. Two factor analyses have been carried out. These showed that BDAE measures language functions associated with different localizations and the differently affected among aphasic syndromes. Studies have found high correlation between performance on BDAE and other formal tests, but not with functional assessments, e.g. Holland (1980).

Evaluation The therapist attempting to use the Boston for the first time should be thoroughly prepared, by having read both the manual's directions and the instructions given in the record booklet. Materials are portable but some of the stimuli are small and cluttered, some show American cultural bias and the colours are ambiguous. Scoring can be complicated but provides more information than other such tests and more of a qualitative nature, which could provide a focus for therapy. As a comprehensive battery, it is long and may not be suitable for the more severely aphasic patient or patients with other problems. The Cookie Theft picture is very often used in research to sample connected speech. Overall, this test provides the therapist with a great deal of information but at a cost of lengthy assessment and rather complicated scoring/analysis.

Country of origin USA

Publisher Lea & Febiger, Philadelphia (1972, revised 1983)

References

Beele, K. A., Davies, E. and Muller, D. (1984). 'Therapists' views on the clinical usefulness of four aphasia tests'. *British Journal of Disorders of Communication*, 19, 169–78.

Borod, J. C., Goodglass, H. and Kaplan, E. (1980). 'Normative data on the Boston Diagnostic Aphasia Examination, Parietal Lobe Battery, and the Boston Naming Test'. *Journal of Clinical Neuropsychology*, 2, 209–15.

Davis, G. A. (1983). *A Survey of Adult Aphasia*. Englewood Cliffs, NJ: Prentice-Hall.

Goodglass, H. and Kaplan, E. (1972). *The Assessment of Aphasia and Related Disorders*. Philadelphia: Lea & Febiger.

Holland, A. L. (1980). *Communicative Abilities in Daily Living*. Baltimore: University Park Press.

Muller, D., Munro, S. M. and Code, C. (1981). *Language Assessment for Remediation*. London: Croom Helm.

Ulatowska, H. K., Macaluso-Haynes, S. and Mendel-Richardson, S. (1976). 'The assessment of communicative competence in aphasia'. In R. H. Brookshire (ed.), *Clinical Aphasiology Conference Proceedings*. Minneapolis: BRK.

Linda Armstrong

BOSTON NAMING TEST (BNT)

Test authors   E. Kaplan, H. Goodglass and S. Weintraub

Purpose   This is a 'wide-ranging naming vocabulary test'. It is used to identify the extent and type of errors made by patients in confrontation picture-naming, as a paradigm for word-finding difficulties experienced in spontaneous speech.

Subject population   Children $5\frac{1}{2}$–$10\frac{1}{2}$ years, adult aphasic patients, demented patients, patients presenting with anomia

Administration time   20 seconds are allowed for naming response, 20 seconds for response following stimulus and phonemic cues (if these require to be given). Administration time will show individual variation and will depend upon whether the patient needs cues. A normal communicator can complete the test in less than 5 minutes, but it may take up to 45 minutes with neurologically impaired patients (Williams *et al.* 1989).

Materials   Test stimuli presented in a flip-over fashion, with instructions for administration and record forms. The latter contain standardization details.

Structure and administration   The test consists of sixty black-and-white line drawings, graded in difficulty. It was developed from an 85-item experimental version which is widely used in research literature. Subjects are required to give a one-word name for each stimulus and are offered standard cues if they cannot name spontaneously or name incorrectly. A stimulus cue is given first, if the picture is not recognized or misperceived, e.g. for item 14 (mushroom) – 'It's something to eat'. A phonemic cue (the opening sound of the target) is given if the stimulus cue fails to elicit the correct response, e.g. for mushroom – 'mu'. It is suggested that the test is started at item 1 with aphasic patients but at 30 with adults. Testing is discontinued after six consecutive failures.

Scoring and interpretation   Responses are scored as correct if named without assistance or following stimulus cue; therefore maximum potential score is 60. Responses made are noted on the record form so that naming behaviour and the effectiveness of the different cues can be evaluated. Only quantitative information is scored. Goodglass (1980) describes types of naming errors made by normal elderly, aphasic and institutionalized subjects.

Technical details

Standardization   Preliminary norms are given by the authors for children (age 5½–10½), normal adults (age 18–59) and aphasics (severity rating, not ages given). References to several studies which have used the 85-item version of the test with healthy elderly people are given in Williams *et al.* (1989). In an unpublished study by Gordon (1986), the mean score achieved by a group of normal elderly British people on the published version was 43 (age 73–84). The range of scores was 29–57. Van Gorp *et al.* (1986) also used the present version with older subjects and found that scores declined only slightly with age. They did, however, find more variation in the performance of the higher age groups. More work is required to standardize the test on a British elderly population. Some work has also been done in extending the normative data for children, e.g. Kindlen and Garrison (1984), who used the longer version, and Cohen *et al.* (1988) who provide normative data for 6–12-year-olds and compared performance of two types of dyslexic children and a left-temporal-lobe tumour group. Further studies have provided data on performance on the Boston Naming Test (BNT) by demented subjects, such as Williams *et al.* (1989), Huff *et al.* (1986), Knesevich *et al.* (1986).

Reliability   No information on reliability is given by the authors. Huff *et al.* (1986) developed two equivalent shorter forms of the 85-item test. Williams *et al.* (1989) constructed three 30-item shortened versions of the 60-item test and found high significant correlations between the versions. Coefficient alphas showed high internal consistency of all versions, with the full version being highest.

Validity   No information on validity is given by the authors. In Gordon (1986) correlation between scores on this test and the Graded Naming Test were computed for normal elderly subjects, r = 0.81, showing high positive correlation between scores on these two naming tests. Thompson and Heaton (1989) found high positive correlation between the BNT and other language measures, especially the vocabulary subtest of the WAIS-R. Halperin *et al.* (1989) looked at what the 'BNT actually measures' by comparing performance on it with performance on other language and memory tests by children aged 6–12 years.

Evaluation   Although this is an American test, it contains a few items which have a strong cultural bias (e.g. item 19 – pretzel). The stimuli have more functional relevance than those of some other naming tests and may therefore represent more closely actual level and type of word-finding difficulties. Of its kind, it offers a good assessment of picture-naming difficulties and is widely used. Nevertheless, the shortcoming of using

197

picture-naming as a paradigm of word-finding should not be under-estimated nor should the non-linguistic factors which influence naming ability.

Country of origin USA

Publisher Lea & Febiger, Philadelphia (1983)

References

Cohen, M., Town, P. and Buff, A. (1988). 'Neurodevelopmental differences in confrontation naming in children'. *Developmental Neuropsychology*, 4, 75–81.

Goodglass, H. (1980). 'Naming disorders in aphasia and ageing'. In L. K. Obler and M. L. Albert (eds), *Language and Communication in the Elderly: clinical, therapeutic and experimental issues.* Boston, Mass: D.C. Heath.

Gordon, L. (1986). 'A comparative study of confrontation naming skills in normal elderly and demented elderly people'. Unpublished.

Halperin, J. M., Healey, J. M., Zeitchik, E., Ludman, W. L. and Weinstein, L. (1989). 'Developmental aspects of linguistic and mnestic abilities in normal children'. *Journal of Clinical and Experimental Neuropsychology*, 11, 518–28.

Huff, F. J., Collins, C., Corkin, S. and Rosen, T. J. (1986). 'Equivalent forms of the Boston Naming Test'. *Journal of Clinical and Experimental Neuropsychology*, 8, 556–62.

Kaplan, E., Goodglass, H. and Weintraub, S. (1983). *Boston Naming Test.* Philadelphia: Lea & Febiger.

Kindlen, D. J. and Garrison, W. (1984). 'The Boston Naming Test: norm data and cue utilization in a sample of normal 6 and 7 year old children'. *Brain and Language*, 21, 255–9.

Knesevich, J. W., LaBarge, E. and Edwards, D. (1986). 'Predictive value of the Boston Naming Test in mild senile dementia of the Alzheimer type'. *Psychiatry Research*, 19, 155–61.

Thompson, L. L. and Heaton, R. K. (1989). 'Comparison of different versions of the Boston Naming Test'. *Clinical Neuropsychologist*, 3, 184–92.

Van Gorp, W. G., Satz, P., Kiersch, M. E. and Hendry, R. (1986). 'Normative data on the Boston Naming Test for a group of normal older adults'. *Journal of Clinical and Experimental Neuropsychology*, 8, 702–5.

Williams, B. W., Mack, W. and Henderson, V. W. (1989). 'Boston Naming Test in Alzheimer's Disease'. *Neuropsychologia*, 27, 1073–9.

Linda Armstrong

BRISTOL LANGUAGE DEVELOPMENT SCALES (BLADES)

Test author Mary Gutfreund, Maureen Harrison and Gordon Wells

Purpose Blades is a developmental-language assessment package, giving pragmatic, semantic and syntactic analyses of recorded and transcribed language samples. The analyses categories are based on data from the Bristol Language Projects (Wells, 1985), one of the most representative and complete databases available.

Subject population   Children aged between 15 months and 5 years

Administration time   Variable

Materials   Contains a manual, record forms and therapy-planner forms.

Structure and administration   It is suggested that a 30-minute language sample is recorded in six 5-minute periods to ensure a variety of contexts, and that this is transcribed in English orthography, glossing meaning and using particular punctuation conventions. The three analyses – pragmatic, semantic and syntactic – are all carried out on the same sample, ensuring that a maximum amount of information is gained from one recording and transcription. Two principal scales are presented – the Main Scale, reflecting the developmental level reached, used for determining whether there is a problem, and for checking progress; and the Therapy Planning Form, giving further examples and details, used for spotting gaps in a child's performance and planning therapeutic intervention. There is also a syntax-free form to measure symbolic communication in children whose language is not entirely spoken English, such as users of British Sign Language.

Scoring and interpretation   As well as qualitative data, the analyses give an overall stage measure or level which translates into an age score, and diagrams indicating the order in which items emerged in normal children are presented to help therapy-planning.

Technical details

Standardization   The scales are based on data from a balanced, longitudinal sample of 128 Bristol children, between the ages of 15 and 60 months, collected at three-month intervals using naturalistic sampling methods and automatically timed microphones.

Reliability   Good levels of reliability were achieved in the original Bristol study (Wells, 1985) but no test–retest or inter-/intra-user reliability measures are presented for the scales themselves, although a bibliographic reference is made to a research report. Reliability is likely to be a problem, judging by the amount of work needed to establish reliability of transcription and coding in the main study.

Validity   Validity and test procedures were subjected to 12 months' testing by experienced and naïve coders on a variety of recordings from a variety of sources (BLADES manual, introduction, unnumbered page) but no further information is given in the manual.

Evaluation   The intention is to make BLADES accessible to less linguistically sophisticated users than other language analyses, and to provide a clinically useful description of a child's language. The scales have been piloted on clinical data, but no details are given in the manual.

Country of origin   UK

References

Wells, G. (1985). *Language Development in the Pre-school Years.* Cambridge: Cambridge University Press.

Elspeth McCartney

BRITISH PICTURE VOCABULARY SCALE (BPVS)

Test authors   L. M. Dunn, D. Pantile and C. Whetton

Purpose   This is a test of a hearing vocabulary for standard English. It is also an achievement test in that it makes an assessment of the extent of vocabulary acquisition. This can be useful for a variety of groups: preschool children, early and general school use, foreign-language students, clinical use with non-readers, autistic and even psychotic individuals. The subject should have no hearing difficulties.

Subject population   2-year-olds to adults

Administration time   The text takes a maximum of five minutes for 5- and 6-year-olds on the short form. Four-year olds are more variable. Scoring time is under a minute.

Materials   There is a (verbose) manual including a large number of tables. There are booklets of pictures and record forms for the long and short forms and a plastic stand to present the pictures. The BPVS is contained in a convenient box.

Structure and administration   Those under 8 years are given training pictures, but I find that this is unnecessary even for most 5-year-olds. The task is to point to one out of four pictures to indicate the word spoken by the examiner. The short form has a total of 32 items, and the long form, 150 items. As most will use the short form, only this will be described here. The object in testing is to find the critical range that provides maximum discrimination among those of similar ability. One begins at different points, depending on age, but moves further back if the items are too difficult. The basal point is where there are 6 consecutive correct responses and the ceiling is where out of 6 consecutive responses there are 4 errors.

Scoring and interpretation As an example, suppose the last item administered for the ceiling was the 22nd item and the total number of errors was 6; these errors comprised the 4 within the ceiling region and 2 within the region between the basal and ceiling regions. The raw score is 22 minus 6 which is 16. From the raw score the age equivalents and percentiles can be looked up.

Technical details

Standardization The test was developed from the American Peabody Picture Vocabulary Test. A pool of 424 items (excluding American terms) was given to 1,401 subjects ranging from 2 to 16 years, from which the short and long forms of the test were derived. The short form (mainly) was given to a representative sample of over 3,000 children in the UK.

Reliability Split-half reliabilities ranged from 0.75 to 0.86 for each year group from 3 to 6 years. But for 17-year-olds reliability goes down to 0.41 on the short form, due to the small number of items. There are no measures of test–retest reliability.

Validity The content validity is good in that there are 18 categories covered to ensure a breadth of vocabulary (e.g. animals, actions). But no data are provided on direct tests of validity.

Evaluation As pointed out in the manual, this is a test of hearing vocabulary by selecting pictures. It is not the same as the subject giving a definition of a word as in the Stanford-Binet, Wechsler and BAS scales. This is a distinction between measuring receptive language in the case of the BPVS and measuring expressive language. The test is well constructed to give a quick and efficient measure of current vocabulary level. Further research is needed to establish the connection between this test and intelligence tests. As other research has established strong connections between IQ and other vocabulary tests (including the Peabody from which the BPVS is derived), it is likely that a strong connection would be found. This does not mean that it should be treated as an IQ test, as testing vocabulary is only a limited aspect of cognitive abilities.

Country of origin   UK

Publisher   NFER-NELSON, Windsor (1982)

References

Binet, A. and Simon, T. (1916). *The Development of Intelligence in Children* (translated by E. S. Kite). Vineland, NJ: The Training School.

Dunn, L. M. (1981). *Peabody Picture Vocabulary Test – Revised Manual.* Circle Pines, MN: American Guidance Service.

Elliott, C. D. (1983). *The British Ability Scales. Manual 2: Technical and Statistical Information.* Windsor: NFER-NELSON.

Wechsler, D. (1974). *Wechsler Intelligence Scale for Children – Revised.* New York: The Psychological Corporation.

John R. Beech

CARROW ELICITED LANGUAGE INVENTORY (CELI)

Test author   Elizabeth Carrow-Woolfolk

Purpose   CELI aims to provide a measure of a child's productive control of grammar by eliciting imitations of sentences. It aims to identify children with language disorders and to determine which specific structures are contributing to the child's inadequate linguistic performance. It is used with children between 3 years and 7 years 11 months, but the test manual suggests that there is an effective ceiling of 6 years 7 months.

Materials   Manual, training guide, test forms, training audio cassette.

Structure and administration   The test materials consist of 52 phrase and sentence stimuli containing a range of syntactic constructions and grammatical morphemes presented for a child to imitate directly. The average time taken for administration, transcription and scoring is 45 minutes. Test procedures are clearly described: scoring conventions are clear but no underlying syntactic rationale is stated. There is a separate protocol for assessing verb errors.

Technical details

Standardization   The test was piloted, then standardized on 475 white middle-class monolingual children in Houston, Texas.

Reliability   A test–retest coefficient of 0.98 was obtained on 25 children selected at random and retested after a period of two weeks. Inter-examiner reliability was measured by (i) correlating the administration, transcription and scoring of two examiners with ten randomly selected tapes; the coefficient was 0.98: and (2) correlating the administration, transcription and scoring of the CELI by two examiners on 20 children, 10 of whom were designated language-disordered, with a resulting coefficient of 0.99.

McCauley and Swisher (1984) do not accept this evidence as adequate, perhaps because no actual measure of the significance of these results is given.

Validity   Miller (1981) comments on the problems inherent in using elicited imitation as a measure of syntactic production. McCauley and Swisher (1984) accept the evidence in the CELI manual for concurrent validity, as the CELI can differentiate between language-disordered children and children with normal language; but not the evidence on item analysis, perhaps because non-discriminating items remained to allow broad coverage of grammatical categories.

Reviews   Nelson and Weber-Olsen (1980) found that CELI items could predict morpheme difficulty in language-impaired children only when contextual support was offered. Howell *et al.* (1981) found that CELI differentiated powerfully between children aged $4^{1}/_{4}$–$5^{1}/_{4}$ referred for speech and language therapy and control children, but mainly because 11 of the 19 referred children scored below the test floor, and little information on syntactic abilities was gleaned. Hawkins and Spencer (1985) compared CELI results with LARSP results for one 5-year-old child referred for language delay, and concluded that LARSP gave a more accurate reflection of his syntactic abilities in part due to the CELI emphasis on scoring morphological errors, rather than syntactic structures.

Evaluation   CELI appears to be good at discriminating between language-impaired and other children, but may not give a good account of a child's grammatical ability. The status of elicited imitation for children acquiring language is equivocal, and although some processing does go on, the relationship between sentences elicited by imitation and produced spontaneously is not clear. The emphasis on morphological (word-level) errors may underestimate a child's ability.

Country of origin   USA

Publisher   DLM Teaching Resources, Allen, Texas (1974)

References

Hawkins, P. and Spencer, H. (1985). 'Imitative versus spontaneous language assessment: a comparison of CELI and LARSP'. *British Journal of Disorders of Communication*, 20, 191–200.

Howell, J., Skinner, C., Gray, M. and Broomfield, S. (1981). 'A study of comparative effectiveness of different language tests with two groups of children'. *British Journal of Disorders of Communication*, 16, 31–42.

McCauley, R. J. and Swisher, L. (1984). 'Psychometric review of language and articulation tests'. *Journal of Speech and Hearing Disorders*, 49, 34–42.

Miller, J. (1981). *Assessing Language Production in Children*. London: Edward Arnold.

Nelson, L. K. and Weber-Olsen, M. (1980). 'The Elicited Language Inventory and the influence of contextual cues'. *Journal of Speech and Hearing Disorders*, 45, 549–63.

Elspeth McCartney

CASP

Purpose   To provide a functional assessment of the communication skills of adults with severe to mild mental handicap, in relation to their environment and living style. It is not suitable for the profoundly handicapped, nor those with severe visual disability.

It can be used as a screening assessment and provides a within-population comparison.

Administration time   Variable

Structure and administration   CASP should be completed by the carer/ key worker who knows the client well, and speech and language therapist, jointly.

There are three parts, with corresponding recording forms.

Part I – the carer's assessment   This is a questionnaire, dealing with how the client uses his or her communication skills, together with some basic information about his or her daily life and environment.

Part II – the therapist's assessment   This section may be scored and the scores transferred on to the raw score and percentile chart in Part III. Part II consists of 8 sections:

1   Event knowledge; responses are elicited during normal conversation
2   Hearing and Auditory Discrimination Skills
3   Vocabulary (Comprehension and Expression)
4   Comprehension of Functional Use of Everyday Objects
5   Comprehension and Sentence Level
6   Comprehension and Expression at Sentence Level

Responses are elicited using specific instructions and (mainly) photographs from the manual, e.g.

- 'Which one do you cut with'
- 'Put the smallest coin beside the purse'
- 'Show me the man giving the lady the book'
  (The Comprehension and Sentence Level material is not necessarily developmentally ordered, but based on the concept of information-carrying words (Masidlover *et al.*, 1982).)

7   Communicative Functions requires the examiner to observe the client in different situations, and record aspects of conversational competence and communicative functions.

8   This section, which is not scored, provides a summary of the clients' expressive skills (speech, gesture, sign, symbol-use or aided communication).

Appendices 1–4 provide information on understanding of some verbal concepts, recognition of a few 'social-sight' words and signs, the clients' phonology (not scored), oromuscular skills, and manual dexterity in imitation of gesture.

Part III – the joint assessment   The carer and the speech and language therapist work together, filling in the summary of assessments, and involving the client wherever possible. The raw scores from the subtests in part II can be translated into percentiles and the profile thus obtained. Then the speech and language therapist and carer together summarize the client's strengths (this completed page may also be photocopied for inclusion in the client's hospital/centre notes) in terms of Skills, Activities, and Resources, from information gained from Parts I and II.

The Communication Environment Rating Scale is completed, which gives a broad outline of whether the client's different environments are enabling/encouraging him or her to *use* his or her communication skills.

Finally, Priorities for Change are agreed. These would be specific targets in the areas of:

- further assessments
- particular skills which are required for more effective communication
- particular aspects of the environment which it would be beneficial to change

Technical details

Validity and reliability   Three clinical trials and tests of internal and external validity and reliability (test–retest and inter-rater) involving Carers' Assessment and various sections of the Therapist's Assessment are detailed in the manual. The validity of CASP was supported and its reliability was high.

Evaluation   This is an extremely well laid-out assessment; the manual and recording forms are clear and easy to follow.

It does indeed provide, as it purports to do, a profile of the functional communication skills of adults with mental handicap, and combines both the carer and the speech and language therapist to do so. This approach must be welcomed by all speech and language therapists who work with this client group.

Speech and language therapists may wish that the sections relating to Communicative Functions (i.e. Part I Section 1 and Part II Section 7) were more detailed, particularly in the area of conversational competence and management of discourse. Few such assessments exist in sufficient detail.

CASP provides a welcome basis for discussion between carers and the speech and language therapist, concerning the communication environment and the possibilities of changing it for the better. Users of CASP might also wish to consult INTECOM (Jones, 1990) which has a similar philosophy but which then continues further into staff training.

Part III of CASP ensures that the assessment is followed up by *action* which all parties 'own'.

Overall, a most valuable tool for practitioners with this client group.

Country of origin   UK

Publisher   Speech Profiles Ltd (1988)

References

Jones, S. (1990). *Intecom.* Windsor: NFER-NELSON.
Masidlover, M. *et al.* (1982). *Derbyshire Language Scheme.* Derbyshire County Council

Beth McCaig

THE DERBYSHIRE LANGUAGE SCHEME, 1987 (REVISED)

Test authors   W. Knowles and M. Masidlover

Purpose   This language scheme is a teaching programme designed to improve the functional language skills of children with learning difficulties and delayed language development. It assesses comprehension and expressive-language levels following normal developmental stages in detail.

The results are designed so that treatment objectives can be planned.

Subject population   Children aged 3 upwards with language and learning difficulties

Administration time   Rapid Screening Test – 5–8 minutes; Detailed Test of Comprehension – 20 minutes; Expressive Sample – no time given as it is seen as an on-going process – test and teach; scoring – simple scoring of comprehension, expressive sample and cross-referencing. This process can be lengthy.

Materials   These include a user's-guide manual, assessment booklet, assessment and progress-record forms, class charts and two teaching manuals.

Structure and administration   This is a criterion-referenced test. The authors recommend that testing is carried out by the person who will remediate the child. The Rapid Screening Test assesses five items as a sample of comprehension to allow entry at the appropriate point into the Detailed Test of Comprehension. Items are presented in developmental sequence from single words to complex sentence, using large toys, miniatures or picture materials. The test is administered as a 'play' situation with opportunity for role reversal. This allows for sampling of functional communication in a structured setting. Variation in vocabulary items and instructions are allowed to maximize the child's performance and to minimize the effect of vocabulary or other attention problems.

Scoring and interpretation   The Detailed Test of Comprehension is scored as correct or incorrect responses non-verbally, i.e. by pointing or manipulation. This yields an overall score to be compared with the stated pass mark for each section. The Expressive Language Sample is analysed in several ways: by vocabulary count at a single-word level; by sentence structure expressed as semantic relations for the simple sentences; by elements of syntactic structure for the complex sentences. All information is entered on the assessment-summary table. All data are transferred to the progress-record chart or class chart for interpretation, planning and implementation of the remediation programme.

Technical details

A criterion-referenced test with some comparative norms from the child-language (Bloom *et al.*, 1975; Wells, 1980; Miller, 1981).

Evaluation   As an assessment the Derbyshire Language Scheme provides a baseline of the child's communicative abilities in a natural context. The information gained gives direct access to a wealth of teaching ideas. It has wide clinical utility and has been used successfully with its stated client groups. It avoids the problems of some published tests of comprehension by being interactive, flexible in its choice of play material and being geared to the needs of children with learning difficulties. Its limitations include: the complex and time-consuming form-filling; transfer of information from the assessment to teaching phases; the use of both semantic and syntactic terminology in analysing expressive language. There is little research into its uses or efficacy. However, the assessment can be adapted for signed input and its popularity should encourage further research and development.

Country of origin   UK

Publisher   Educational Psychology Service, Derbyshire County Council, Ripley

References

Bloom, L., Lightbown, P. and Hood, L. (1975). 'Structure and variation in child language'. *Monographs of the Society for Research into Child Development,* no. 160.

Miller, J. (1981). *Assessing Language Production in Children.* Baltimore: University Park Press.

Wells, E. (1980). 'Syntactic and semantic developmental chart'. Unpublished, School of Education, Bristol University.

Julie Dockrell

THE EDINBURGH ARTICULATION TEST

Test authors   A. Anthony, D. Bogle, T. Ingram and M. McIsaac

Purpose   The articulation test is a standard traditional speech-and-language-therapy procedure. The Edinburgh Articulation Test (hereafter EAT) is a unique version of its type. Its uniqueness lies in its construction and its assessment procedures. It does, however, employ the typical elicitation technique of a picture-naming game and involves an assessment primarily based on the analysis of a child's pronunciation errors.

Subject population   Children aged 3–6 years

208

Administration time   15 minutes approximately; scoring time: 20 minutes

Structure and administration   A set of 41 pictures is used to elicit 41 words which include the 68 phonological items included in the test. These 68 items are all consonants in word-initial, within-word and word-final positions as singletons, in 2- and 3-element clusters. The words are monosyllabic and disyllabic for the most part but there are three trisyllabic words. A test of articulation must include a majority of phonological segments, sequences and structures which most reliably reveal the developmental status of a child's articulatory skills. The EAT does this by including items that were found in an extensive pilot study to be good discriminators between children at different stages in their articulatory development. Unlike other articulation tests the EAT does not attempt to test every consonant phoneme in all word positions. Instead, again on the basis of the pilot study, it tests reliable representatives of classes of phonemes and clusters that are known to share a common pattern of development. In selecting items for inclusion in the test, possible phonotactic structures were also considered. These factors render the EAT unique in its construction and arguably more reliable in the assessment of the maturation of articulatory skills.

Scoring and interpretation   The EAT once again combines tradition and innovation. The first stage in scoring is the traditional Quantitative Assessment which evaluates the child's pronunciation of the 68 items as right/wrong. The total number of right items can be compared against those of a normal population and a standard score obtained. If the standard score is one deviation below the norm (= 15 points) then further investigations are advisable. These will include the second stage in scoring the EAT: the Qualitative Assessment. Here the child's pronunciations of the test items are compared with the pronunciations provided by the normal standardization sample. These are classified into developmental categories: almost mature; immature; very immature; atypical. It is thus possible to gauge the articulatory maturity of a child's so-called error pronunciations and in re-testing to monitor the changes that occur over time (Grunwell, 1983). The Qualitative Assessment is thereby a most valuable analytical assessment tool for a speech and language therapist. It also provides clinicians with comprehensive information about the patterns of normal articulatory development.

Technical details

Standardization   The EAT was standardized on a population of 510 Edinburgh children in the late 1960s. Subsequent unpublished investigations carried out by the author in Birmingham in the mid-1970s and in Grimsby in the mid-1980s have indicated that it remains a reliable tool for assessing the articulatory development of British English-speaking children between the ages of 3 and 6. While sex, birth rank and socioeconomic class were found to have some relationship to articulatory maturity in the original standardization sample, these factors were not statistically significant. Therefore the only factor considered in arriving at a standard score is age.

Reliability The original EAT was administered using a mixture of pictures and objects. Subsequently, on deciding to publish, the authors produced a picture book which was found to be as reliable as the previous collection of objects and pictures. Unfortunately some of the pictures are not particularly effective in easily eliciting spontaneously the words required. Test-users should therefore feel free to replace these with alternatives or with objects. Another possibility is to use an entirely different set of elicitation materials that includes the 41 EAT words and also will elicit a much larger sample of phonologically representative items that can be used to carry out an extensive and in-depth phonological assessment of a child's speech (Grunwell, 1987). In order to use the EAT effectively the administrator must be able to record the child's pronunciations of the test items in narrow phonetic transcription. Use of the test is thus effectively restricted to speech and language therapists and clinical linguists and phoneticians. No reliability studies are available specifically investigating the EAT.

Validity Performance on the EAT is clearly associated with overall pronunciation abilities and phonological development. In some children it may also be associated with other aspects of language development and indeed general development. No studies are available which match the EAT to language development. However, the EAT is frequently used as a standardized measure in studies of developmental phonological disorders (e.g. Grunwell, 1983).

Country of origin   UK

Publisher   Longman (1971)

References

Grunwell, P. (1983). 'Phonological development in phonological disability'. *Topics in Language Disorders*, 3, 62–76.
Grunwell, P. (1987). *PACS Pictures*. Windsor: NFER-NELSON.

Pam Grunwell

EISENSON'S EXAMINATION FOR APHASIA

Test author   J. Eisenson

Purpose   'To provide the clinician with a guided approach for evaluating possible aphasic language disturbances and other disturbances related to language function ... primarily directed towards obtaining essential information ... useful for the rehabilitation of persons found to be aphasic ... intended to reveal both the assets and deficits of the subject' (p. 21). The author finds it useful in initial assessment and as a measure for patient improvement.

Subject population   Adolescents and adults whose language abilities became impaired after normal language functioning was established, and 'congenital aphasics'.

Administration time   30 minutes to 2 hours, depending on severity of impairment, for the whole examination. Shorter versions may be administered (by using either every second item in the subjects or only the first in each subtest, to screen a patient). No time limit is set.

Materials   Record form with test items in full, summary sheet for individual performance and space for comments. Manual containing background, explanations, instructions and visual test stimuli. Additional everyday objects are needed.

Structure and administration   This test consists of adapted educational achievement tests, graded in difficulty. The Weisenburg and McBride (1935) aphasia-classification system is its theoretical base. Areas assessed are receptive (visual, auditory and tactile agnosias, auditory aphasia and silent reading) and expressive functions (non-verbal and verbal apraxias, automatic speech, spelling, writing, naming, word-finding and arithmetic processes). The subtests are self-explanatory – for some, instructions are given, and for others, only general directions are given and the tester must use ingenuity to explain the task to the patient. The test may be given over more than one sitting if necessary. The author is extremely flexible in how the test may be administered, e.g. in the first section (visual agnosia), in subtest 1-a (Recognition of Common Objects), the patient is 'asked to do one of the following: name objects to which examiner points; point to object named by examiner; demonstrate the object's use; or select the name from choices given orally by examiner'.

Scoring and interpretation   Most of the items are scored on a pass/fail basis but qualitative information is also taken into account, so that a profile of the individual is built up on a five-point scale of dysfunction. The examiner should take clinical notes of noteworthy behaviour.

Technical details

Standardization A standardization procedure was felt by the author to be unnecessary. He states: 'Aphasic patients are characteristically too inconsistent in their responses to permit formal scoring standards to be developed and meaningfully applied' (p. 31). Reading and spelling tests contain educationally standardized materials.

Reliability No information given by the author.

Validity No information given.

Evaluation This test is based on educational assessment. It is of American origin and includes culturally biased and out-of-date pictures and words. It has strength in its emphasis on quality of response, rather than on number of errors alone. It presents as the type of assessment constructed locally by clinicians and students as an 'informal assessment' for patients in the initial stages of recovery. It is not used currently in research nor by therapists, although its format is very familiar and seen in more modern and theoretically oriented formal assessments. Davis (1983) notes that it is 'of historical significance'.

Country of origin USA

Publisher The Psychological Corporation

References

Davis, G. A. (1983). *A Survey of Adult Aphasia.* Englewood Cliffs, NJ: Prentice-Hall.

Eisenson, J. (1954) *Examining for Aphasia: a manual for the examination of aphasia and related disturbances.* New York: Psychological Corp.

Eisenson, J. (1973). *Adult Aphasia: assessment and treatment.* New York: Appleton-Century-Crofts.

Weisenburg, T. and McBride, K. (1935). *Aphasia: a clinical and psychological study.* New York: Commonwealth Fund.

Linda Armstrong

FRENCHAY APHASIA SCREENING TEST (FAST)

Test authors   P. Enderby, V. Wood and D. Wade

Purpose   This is a short, simple, standardized test for use in the identification of aphasia. Its authors do not claim that it aids in identifying specific areas of dysfunction, planning treatment or measuring change. Their aim is to provide doctors assessing acute stroke patients with a diagnostic tool which may be of use both in patient management, including referral to speech and language therapy, and in research.

Subject population   Adults

Administration time   3–10 minutes

Structure and administration   The test equipment consists of an eight-page manual, including administration form, a test card with printed instruction labels attached, and a number of gummed score-summary forms, enclosed in a transparent plastic carrying folder.

The four major facets of language are tested: comprehension of speech, expression, comprehension of reading, and writing. Comprehension of both speech and reading is tested through a set of graded instructions relating to two pictures. Expression is tested by asking the subject to describe, in writing and in speech, one of the test pictures, and also by a test of verbal fluency (naming as many animals as possible in one minute). Scoring instructions are given on the administration form.

Technical details

Standardization   The test was standardized on 123 non-aphasic people covering a wide age range, of whom 25 per cent were aged over 70. Fifty stroke patients, 20 of whom were aphasic, were also assessed within 36 days of their acute dense stroke. The age range of the aphasic sample is not specified. The authors claim that the presence or absence of aphasia may be established with reference to either normal or aphasic cut-off points. Among the younger (under-60) age group, the majority of normals scored 29 or 30/30, whereas in older normals there was a wider spread of scores, with a significant minority of over 70-year-olds scoring 26 or 27/30. The cut-off values derived from these results are 27/30 (age under 60), and 25/30 (age 61+). In this study, no subject later classified as aphasic scored higher than 23.

The test was successful in identifying all the aphasic subjects, and there were no false negatives. Fourteen of the subjects were incorrectly identified as aphasic due to visual neglect, hemianopia, hemiplegia, confusion or poor pre-morbid command of English.

An abbreviated form of the test, omitting the reading and writing sections, was also standardized. This resulted in a decrease in false positive identifications, but its use would prevent the detection of dyslexic or dysgraphic deficits.

Reliability   There is good reliability, both inter-tester and test–retest.

Validity   In the authors' study, the test was successful in identifying all the aphasic subjects, including two whose language disorder had not been detected by the doctor responsible for their management. In common with other aphasia tests, there is a risk of over-inclusiveness, as patients with dementia or acute confusion, visual neglect, severe dysarthria, pre-morbid illiteracy or poor command of English may be identified as having a language disorder.

Evaluation   The use of cut-off points in scoring could result in a failure to identify high-level language deficits in the pre-morbidly highly articulate patient. However, such patients may also go undetected if a screening test is not routinely used.

No grand claims are made for this test, nor does it fulfil them. However, it may be of use in determining which patients should be referred to speech and language therapy for a more detailed assessment.

Country of origin   UK

Publisher   NFER-NELSON, Windsor (1987)

Carole Pound, Jenny Sheridan and Judith Williams

FRENCHAY DYSARTHRIA ASSESSMENT

Test author   P. Enderby

Purpose   This is a well-established standardized clinical test used by speech and language therapists for the differential diagnosis of dysarthria. (The term 'dysarthria' is used to describe speech abnormalities caused by neuromuscular disorders.)

Subject population   12 years to adult

Administration time   Non-computerized administration and scoring time: 30–40 minutes

214

Materials Manual, scoring forms pad, or Apple disk pack (with manual and scoring forms). The computer interpretation package for this assessment is compatible with Apple II, II Plus and IIe computers. The software will generate an instant profile from scores entered by the speech and language therapist.

Structure and administration The following equipment is required for the test: test manual, scoring form, tongue depressor, stopwatch, tape recorder, glass of water, word and sentence cards.

The test is divided into ten major sections: Reflex, Respiration, Lips, Jaws, Soft Palate, Laryngeal, Tongue, Intelligibility, Influencing Factors (hearing, sight, teeth, language, mood, posture) and Other Factors. The first eight sections contain subtests and require the therapist to analyse the behaviour of each component in isolation to examine the relative abilities and disabilities. Only the second attempt of the specified test should be scored, the first attempt being for practice purposes.

A nine-point rating scale is used to score the patient's responses for each subtest and the results are charted on a bar graph on the scoring form and this can be scored during the test. An additional section of the form enables the examiner to comment on influencing factors that may affect the speech disorder, or the recovery.

1 Reflex: this is an assessment to elicit whether the patient has difficulty or a degree of difficulty with the cough reflex, or swallowing, or whether there is dribbling or drooling.
2 Respiration: this is an observation of the patient's respiration at rest and in speech.
3 Lips: an assessment of the position of lips when at rest, when spread, when sealed and during alternating exaggerated movements and during speech.
4 Jaw: an assessment at rest and during speech.
5 Soft Palate: observation of patient when eating and drinking to discover whether food or drink comes down the nose, and an exercise to demonstrate patient's palatal movement. Speech – assessment of nasal resonance and nasal emission in conversation.
6 Laryngeal: there is a timed voice exercise with assessment of pitch and volume. In speech, the clarity of phonation and appropriateness of volume and pitch in conversation are noted.
7 Tongue: observations of the position of the tongue at rest, when protruded, elevated, during lateral movements outside the lips, during alternative quick movements and tongue movements in conversation are noted.
8 Intelligibility: (a) from 50 selected words, 12 are chosen at random and then the therapist writes down the word as understood when articu-

lated by the patient. After the test, the words are checked against cards; (b) from 50 selected sentence cards, 12 are chosen at random and treated in the same manner as the above exercise; (c) the patient is then engaged in conversation for about five minutes.

9 Influencing Factors: these include assessments of hearing, sight, teeth, language, patient's mood and posture.

10 Other Factors: (a) rate a recording of the patient's conversation in order to judge speed of patient's speech; (b) sensation: a test of sensation of the patient's lips and tongue.

Technical details

Standardization   Standardizatons were based on 46 normal healthy adults ranging in age from 23 to 64 years. Subsequently, this test was administered to an additional 148 normal subjects, 111 ranging in age from 15 to 59 years, with the remaining 37 ranging in age from 60 to 97 years. In the younger group 94.6 per cent achieved a top grade of 9, 4.6 per cent achieved a grade of 8, and less than 1 per cent achieved a grade of 7 or less. The lowest overall total score was 172 out of a possible maximum score of 180. The older group showed results similar to the younger group; 90.8 per cent scored the top grade of 9, and 8.9 per cent scored a grade of 8.

Reliability   Eight speech and language therapists who were unfamiliar with the Frenchay Dysarthria Assessment had three hours' training in the test procedure. Then, these testers independently scored 113 dysarthric subjects (from videotapes) presenting a broad range of type and degree of speech disability. In addition, three live subjects were examined by an independent clinician in front of the eight speech and language therapists who recorded their results. The widest range of scores by judges on any individual patient was 15 per cent of the overall score, and the majority of the patients' scores were clustered more closely. A product-moment correlation on each item between testers yielded high inter-tester coefficients.

Validity   Certain identifiable features of dysarthric speech are directly attributable to the underlying neurological condition. Validation was needed to discover whether there were patterns associated with specific neurological conditions, or whether the patterns just showed discrimination between individual patients regardless of pathology.

Results of a study in which the Frenchay Dysarthria Assessment was administered to 85 dysarthric patients with confirmed medical diagnosis showed:

1   upper motor-neurone lesion: 30
2   mixed upper and lower motor-neurone lesions: 13

3   extrapyramidal disorders: 18
4   cerebellar dysfunction: 14
5   lower motor-neurone lesion: 10

Investigations of the clinical validity of the Frenchay Dysarthria Assessment resulted from descriptive reports made by therapists from clinics throughout the United Kingdom who submitted test results for analysis. Enderby provided the therapists with a description of a patient on the basis of their test scores. Of the 112 analysed case reports, 89.3 per cent were found accurate by the patient's therapist. Thus, from a blind analysis of only the Frenchay Dysarthria Assessment scores, an independent diagnosis was accurate in 89 per cent of the scores.

Country of origin   UK

Publisher   NFER-NELSON, Windsor (1988)

GOLDMAN-FRISTOE-WOODCOCK AUDITORY SKILLS TEST BATTERY

Test authors   R. Goldman, M. Fristoe and R. W. Woodcock

Purpose   To diagnose an individual's ability to hear clearly under difficult conditions. Used for instructional planning

Subject population   3–85 years

Administration time   About 15 minutes for each subtest

Materials   Each section of the battery is packaged in a plastic file containing a flip-over booklet (easel-style) of stimulus pictures, a cassette tape-recording of certain of the stimulus-test items and a pad of score-sheets.

Structure and administration   This complex collection of tests is aptly named a battery. There are twelve areas of measurement of auditory skills. These are:

- Auditory Selective Attention Test
- Diagnostic Auditory Discrimination Test
- Auditory Memory Tests:
  - Recognition Memory
  - Memory for Content
  - Memory for Sequence

- Sound Symbol Tests
  - Sound Mimicry
  - Sound Recognition
  - Sound Analysis
  - Sound Blending
  - Sound–Symbol Association
  - Reading of Symbols
  - Spelling of Sounds

The Auditory Selective Attention Test measures a child's ability to perform a listening task in the presence of competing noise, which is created by playing the cassette recording. After a fairly lengthy training section to acquaint the testee with the materials, the child is required in the test to point to one of a set of four pictures named on the recording. The four words in each set consist of two minimal pairs; for example *pat, patch, chair, tear.* There are 110 items in the test divided into four subsets according to the type of noise against which the test items are said. The four subtests are designated as follows: Quiet; Fan-Like Noise; Cafeteria Noise; Voice (that is, continuous speech background). These are said to represent the major types of distractions that face people in everyday listening situations.

The Diagnostic Auditory Discrimination Test measures a child's ability to discriminate between speech sounds and in addition pinpoints any sound confusions. There are three parts to the test, each with their own training section. Part I involves the discrimination of 100 minimal pairs; the words are contrasted by either initial or final consonants; for example *tack/shack*; *tack/tag.* It has to be noted that many of the items on this section and indeed throughout the whole battery are culturally biased and would probably be unusable outside of an American English context; for example *base* (as in baseball) paired with *vase* (presumably pronounced /veɪs/). The test requires the testee to point to one of the two pictures according to the word spoken by the tape-recorded voice. Part I is diagnostic in that if a child evidences speech-sound discrimination difficulties, then Parts II and III should be administered to investigate those difficulties further. These each contain another 100 minimal pair items.

The Auditory Memory Tests measure aspects of short-term retention of information. There are three tests:

Test 1 – Recognition Memory measures the ability to recognize whether or not a given word has been heard in the immediate past. The test consists of 110 words divided into five lists of 22 words each. The test section is preceded by a training section. The test is presented on a pre-recorded tape.

Test 2 – Memory for Content   measures the ability to recognize a set of elements that occurred in a recent auditory event. As with the other tests there is a training section. The child listens to a list of words while facing a blank page. Immediately after the list has finished, the examiner turns to the response page and the child is asked to point to the pictures that were not named in the list. The lists range in length from two items with 4 pictures on the response page to nine items with 11 pictures on the response page. There are 16 lists.

Test 3 – Memory for Sequence   measures the ability to remember the order of a set of recent auditory events. There is a training section preceding the test section. The testee listens to a pre-recorded list of words and is then required to put a set of picture cards into the same order as the list by placing them in pockets on a page. The lists range from 2 to 8 words long and there are 14 items.

Sound Symbol Tests   measure a range of abilities which underlie the development of particular oral and written language skills. There are seven tests:

Test 1 – Sound Mimicry   measures the ability to initiate syllables presented auditorily. The testee hears a nonsense word twice and is then required to repeat it. There are 55 nonsense words ranging from one to three syllables in length and including a range of syllable types: VC, CV, CCV, VCC, CVC, CVCC, CCVC, CCVCC.

Test 2 – Sound Recognition   measures the ability to identify a familiar word when it is presented as a sequence of isolated phonemes. The child is presented with a set of four pictures the names of which have some phonemes in common; for example *back, bag, cat, eat.* The child hears /k_a_t/ and is required to select the picture that the sounds would name if integrated into a word. There are 30 test items.

Test 3 – Sound Analysis   measures the ability to identify the phonemic components of syllables. There is a training section. The test section consists of 28 two- or three-phoneme nonsense syllables pre-recorded on tape. The testee is required to repeat the first, middle or last sound of each syllable as instructed.

Test 4 – Sound Blending   measures the ability to blend 2–7 isolated sounds into familiar words. The testee is presented with a series of isolated phonemes and is requested to say the word that these phonemes would compose when blended. There are 33 items ranging in difficulty from *ice* to *quarts.*

Test 5 – Sound–Symbol Association assesses the ability to learn new associations between unfamiliar auditory and visual stimuli. The examiner presents a novel visual figure and 'names' it with a nonsense syllable. The testee is then shown a page of novel figures and is asked to select the figure 'named' with the nonsense syllable. The task becomes progressively more difficult as nine only sound–symbol associations are presented. The test involves 55 identifications.

Test 6 – Reading of Symbols measures the ability to make phoneme-to-grapheme translations. The test contains 70 nonsense words 1–3 syllables long which the testee is required to read aloud. The 70 words contain all the major spellings of the English phonemes. It appears, though the instructions are not entirely clear, that the child is required to 'sound out' the phonemes individually in the correct order and then to 'blend' them to pronounce the nonsense word.

Test 7 – Spelling of Sounds measures the ability to make phoneme-to-grapheme translations. The child hears nonsense words on the pre-recorded tape and is then asked to repeat the word aloud before spelling it by writing it down on a form. Lists of acceptable spellings for the nonsense words are provided. There are 50 words ranging from 1 to 3 syllables in length and containing singletons and consonant clusters.

Scoring and interpretation The results of all the tests in the battery can be assembled on a G-F-W Battery profile which reveals an individual's strengths and weaknesses on the various tests within the battery. This profile, the devisors suggest, can then be used for diagnostic and therapy-planning purposes.

At the end of each flip-over booklet there is a section entitled Manual. This contains administration instructions, guidelines for interpretation and tables of percentile marks and age-equivalent scores.

Technical details

Standardization All of the tests in the battery are standardized on a population ranging from 3 to 19 years and over, with an upper age limit of 85.

Reliability A separate technical manual details the constructions, development and standardization of the whole battery. There are also sections reporting reliability and validity studies.

Country of origin USA

Publisher   American Guidance Service, Circle Pines, MN (1976)

Pam Grunwell

GRADED NAMING TEST (GNT)

Test authors   P. McKenna and E. Warrington

Purpose   To detect degrees of naming deficit before they become clinically evident, by sampling the more vulnerable (low-frequency) items on the boundary of an individual's naming vocabulary

Subject population   Those with insidious word-finding difficulty

Administration time   Less than five minutes for a normal communicator, longer according to speed of naming responses made

Materials   Booklet of picture stimuli, manual and record form

Structure and administration   The test consists of thirty black-and-white pictures to be named to confrontation, graded in difficulty and selected from an initial battery of 61. It is untimed and the tester may 'question' responses in cases of misperception or insufficient response (e.g. superordinate term being given as a naming response).

Scoring and interpretation   Patients score 1 for a correct response and 0 for an incorrect one. Scores indicate present naming vocabulary, not degree of anomia. Equivalent scores are available for the other tests used in the standardization procedure. 'A diagnosis of impaired performance must be based on ... quality of responses ... and whether the present measure of the naming ability is in good accord with other known variables in the particular case.' (p. 6)

Technical details

Standardization   One hundred subjects (aged 20–76) took part in the standardization study, 67 of whom were men. The GNT, subtests of Wechsler Adult Intelligence Scale and two reading tests were given and correlations between scores computed. Common types of naming errors are exemplified.

In Gordon (1986) GNT was administered to a group of healthy elderly people. The mean score for subjects aged 73–84 was 15.2, with a range of 9–24. A very low level of positive correlation between age of subject and

221

naming score was computed – $r = 0.14$, $r^2 = 0.0196$ (not significant). In view of this result and accepted decline in naming with advancing age, it would appear that factors other than naming ability and ageing *per se* affect naming performance on this test, e.g. previous experience, general level of vocabulary.

Reliability Significant correlations were found in the standardization study between scores on GNT and on the reading test, confirming the results of previous studies. Baxter (described in the test manual) found a different order of difficulty and differences in competence in a study in which GNT was administered to another sample of normal subjects. The authors state that the differences are 'likely to be due to an overall lower IQ' (p. 11) in Baxter's population.

Validity Forty-six patients with left hemisphere lesions were tested. Significant differences were found between performance of the earlier normal sample and the validation-study subjects.

Evaluation This test is not felt to be one that could appropriately or usefully be used with older people. Despite the authors' claims that no specialist knowledge is required, the vocabulary tested is certainly not representative of that used in everyday communication, which is that which ought to be tested in elderly people. GNT lacks the very useful adjunct of cueing, which adds much information about the nature of the naming deficit. It is not widely used clinically and is not known to have been used in any published research. It is unusual for people to be referred for speech and language therapy before word-finding difficulties interfere significantly with communication.

Country of origin UK

Publisher NFER-NELSON, Windsor

References

Gordon, L. (1986). 'A comparative study of confrontation naming skills in normal elderly and demented elderly people'. (Unpublished) (Available from Linda Armstrong.)

McKenna, P. and Warrington, E. K. (1983). *Graded Naming Test.* Windsor: NFER-NELSON.

Linda Armstrong

ILLINOIS TEST OF PSYCHOLINGUISTIC ABILITIES (ITPA)

Test authors   S. A. Kirk, J. J. McCarthy and W. Kirk

Purpose   The Illinois Test of Psycholinguistic Abilities was designed to measure input, processing and output abilities that underlie language development. Osgood's (1957a, b) model of psycholinguistic abilities is cited as the basis for composition and organization of the test. The format of the test contains three hypothetical components of communication:

1   channels of communication
2   levels of organization
3   psycholinguistic processes.

These components are addressed in the subtests. The test is designed to be used diagnostically and to indicate strengths and weaknesses which are related to specific abilities assessed by the subtests. It is claimed that remediation programmes can be based on the test findings.

Subject population   Children 2 year 4 months – 10 years 3 months

Materials   The complete set contains an examiner's manual, record forms and picture strips, booklets for subtests and a copy of *Psycholinguistic Learning Disabilities: diagnosis and remediation.*

Structure and administration   The test consists of twelve independent subtests, ten of which are routinely administered and provide an overall language score. The twelve subtests are: auditory reception; visual reception; visual sequential memory; auditory association; auditory sequential memory; visual association; visual closure; verbal expression; grammatical closure; manual expression; auditory closure; sound blending. They should be presented in the prescribed order. The tests were arranged in this order to avoid mental set, to provide maximum interest and to prevent fatigue. The test takes about 45 minutes to complete and can be administered in more than one sitting providing no longer than one week occurs between sittings. The ITPA is a user-friendly test. It is easy to administer and clear guidelines for item presentation and scoring are given. There is an invaluable accompanying publication, *Aids and Precautions in Administering the ITPA.* Any therapist unfamiliar with the test or a particular item should consult this manual. Some of the test items are outdated for the 1990s. In particular, some of the more obscure pictures may well cause problems with certain populations.

Scoring and interpretation   Clear guidelines for scoring correct and

223

incorrect answers are provided. Basal and ceiling data are presented at the start of each test. Various types of scores can be computed from the number of correct responses a child makes for each subtest and the total number of correct responses on the entire test: scaled scores; psycholinguistic ages; psycholinguistic quotients; and percentage scores. The manuals provide detailed information about profiling and interpretation.

Technical details

Standardization   962 children were administered the revised ITPA and thus comprise the normative group. Although the test was designed for children with learning difficulties (Paraskevopoulus and Kirk, 1985), children who were having problems in school were systematically excluded. 'Only those children demonstrating average intellectual functioning, average school achievement, average characteristics of personal social adjustment, sensory motor integration, and coming from predominantly English speaking families' (Paraskevopoulus and Kirk, 1985) were included in the norm groups. The sample was taken from the Midwest (USA) with a slight bias towards middle-class membership.

Reliability   Internal consistency varies with age and subtest from 0.51 to 0.96. Some subtests are noticeably less reliable than others, e.g. verbal expression, grammatic closure and visual closure. Only four of the twelve subtests have any reliability coefficients at or above 0.90. The composite reliability coefficients are above 0.90 for 6 of the 8 age levels. However, most of the discussion on uses and interpretation of the ITPA refers to the subtest scores and not the composite score. The five-month stability coefficients for the composite scores range from 0.91 (4 years) to 0.86 (8 years). However, individual subtest stabilities are significantly less reliable (0.28 to 0.93).

Validity   There are no estimates of predictive validity using teacher ratings or school achievement for the revised edition. More important, there is no evidence of validity with other measures of language for the revised edition (see Salvia and Ysseldyke, 1985). When intelligence is controlled for only the grammatic closure, subtest correlates with reading ability and spelling (Newcomer and Hammill, 1975).

Evaluation   The ITPA remains a highly controversial test (see Sugden, 1989). Salvia and Ysseldyke (1985) conclude that the test has inadequate norms, poor reliability and questionable validity (p. 261). However, during the 1960s and early 1970s the ITPA was one of the core tests of the ability-training approaches. While many of the tests and much of the theoretical work surrounding this approach has been discredited (Coles, 1978), the test still has considerable appeal. This appeal appears to rest on the link between assessment and remediation. A meta-analysis (Kavale, 1981) indicated that there was an effect of psycholinguistic training on the variables measured by the ITPA but whether this bears any relation to normal language functioning or academic achievement must be questioned (Hammill and Larson, 1978). There has been a general move away from tests based on the skills required to complete a particular task. Irrespective of the theoretical orientation, therapists must be aware that the ITPA has not been reliably standardized on 'non-average' children.

Country of origin USA

Publisher NFER-NELSON, Windsor (1982)

References

Coles, G. S. (1978). 'The learning disabilities test battery: empirical and social issues'. *Harvard Educational Review*, 48, 313–40.

Hammill, D. D. and Larson, S. C. (1978). 'The effectiveness of psycholinguistic training: a reaffirmation of position'. *Exceptional Children*, 44, 402–14.

Kavale, K. A. (1981). 'Functions of the Illinois Test of Psycholinguistic Abilities (ITPA): are they trainable?' *Exceptional Children*, 47, 496–510.

Newcomer, P. and Hammill, D. (1975). 'ITPA and academic achievement'. *Reading Teacher*, 28, 731–41.

Osgood, C. E. (1957a). 'Motivational dynamics of language behaviour'. In M. R. Jones (ed.), *Nebraska Symposium on Motivation*. Lincoln, NB: University of Nebraska.

Osgood, C. E. (1957b). 'A behaviouristic analysis of perception and language as cognitive phenomena'. In *Contemporary Approaches to Cognition*, 75–118. Cambridge, Mass: Harvard University Press.

Paraskevopoulus, J. N. and Kirk, S. A. (1985). *The Development and Psychometric Characteristics of the Revised Illinois Test of Psycholinguistic Abilities*. Champaign: University of Illinois Press.

Salvia, J. and Ysseldyke, J. (1985). *Assessment in Speech and Remedial Education* (3rd edn). Boston: Houghton Mifflin.

Sugden, D. (1989). 'Special education and the learning process'. In D. Sugden (ed.), *Cognitive Approaches in Special Education*. London: Falmer Press.

Julie Dockrell

LANGUAGE ASSESSMENT, REMEDIATION AND SCREENING PROCEDURE (LARSP)

Test authors D. Crystal, P. Fletcher and M. Garman (1989), The *Grammatical Analysis of Language Disability* (2nd edn).

225

Purpose and design   First published in 1976, but piloted extensively before that date, LARSP constitutes a linguistic profiling procedure resulting in a single-page chart on which patterns of grammatical output can be summarized. The syntactic framework is taken from the descriptive contemporary English grammar of Quirk and colleagues (Quirk *et al.*, 1972), justified because the terminology was familiar to users and because the levels of analysis (clause, phrase and word level) were workable and could demonstrate syntactic patterns used by clinical cases.

The recommended language sample is around 30 minutes of adult–child dialogue, ideally 15 minutes of free play and 15 minutes of discussion on a topic that is not part of the immediate situation, in order to record a range of syntactic structures. An individual child's profile can be placed against that of normally developing children, giving a grammatical stage and an approximate age level. Differences in patterns of syntactic use are clearly evident: for example, children who use a preponderance of clausal elements but little phrase structure, or children who use word inflections but with little phrase- and clause-level development. From such patterns intervention targets can be selected and therapeutic strategies hypothesized. A great deal of clinical work has resulted from the use of this procedure, much of it summarized in Crystal (1979).

Subject population   Children between approximately 3 and 7 years

Technical details

Standardization   LARSP was not standardized on normally developing children; stages and ages were gleaned from the child-language literature. A computerized normative study of 3–7-year-old British children has been undertaken (Fletcher *et al.*, 1986; Johnson, 1986).

Reliability   No reliability data are presented. Transcription variance is discussed by Fletcher and Garman (1988), and segmentation procedures to increase inter-transcriber reliability for complex data, by Garman (1989).

Validity and evaluation   Validity is not discussed in the LARSP procedures, and there are few studies on normal children or with external validity criteria. Klee and Paul (1981) compare LARSP with five other structural-analysis procedures for one 3 years 5 months-old child with speech difficulties; Klee and Fitzgerald (1985) have compared LARSP with MLU (mean length of utterance) for 18 normally developing children, and Hawkins and Spencer (1985) compared it with the Carrow Elicited Language Inventory (see review, this volume).

ㆍA comprehensive linguistic review of the 1982 version is given by Connolly (1984) with a reply by Crystal (1984).

Country of origin   UK

Publisher   Cole & Whurr, London

References

Connolly, J. (1984). 'A commentary on the LARSP procedure'. *British Journal of Disorders of Communication*, 19, 63–71.

Crystal, D. (1979). *Working with LARSP*. London: Edward Arnold.

Crystal, D. (1984). 'Suffering a RELARSP'.ㆍ *British Journal of Disorders of Communication*, 19, 72–77.

Crystal, D., Fletcher, P. and Garman, M. (1989) *The Grammatical Analysis of Language Disability* (2nd edn). London: Cole & Whurr.

Fletcher, P. and Garman, M. (1988). 'LARSPing by numbers'. *British Journal of Disorders of Communication*, 23, 309–321.

Fletcher, P., Garman, M., Johnson, M., Schelletter, C. and Stodel, L. (1986). 'Towards a grammatically-based characterisation of normal and abnormal language development in preschool and school-age children'. *Proceedings of the Child Language Seminar*. Durham: University of Durham.

Garman, M. (1989). 'The role of linguistics in speech therapy: assessment and interpretation'. In P. Grunwell and A. James (eds), *The Functional Evaluation of Language Disorders*. London: Croom Helm.

Hawkins, P. and Spencer, H. (1985). 'Imitative versus spontaneous language assessment: a comparison of CELI and LARSP'. *British Journal of Disorders of Communication*, 20, 191–203.

Johnson, M. (1986). 'Transcription and computer analysis of child language'. *Proceedings of the Child Language Seminar*. Durham: University of Durham.

Klee, T. K. and Fitzgerald, M. D. (1985) 'The relation between grammatical development and mean length of utterance in morphemes'. *Journal of Child Language*, 12, 251–68.

Klee, T. K. and Paul, R. (1981). 'A comparison of six structural analysis procedures: a case study'. In J. F. Miller (ed.), *Assessing Language Production in Children: experimental procedures*. London: Edward Arnold.

Quirk, R., Greenbaum, S., Leech, G. and Svartvic, J. (1972). *A Grammar of Contemporary English*. London: Longman.

Elspeth McCartney

METAPHON RESOURCE PACK (MRP)

Test authors   Elizabeth Dean, Janet Howell, Anne Hill and Daphne Walkers

Purpose   The Metaphon Resource Pack (MRP) is designed to provide materials for the assessment and remediation of phonological disorders in children. Specifically it aims:

227

- to facilitate the collection of a speech sample for a phonological assessment
- to provide an analytical framework within which to carry out a phonological assessment
- to provide judgements about the nature of a child's phonological disorder
- to provide the basis for planning intervention programmes and appropriate remediation strategies

The Metaphon approach to both assessment and remediation is specifically designed for children with developmental phonological learning disorders without any identifiable medical, psychological or environmental cause for their linguistic disability.

Subject population   Children aged $3\frac{1}{2}$–7

Administration time   Screening assessment – 15 minutes to administer; 15 minutes to score

Structure and administration   The MRP is made up of six different items:

- manual
- screening-assessment pictures
- screening-assessment record forms
- process-specific picture book
- process-specific record booklets
- monitoring pictures

These materials comprise three related assessment procedures: screening assessment, process-specific probes and the monitoring procedure. These are described in the manual. In addition, in the last section of the manual there is a description of the principles of Metaphon therapy and practical examples of remediation strategies are outlined.

The analytical framework used throughout the MRP for structuring the assessment procedures and the remediation strategies is phonological process analysis. The processes chosen for this framework are nine patterns that entail systemic simplifications and four that entail structural simplifications. These processes include those that occur in normal development of phonology and those that have been frequently encountered in a clinical setting. The systemic simplifications are:

- velar fronting
- palato-alveolar fronting
- fronting of interdental fricatives
- backing of alveolar stops (not a normal process)

228

- stopping of fricatives
- stopping of affricates
- context-sensitive voicing of initial segments
- word-final devoicing
- liquid/glide simplification

The structural simplifications are:

- deletion (or glottal replacement) of word-initial consonants
- deletion (or glottal replacement) of word-final consonants
- initial cluster reduction/deletion
- final cluster reduction/deletion

It is unfortunate that deletion and glottal-replacement processes are conflated. They are arguably different phonological patterns with different therapeutic and developmental implications. (Grunwell, 1985).

The MRP primary and ultimate aim is to provide the information base required to develop a Metaphon therapy programme. In the context of this volume, however, this review will concentrate upon the assessment procedures that are in fact the major components of MRP.

Screening assessment procedure is designed to provide an overview of the phonological processes present in a child's speech patterns. It comprises a picture book and a record form. The picture book contains line drawings representing 44 monosyllabic words and an additional 26 optional multisyllabic words. The procedure is thus basically intended to investigate word-initial and word-final processes. The words included in the sample have been selected to exemplify the 13 identified processes but also to avoid items that may be used in minimal-pair therapy. One picture may elicit more than one word. The intention is that the words will be elicited spontaneously by the pictures or by recommended prompts. The administrator/clinician is instructed to make a live transcription of the child's response on the record form.

The record form also provides for an analysis of the phonological processes occurring in the words in a series of tables which score the number of occurrences against the number of possible occurrences for each of the thirteen processes.

Unfortunately, the tables contain only a representative selection of the words that might exhibit the occurrence of a process. None of the optional items are included and not all of the monosyllabic words. For example, on the table analysing word-final stopping of fricatives, *knife, path, glass, stairs* are missing; none of the liquids or glides occurring in clusters are included in the analysis of liquid simplifications. Valuable data that may reveal variability and/or progressive change is therefore not being analysed. The manual is, however, helpful on how to handle the co-occurrence of processes and the implications of this phenomenon for therapy. On the other hand, little guidance is provided on how to evaluate unlisted processes or deviations in vowels.

After scoring the occurrence of processes in the screening procedure the clinician is instructed to move on to the process-specific probe procedure when a process occurs on 50 per cent or more of the test items. It is suggested that when a process occurs at less than 50 per cent frequency, then spontaneous elimination is taking place. No evidence is provided to support this claim, except that current research by the authors indicates that this is likely.

Process-specific probes are designed to enable the clinician to examine in more detail the occurrence of processes identified as present in a child's speech patterns by the screening assessment procedure. The materials consist of a picture book containing a set of prompt cards for each of the 13 phonological processes and a record booklet. The words elicited by the pictures examine the processes in syllable-initial, within-word and syllable-final positions. The number of items in each process probe varies. Many of the pictures recur in different probes and are also in the screening procedure.

As with the screening assessment the percentage occurrence of each process is scored. These scores are intended to form the basis of treatment-planning. The process with the highest percentage occurrence is regarded as a high priority for treatment. Clinicians are advised, however, to take into account as well the age of the child and the chronology of phonological processes, as described for example in Grunwell, 1985 and 1987. No developmental information is provided in the MRP itself.

Clinicians are also advised to investigate articulatory imitation and auditory discrimination abilities – two other areas outside of the scope of MRP.

The authors emphasize that the process-specific probes should not be used as a measure of therapy outcome; for this purpose the screening assessment or the monitoring procedure should be used.

The monitoring procedure is designed to provide a means of assessing change in a child's pronunciation patterns. As such, it should be used at regular intervals during treatment. It is intended to elicit multiple tokens of single-word items in a sorting/matching game. The materials consist of 48 sheets of line drawings on different-coloured cards that are to be cut up to produce single-word cards which can be sorted into sets. Photocopiable record sheets are also provided. The words are selected to avoid words used in the two previous procedures and words likely to occur in minimal pairs used in therapy.

The materials are intended to be used in games where a child sorts the cards by colour or item and is required to say each word represented. The aim is to distract the child's attention from speech to the game and thereby during treatment to have a means of monitoring progress. The scoring system includes partial elimination as well as the presence or absence of a process.

Metaphon therapy is an approach to phonological therapy that involves two phases: Phase One is designed to capture the child's interest in sounds and to build up the child's metaphonological skills; Phase Two applies the knowledge and skills gained in Phase One to the communicative context of minimal pair-based phonological therapy.

The manual describes the aims and procedures for these two phases and provides lists of the various activities that the authors have found to be successful in promoting metaphonological and phonological learning. There are two Appendices to this section: Appendix I contains a list of minimal pairs for each process; Appendix II describes briefly an efficacy study of Metaphon therapy carried out on 13 children.

Technical details

Standardization The assessment procedures in MRP are not standardized. The age range as indicated above is $3^{1}/_{2}$–7 though the authors actually state $3^{1}/_{2}$–5; but the materials are usable with children up to 7. The materials have been informally piloted in the authors' clinics.

Reliability No reliability studies have been carried out for these materials, as is common with such informal procedures in speech and language therapy.

Validity A small-scale efficacy study indicates that the Metaphon approach to therapy can achieve its objectives.

Country of origin UK

Publisher NFER-NELSON, Windsor (1990)

Pam Grunwell

References

Grunwell, P. (1985). *Phonological Assessment of Child Speech (PACS)*. Windsor: NFER-NELSON.
Grunwell, P. (1987). *Clinical Phonology*. London: Croom Helm.

MINNESOTA TEST FOR THE DIFFERENTIAL
DIAGNOSIS OF APHASIA (MTDDA)

Test author H. Schuell

Purpose To permit the examiner to observe the level at which language performance breaks down in each of the principal language modalities

Subject population Neurologically stable aphasics

Administration time Over 1½ hours for non-aphasic subjects over 50 years (according to its author). Considerably longer for aphasic people – Davis (1983) suggests an average of 3 hours, with a range of 2–6

Materials Administration manual, scoresheets, test stimuli (two sets of flip-over booklets) and some objects are needed.

Structure and administration The test consists of 47 graded subtests assessing auditory disturbance, visual and reading disturbance, speech and language production, visuomotor and writing disturbance, and numerical ability and arithmetic processes. The original materials were amended for British patients (Davies and Grunwell, 1973). Detailed instructions which must be adhered to are given for each subtest. It can be used with all levels of severity of aphasia.

Scoring and interpretation Mainly a pass/fail scoring system. Error scores are entered on a graph, which gives a patient profile. These profiles classify patients (seven major categories have been found by the author) and are claimed to have prognostic value.

Technical details

Standardization Non-aphasic subjects were used in the standardization procedure. Schuell and co-workers found that occasional random errors were made, more errors were made by non-aphasics over 50 years than those under 50 and the former group were slower in response. Davies and Grunwell's (1973) normal subjects also made occasional errors but they did find statistically significant differences between aphasic and non-aphasic populations. Walker (1982) administered the full version of MTDDA to healthy elderly Scottish people, which provides a base for therapists working with older aphasic people.

Reliability Schuell found reliability in test–retest profiles, although these were used to measure recovery, not to examine reliability.

Validity   MTDDA was developed from the 1950s onwards – it must have some face validity to have remained in use until today (Eisenson's Examination for Aphasia (see pp. 210–212) has not). Construct validity was indicated by a factor analysis of the test (Schuell, Jenkins and Carroll, 1962).

Evaluation   MTDDA, in its original form, is very time-consuming to administer, especially if the much-maligned but often practised model of once-weekly intervention is followed. Shortened versions are available. The first was constructed by Schuell herself (1957) by selection of tests considered to have high diagnostic and prognostic value. It was not later used by the author, who argued for the need for comprehensive assessment. Thompson and Enderby (1979) found many of the items to be redundant (too easy) and Powell *et al.* (1980) reduced the number of subtests to four and used this to detect aphasia rather than to classify types of aphasia. The shortened version devised by Thompson and Enderby, which provides a shorter test with British norms and materials, is probably the one used most frequently in Britain today. The test is not used as much for classification as for measurement of communication ability/disability, planning treatment-planning and progress-monitoring.

Davis (1983) describes MTDDA as the 'archetypical test for aphasia' (p. 155), the first of its kind. It has anticipated the content and structure of most subsequent batteries.

Country of origin   USA

Publisher   University of Minnesota Press

References

Davies, C. and Grunwell, P. (1973). 'British amendments to an American test for aphasia'. *British Journal of Disorders of Communication*, 8, 89–98.

Davis, G. A. (1983). *A Survey of Adult Aphasia*. Englewood Cliffs, NJ: Prentice-Hall.

Jenkins, J. J., Jimenez-Pabon, E., Shaw, R. E. and Sefer, J. W. (1975). *Schuell's Aphasia in Adults* (2nd edn). Hagerstown, MD.: Harper & Row.

Powell, G. E., Bailey, S. and Clark, E. (1980). 'A very short version of the Minnesota Aphasia Test'. *British Journal of Social and Clinical Psychology*, 19, 189–94.

Schuell, H. (1957). 'A short examination for aphasia'. *Neurology*, 7, 625–34.

Schuell, H. (1965). *The Minnesota Test for the Differential Diagnosis of Aphasia.* Minneapolis: University of Minnesota Press.

Schuell, H. M., Jenkins, J. J. and Carroll, J. B. (1962). 'A factor analysis of the Minnesota Test for the Differential Diagnosis of Aphasia'. *Journal of Speech and Hearing Research*, 5, 349–69.

Thompson, J. and Enderby, P. (1979). 'Is all your Schuell really necessary?' *British Journal of Disorders of Communication*, 14, 195–201.

Walker, S. (1982). 'Communication as a changing function of age'. In M. Edwards (ed.), *Communication Changes in Elderly People*. London: College of Speech Therapists' Monograph.

Walker, S. (1982). 'Investigation of the Communication of Elderly Subjects'. M.Phil. thesis. University of Sheffield.

Linda Armstrong

PORCH INDEX OF COMMUNICATIVE ABILITY (PICA)

Test author   Bruce E. Porch

Purpose   To assess and quantify aphasics' basic communication abilities

Subject population   Adult aphasics (children's version PICAC published 1974) (3–12-year old)

Main users   Speech and language therapists, clinical psychologists

Administration time   1 hour approximately

Structure and administration   The *Porch Index of Communicative Ability* was designed to assess and quantify spoken, written and gestural responses following brain injury. Comprising 18 subtests – 4 verbal, 8 gestural and 6 graphic, it samples various tests of ability in each modality. Since the same 10 everyday objects are used throughout the battery, the subtest order is structured to give the patient minimal information in the early stages. PICA is a test of decreasing complexity; at the end of each modality battery, the patient is asked only to match identical items.

Scoring and interpretation   Each of the 180 responses is evaluated on a 16-category scale, describing its degree of accuracy, promptness, responsiveness, completedness and efficiency. The scale ranges from 'complex response' (score 16), to 'no response' (score 1), with a score at least 6 for any attempt to respond. The assessor can then complete three scores: the mean scores for each subtest, the mean scores for gestural, verbal and graphic modalities and the overall response level – an average of all subtest means and, according to Porch, the best single index to the patient's communication ability.

Technical details

Standardization   150 patients, 86 male and 64 female, mean age 60½ years, with varying degrees of communication problems, were tested over a 2-year period. Manual volume 1 gives comprehensive details of the clinical sample.

Reliability   There is high reliability, both test–retest and inter-tester.

Validity   The logic of the construct validity is widely accepted but there is controversy about the statistical data (vol. 2) and the predictive claims based on it.

Evaluation   The manuals give explicit details of the standard test environment, administration, scoring and interpretation of results. These are presented graphically to give a test profile. The scoring system is the most difficult aspect of the PICA and a 40-hour workshop or supervised training to ensure accuracy and inter-tester reliability is strongly advised.

The finely graded scoring system has two main advantages: it enables a clinician to measure variation on early retest and describes communicative behaviour in language accessible to a wide audience. The 16-point scale can be used in combination with specific language assessments to provide additional response information. Testers need frequent practice in observing and scoring, however, to maintain speed and accuracy.

Patients with moderate/severe receptive problems can become confused as they are constantly presented with the same 10 items and, in certain subtests, required to perform identical tasks.

PICA was used more widely in the UK in the 1970s/early 1980s than it is today. It has some shortcomings, but samples basic communication abilities, with no educational experience or intelligence bias, and also demands acute observation by the clinician as an integral part of the test. It is a useful clinical tool.

Country of origin   USA

Publisher   Consulting Psychologists Press (1967, revised 1971)

References

Byng, S., Kay, J., Edmundson, A. and Scott, C. (1990). 'Aphasia tests reconsidered'. *Aphasiology*, 4: 1, 67–92.

Martin, A. D. (1977). 'Aphasia testing, a second look at PICA', *Journal of Speech and Hearing Disorders*, 42, 547–61.

Spreen, O. and Risser, A. (1981). 'Assessment of aphasia'. In M. Taylor Sarno (ed.), *Acquired Aphasia*, 106–9. New York: Academic Press.

Carole Pound, Jenny Sheridan and Judith Williams

THE PRAGMATICS PROFILE OF EARLY
COMMUNICATION SKILLS

Test authors   H. Dewart and S. Summers

Purpose   The Pragmatics Profile provides a structured set of questions to be asked of parents, carers, etc., to elicit and code specific examples of the communicative behaviours commonly seen in preschool children. The areas assessed are communicative intentions, response to communication, interaction and conversation, and contextual variation.

Materials   Manual, including profile to be photocopied

Scoring and interpretation   The profile is in the form of a structured interview schedule, carried out in an informal way with a relevant informant, such as a parent or carer. Information is qualitative, giving a picture of the child's current communication status as perceived by the informant, and an indication of the variation in communication due to context. Respondents are encouraged to describe the child's communication in their own words; examples are provided as prompts only if necessary, and the use of such prompts is noted. Respondents' own words are recorded if possible, and the information gleaned is summarized in terms, for example, of the range, nature and extent of behaviours used in the various sections.

Technical details

Standardization   No mention is made of standardization in the manual. The profile was constructed using research information on early child communicative behaviours and the authors' personal experience, and a pilot version was used by speech and language therapists with feedback to the authors.

Reliability   This is not mentioned, although users are advised to note differences between informants (p. 13) and to investigate further if responses seem 'unrealistic or inconsistent' (p. 9).

Validity   Validity is not mentioned in the manual. The main check on the validity of respondents' answers is that they are asked to give examples to substantiate each point. One undergraduate research project (Hinds, 1985) is mentioned which suggested that children referred to as 'language-delayed' differed in the range of communicative intentions shown from a group of 3-year olds developing language normally; no other details are given.

236

Evaluation A clinical review of the Pragmatics Profile is given by Miller (1990).

Country of origin UK

Publisher NFER-NELSON, Windsor

References

Hinds, S. (1985). 'Assessing pragmatic development in young children: a protocol for a parental interview'. Unpublished B.Sc. project, Central School of Speech and Drama, London.

Miller, N. (1990). 'Review of the Pragmatics Profile by Dewart and Summers'. *Clinical Linguistics and Phonetics*, 4, 179–82.

Elspeth McCartney

PVC (PRE-VERBAL COMMUNICATION) SCHEDULE

Test authors C. Kiernan and B. Reid

Purpose To assess the communication skills of children and adults who are severely mentally handicapped, who have little or no formal visual/sign/symbol skills, and who are potential candidates for speech or non-verbal communication programmes.

Administration time Over 2 hours, but does not need to be completed at one sitting

Structure and administration PVCS should be completed by anyone who knows the client well. The schedule is (largely) a check-list of 195 items of described behaviour within 27 sections.

The examiner records either Yes/No or Usually/Rarely/Never to the test items. (The two sections on motor and vocal imitation are conducted and scored differently.)

There are two main groups of sections:

1   pre-communicative behaviours, e.g. Section 5: Social Interaction without Communication. Item 1: Watches other people with interest
2   informal communicative behaviours (intentional and non-verbal behaviours), e.g. Section 17: Communication through Gestures. Item 9: Waves goodbye to indicate that she wants another person to go away.

There are two smaller groups of sections:

3   imitation – motor and vocal
4   formal communication skills: early understanding and use of commun-
    ication through speech, sign or symbol

In the full-form PVCS, all items are scored. The short-form PVCS may be
completed where the client is known to have adequate visual and hearing
skills, fine motor skills and vocalization. This short-form looks at functional
communication; items have been extracted from the full battery and are
grouped in categories:

–   attention seeking
–   need satisfaction
–   simple negation
–   positive interaction
–   negative interaction
–   shared attention

The short-form also includes the motor and vocal-imitation sections and
the two sections – Understanding of Non-Vocal Communication and
Understanding of Vocalization and Speech.
   The picture gained (from full- or short-form), of the client's strengths
and needs, is used for programme-planning.

Technical details

Reliability and validity   A limited inter-rater reliability study was
performed (Kiernan, Reid and McConachie, 1987) and showed such
reliability to be between 50.5 per cent and 97.8 per cent for individual
check-list items. All items were included in the PVCS full-form. The
authors justify the inclusion of the lower-reliability items on the grounds
that these were (a) needed for programme-planning, and (b) would
provide a forum for discussion of reasons for disagreement.
   Given the descriptive nature of the items and the highly situational
nature of the likely occurrence of the behaviours, this decision seems
justified. However, the schedule-user should be aware that such disputes
between carers are likely.
   The short-form PVCS items are all reported to have high reliability and
validity and can be used to assess development over time, e.g. results of an
intervention programme.

Evaluation   PVCS is a detailed, thorough, check-list for a subsection of
the handicapped population for whom few assessments exist.
   It is of practical value in its stated purpose, i.e. to delineate the
communicative and pre-communicative, intentional and non-intentional
behaviours of severely mentally handicapped individuals, and then to use

this to assist in planning a functional therapeutic programme. It also has further value in enabling, e.g. the speech and language therapist/psychologist and the regular carer to discuss constructively and in detail the client's skills and needs, and provide the basis of further staff (carer) training.

Professionals wishing to compare PVCS with another assessment which takes a similar check-list approach should consult Kathy Gerard's 'Check-list of communicative competence: 0–2 years'.

One basic problem with PVCS is that of any check-list – it suggests first what the client ought to do and then checks whether he or she does/can. This may mean that the examiner may not pick up on an item of communicative behaviour the client *has* got, because it does not appear in the check-list. A different starting point in examining early communicative and pre-communicative behaviours is taken by the Affective Communication Assessment.

PVCS is likely to be used by clinicians for only a limited number of their clients, largely because the number of clients it is designed for is limited. However, for this difficult-to-assess population it is a valuable and comprehensive tool.

Country of origin   UK

Publisher   NFER-NELSON, Windsor

References

Coupe, Barton, Barber, Collins, Levy and Murphy (1985). 'Affective communication assessment'. Manchester Language Development Working Party; Schools Council Project.
Gerard, K. A. (1986). 'Checklist of communicative competence: 0–2 years'. Kathryn Gerard, 3 Perry Mansions, 113 Catford Hill, London SE6 4PP.

Beth McCaig

RECEPTIVE-EXPRESSIVE EMERGENT LANGUAGE SCALE (REEL)

Test authors   K. R. Bzoch and R. League

Purpose   The test aims to identify language levels in very young children. An outline of normal stages of language development from birth to 3 is given, and a glossary provided. The test results in the allocation of expressive (ELA), receptive (RLA) and combined (CLA) language ages, and these scores are designed to be useful in 'diagnosing and studying a variety of impairments, and in planning effective treatment programmes' (p. 13).

Subject population   Children up to 3 years old

Materials   Handbook (*Assessing Language Skills in Infancy*. (1970). Austin, Texas: PRO-ED) and forms.

Structure and administration   Instructions on how to administer the test are not very specific. The assessor interviews a knowledgeable carer about the child's communication, asking general questions and then specific questions based on the test form. If possible, the assessor also observes the child, but a brief interview (10–20 minutes) is usually sufficient to obtain a result. Detailed questions about receptive and expressive ability are available, corresponding to 1-month (first year of life), 2-month (second year) and 3-month (third year) intervals in normal child development.

Technical details

Standardization   A longitudinal study was carried out on 50 normal children at the University of Florida. No handicapped children were included, and no sex-balance or social-class data are given.

Reliability   The test handbook reports that graduate students untrained in the administration of the REEL or other assessments repeatedly tested 28 infants from 'linguistically stimulating' environments with 90–100 per cent inter-examiner agreement to a criterion of $+/-$ one age interval, and an intra-subject language-quotient correlation of 0.71.

Validity   Brief accounts are given in the handbook of a cross-sectional study of 50 infants balanced by sex in the University of Florida, and of a small-scale replication using 27 'well babies' in Alabama. In the Florida study, Receptive and Combined Language Age scores were within $+/-$ one age interval of the children's actual ages, and 90 per cent of Expressive Language Age scores were also within this range. Four of the five infants with low ELA scores later tested as within these limits without intervention.

Mahoney (1984) investigated the validity of the REEL with young mentally handicapped children, and found that the REEL results were generally consistent with the children's communicative behaviour, and that the construct validity appeared greater for 2- and 3-year-old children than for 1-year-olds.

Evaluation   Wnuk (1987) reviews earlier work by Bannatyne (1972), Johnson (1973) and Proger (1971) that comments upon the REEL. These authors criticize the standardization, reliability and validity measures as inadequate, as the standardization sample was too small and too homogeneous; no work was carried out with children with known developmental problems and no relationship with other measures of language was reported (partly remedied by Mahoney, 1984); and insufficient detail was given about reliability, especially as rapid development can be expected in infant communication skills. No action was suggested if the child did prove to be delayed.

On the other hand, the recognition that early communication skills can best be assessed by those who have access to a child in a range of naturalistic contexts is commendable. Wnuk (1987) concludes that the REEL should only be used as a screening device, but could 'help define broad curriculum considerations in early intervention programs' (p. 96).

Country of origin   USA

Publisher   PRO-ED, Austin, Texas (1970)

References

Bannatyne, A. (1972). 'Review of the Bzoch-League Receptive-Expressive Emergent Language Scale'. *Journal of Learning Disabilities*, 5, 512.
Johnson, D. L. (1973). 'Review of the Bzoch-League Receptive-Expressive Emergent Language Scale'. *Journal of Personality Assessments*, 37, 581-2.
Mahoney, G. (1984). 'The validity of the Receptive-Expressive Emergent Language Scale with mentally retarded children'. *Journal of the Division for Early Childhood*, Fall 1984, 86-94.
Proger, B. B. (1971). 'Test review no. 8 Receptive-Expressive Emergent Language Scale'. *Journal of Special Education*, 5, 383-8.
Wnuk, L. (1987). 'A review of the Bzoch-League Receptive-Expressive Emergent Language Scale and the Test for Auditory Comprehension of Language'. *Canadian Journal for Exceptional Children*, 3, 95-8.

Elspeth McCartney

SENTENCE COMPREHENSION TEST (SCT) (REVISED VERSION, INCLUDING PUNJABI BILINGUAL VERSION)

Test authors   K. Wheldall, P. Mittler and A. Hobsbaum (Punjabi bilingual version: D. Gibbs, D. Duncan, S. Saund and K. Wheldall)

Purpose   The test aims to assess a child's understanding of the syntax of spoken language while minimizing contextual cues. This edition has been extended for use with bilingual Punjabi-speaking children (Duncan *et al.*, 1985) and has been redrawn to avoid cultural and gender bias.

Subject population   Children 3–5 years.

Administration time   10–15 minutes (Punjabi version administered by fluent Punjabi speaker only)

Materials   There is a manual, a picture booklet which is used for both the English and Punjabi versions and separate record sheets for each version.

Structure and administration   The picture booklet presents 4 pictures per page; these offer alternative grammatical interpretations for the child's response to the target sentence spoken by the examiner. The alternative picture referents are systematically varied from the target referent to provide information about the child's error pattern. The test consists of 10 subtests, each testing a different grammatical structure – simple intransitive, simple transitive, intransitive with adjective, plural, past tense, future, negative, prepositions, embedded phrase, passive. The child responds by pointing to the picture matching the target sentence; no verbal response is required. All subtests are attempted. The Punjabi version is administered as above but on two occasions, preferably a few days apart, with Punjabi first, second presentation English. The final subtest is omitted as the passive form is not used in spoken Punjabi.

Scoring and interpretation   The child's response is recorded on the record form allowing a correct score to be calculated for each subtest plus an overall score. Type of error is also noted and patterns identified for future remediation. The authors suggest retesting children with receptive problems before reaching conclusions based on this test despite obtaining significant results on the retest-reliability coefficient and from correlations between total and subtest scores. Comparison of an individual's score on the Punjabi and English version must be viewed with caution. More data are required for a reliable indicator of development.

Technical details

Standardization   Standardization data of the revised English version are presented on a sample of 230 children aged 3–5 years balanced for sex and social background; however, no information is available on cognitive level. Data for the Punjabi version are based on a sample of 172 children aged $3^1/_2$–$5^1/_2$ gearning Enlish as a second language. They were not tested on BPVS (Dunn *et al.*, 1982) or balanced for social class in the same way as the English sample as this was not possible or appropriate.

Reliability   Test–retest reliability was sampled on 50 children aged 3–5, ten in each 6-month interval, with equal numbers of boys and girls. The Revised SCT and BPVS (Dunn *et al.*, 1982) were administered and the SCT repeated two weeks later. Test–retest reliability for this sample was 0.74 for total score and 0.77 for number of tests passed, p < 0.001 which is not as high as the pilot study but the items have been reduced from 60 to 40. Both methods of scoring are thus acceptable alternatives. The revised edition also showed a high correlation with both chronological age (0.58 total, 0.54 subtests passed, p < 0.001) and BPVS score (0.78 total, 0.72 subtests passed, p < 0.001).

Evaluation   The SCT has developed since 1979 (Mittler *et al.*, 1977; Wheldall *et al.*, 1977). It is useful as a screening test to alert the examiner to investigate further the child's receptive problems. The standardization is tentative and does not allow scores to be quoted as comprehension ages. It does allow some patterns of error to be highlighted and remediated. More detailed assessment, standardization and further research is needed for both the English and Punjabi versions.

Country of origin   UK

Publisher   NFER-NELSON, Windsor (1987)

References

Duncan, D. M., Gibbs, D. A. Noor, N. S. and Whittaker, H. M. (1985). 'Bilingual acquisition of L1 Punjabi and L2 English by Sandwell primary school children'. *ITL Review of Applied Linguistics*, 70, 1–32.

Dunn, L. M., Pantile, D. and Whetton, C. (1982). *The British Picture Vocabulary Scale.* Windsor: NFER-NELSON.

Mittler, P., Jeffree, D., Wheldall, K. and Berry, P. (1977). 'Assessment and remediation of language comprehension and production in severely subnormal children'. *Collected Original Resources in Education,* 1: 2, 2572–799.

Wheldall, K. and Martin, B. (1977). 'Socio-environmental influences on the receptive language development of young children'. *Collected Original Resources in Education,* 1: 3, 3130–59.

Julie Dockrell

THE STUTTERING PREDICTION INSTRUMENT FOR YOUNG CHILDREN

Test author   G. D. Riley

Purpose   The Stuttering Prediction Instrument (SPI) was devised by Riley to assist clinicians in determining the severity and potential chronicity of childhood dysfluency

Subject population   Children 3–11 years

Structure and administration   The instrument is divided into five sections:

1   History: the parent interview comprises four questions. The first three are concerned with the onset and severity of the stuttering behaviour and the fourth deals with any family history of stuttering.
2   Reactions: this set of questions investigates the parents, the environment, and the child's reaction to the stuttering behaviour.
3   Part-word repetitions: the most severe examples of part-word repetitions are scored with regard to the number and the quality of the repeated sounds or syllables.
4   Prolongations: three types of prolongations: vowel prolongations, phonatory arrest and articulatory posturing are considered and recorded separately but only the highest scored prolongation contributes to the total score.
5   Frequency: the frequency count is accomplished by counting the number of stuttering events per 100 words of conversational speech.

The clinician obtains a speech sample from the child for analysis using picture plates provided in the manual.

Scoring and interpretation   The scores for sections 2–5 are added together to give a total which is used as an indicator of potential chronicity.

Technical details

Standardization   The SPI has been standardized on approximately 100 stuttering children. These children were followed up and the data of those whose dysfluency had not become chronic were analysed separately in order to establish a reference or cut-off point for the predictive judgement of chronicity.

Validity   It has not been validated independently to what extent this test really identifies children who will become chronic stammerers.

Evaluation   This is undoubtedly a useful assessment tool for a clinician, especially as a preliminary screening device. It provides us with the beginnings of an objective means for assessing the chronicity of stammering. However, the information provided is limited and certain issues are not addressed, such as the interaction of the stammering child within the family and school setting. A significant omission from the parent interview is the child's speech and language development, as research has shown that many stutterers have a history of delay in this sphere which could be a possible indicator of chronicity.

Thus although the SPI fulfils a useful role in the assessment and diagnosis of dysfluency, a clinician would be well advised to incorporate further questioning and investigation into the assessment procedure, in order to obtain a more complete understanding of the nature of the dysfluency and the dynamics surrounding the child speech problem.

Country of origin USA

Lena Rustin

STUTTERING SEVERITY INSTRUMENT FOR CHILDREN AND ADULTS

Test author G. D. Riley

Purpose The Stuttering Severity Instrument (SSI) is a standardized assessment of the quantity and quality of dysfluency, and may be used with either adults or children.

Materials The SSI kit consists of a test form, on the reverse of which is the Frequency Tracking record which enables the clinician to record the number of stuttered words without additional equipment. There are ten plates for the non-reader as well as reading material for the reader. The speech samples are tape-recorded for analysis and the clinician takes note of physical concomitants, rating them from 0 (none) to 5 (severe and painful).

Structure and administration The instrument measures three parameters:

1 frequency of repetition, prolongation of sounds and syllables
2 estimated duration of the longest blocks
3 observable physical concomitants

Each category yields a raw score and the total is converted to a percentile and severity rating.

Evaluation This test serves a useful function within a more comprehensive range of assessments of dysfluency. The numerical score, percentile, severity rating together provide baseline data for a client, against which any changes or progress may be measured during therapy. The descriptions of concomitant behaviours also may be compared throughout the treatment process.

However, the SSI does not address a number of issues which probably have a bearing on severity. The emotional state of clients is not considered, nor the attitudes that they harbour towards the dysfluency in relation to family, school or work and social settings. Furthermore, clients' awareness and insight into their behaviour is not investigated.

The presentation of the SSI is sufficiently clear and straightforward to enable a clinician with a minimum of experience to administer the test and it does not require any technical equipment. This test only measures state of severity at the time of testing and therefore is not a reliable criterion for predicting breakdown of fluency in other situations. However, in conjunction with other measures of social, emotional, and conceptual issues, this procedure can be a valuable clinical asset.

Country of origin   USA

Lena Rustin

STYCAR LANGUAGE TEST

Test author   Mary D. Sheridan

Purpose   To provide clinical information, in normal developmental stages and ages, about a child's reception, comprehension, expression and use of language forms – mime, models, picture and especially spoken-verbal.

Subject population   Normal children from 1–7 years, also older children with developmental delays

Administration time   variable

Structure and administration   The test materials comprise (largely) real objects, toys and pictures, and the manual suggests a wide range of observations and tests which may be performed using the materials. No charts or recording forms are available; the child's performance is recorded descriptively. Throughout, the manual gives details of types and levels of expected responses and age norms; the child's behaviour is interpreted clinically using these.

Close, detailed observation is required by the examiner of the child's ability to use 'language codes' – verbal, gestural and two-dimensional, as well as other symbolic activity – e.g. play, and other aspects of development – e.g. physical manipulation.

The Common Objects Test   (cup, spoon, brush, comb, ball, doll, car, bricks): 11–20 months developmental age. Attention, definition – by use, object permanence, symbolic play levels, verbal and gestural (mime) comprehension and expression are among the more important observations made.

The Miniature Toy Test (dolls, tea-party toys, miniature furniture, toy animals and toy transport) 1½–4 years developmentally. This section evokes 'evidence of progressive understanding and creativity in using language codes'. Thus behaviours shown include categorizations, symbolic play and symbolic understanding, maintenance and shift in attention, eye-hand co-ordination, hearing, alertness, drive, auditory discrimination, general situational understanding, expressive speech and language development, comprehension of spoken instructions, interpersonal relationships and social competence.

The Picture Book Test 3–6 years developmentally. The pictures range from single-object pictures, composite scenes and action pictures to a story sequence. As usual, observations are partly of the child's spontaneous behaviours (e.g. picture description) and partly of elicited responses (e.g. Examiner asks 'Show me some luggage between the car and the house'). Information is obtained about the child's vocabulary, verbal reception, auditory discrimination, hearing, articulation, sequencing of speech units – words and narrative, grammatical usage, sentence construction.

The word lists and other printed test materials Printed letters of the alphabet, numbers, word lists and sentences, are used to test counting, matching hearing, auditory memory, sequencing, certain prosodic features, ability to imitate speech sounds, and 'articulation' (phonology).

In addition to information about age norms and expected responses, the manual also gives details of the likely behaviours of handicapped children, notably mental handicap and deafness.

Evaluation The test materials – real objects, toys and pictures – are deceptively few and simple. The manual suggests how the materials can be used for an *awesomely extensive battery of tests and observations* of the child's ability to communicate and relate to others. The author suggests that the test 'requires considerable experience before its full diagnostic potentialities become apparent' and that the examiner will be 'exercising sophisticated clinical judgement'. Potential users should heed these statements: STYCAR is absolutely not a test for the beginner.

The conducting of the various tests, the interaction with the child and the recording of responses and behaviours, both elicited and spontaneous, would tax most experienced clinicians (especially during the Common Objects Test and the Miniature Toy Test).

The manual gives an outline of ages and stages in the development of spoken language and further detail is included in the sections on administration of the tests. However, it might be difficult for the user to pull this information together and also difficult to match it to the (potential) mass of results from the tests – another indicator that the examiner must be an experienced clinician.

STYCAR examines the child's phonology 'articulation' in some detail towards the end of the test. Now, 15 years after this was formulated, medical users of STYCAR would probably leave this to the speech and language therapist and the speech and language therapist would probably seek more detailed information from specific assessments of phonology (e.g. Edinburgh Articulation Test (Ingram *et al.*, 1971), PACS (Grunwell, 1987).

Other areas in the manual also reflect the age of the test. These are notably

1 comments (p. 17) about sign language, which do not give it true recognition as a proper language

2 very little mention of symbol systems; reflecting that most were in their infancy in 1976

Overall, STYCAR can provide an enormous amount of clinical information in the hands of an examiner with considerable knowledge and experience.

Country of origin   UK

Publisher   NFER-NELSON, Windsor (1976)

References

Grunwell, P. (1987). *The Phonological Assessment of Child Speech (PACS)*. Windsor: NFER-NELSON.

Ingram, T. T. S., Anthony, N., Bogle, D. and McIsaac, M. W. (1971). *The Edinburgh Articulation Test*. Edinburgh: Churchill Livingstone.

Beth McCaig

THE SYMBOLIC PLAY TEST

Test authors   Marianne Lowe and Anthony J. Costello

Purpose   This test has been constructed to assess early concept formation and symbolization. It has been designed to be used in conjunction with other performance and language tests but it is aimed at evaluating the language potential of children who are not developing receptive or expressive language abilities. The child is required to play with miniature toys that represent everyday objects. The child's spontaneous manipulation of the objects is then used as a guide to the level of the child's non-verbal thinking and readiness for verbal language.

Subject population   Chidlren aged 1–3 years

Administration time   10–15 minutes. Scoring time: 2 minutes

Materials   There is a manual, scoresheets, and four sets of toys that easily elicit play abilities from children.

Structure and administration   There are four sets of miniature toys that allow for a progression of play abilities to be demonstrated by the child. The activities selected start with early play where the child enacts daily routines and move to the final section which is not an everyday routine. The toys of the subtest are placed in front of the child, except for Part I which is presented in three stages with some time allowed before the next toys are presented. The manual gives very clear directions for the administration of the test.

Scoring and interpretation   There are 24 items that are scored as either correct or incorrect. The manual gives very clear scoring criteria.

Technical details

Standardization   The initial standardization was carried out on a group of 137 children, ranging in age from 12 to 36 months. Many of the children were tested several times. A total of 241 tests were carried out.

Reliability   Two reliability studies were carried out: the split half and test–retest reliability tests. The split-half reliability study demonstrated correlations that are reasonably high for a short test. The test–retest reliability study shows some ceiling effects to be operating at the extreme age ranges. There are no inter-rater reliability studies but the scoring criteria are clearly explained and the items are easily observable within the testing period; therefore it is assumed that the correlation would be high.

Validity   There is good face validity to the test as the score shows a steady progression with age. Two measures of language were used in the initial construction to validate the test through a correlation with concurrent language ability. Grammatical structure (Reynell Developmental Language Scales, 1969) and a measure of sentence length were compared with the play abilities. The correlation for sentence length was higher. Since the publication of the test it has been used widely in research. These studies have contributed to its validation and highlighted its use in discriminating between language-handicapped and other groups of children. The results of the Symbolic Play Test correlated significantly with the mental age of the Bayley Scales of Infant Development and the Stanford-Binet Intelligence Scale as well as with the comprehension level of the Reynell Developmental Language Scales (Cunningham, 1985).

Evaluation   The Symbolic Play Test is an easy, quick, reliable and valid test to administer and fulfils its aims adequately. Researchers have found a need for a test of play abilities that examines aspects other than symbolic representation. Elaboration and flexibility of play, imaginative play beyond the 3-year-old level (Gould, 1986) and the child's own structuring and planning of play (Gregory and Mogford, 1983) were a few other play elements that were found to be of importance.

Country of origin   UK

Publisher   NFER-NELSON, Windsor

References

Cunningham, C. C. (1985). 'Mental ability, symbolic play and receptive and expressive language of your children with Down's Syndrome'. *Journal of Child Psychology and Psychiatry*, 62: 2, 255–65.

Gould, J. (1986). 'The Lowe and Costello Symbolic Play Test in socially impaired children'. *Journal of Autism and Developmental Disorders*, 16: 2, 199–213.

Gregory, S. and Mogford, K. (1983). 'The development of symbolic play in young deaf children'. In D. R. Rodgers and J. A. Sloboda (eds), *The Acquisition of Symbolic Skills*. New York: Plenum Press.

Kathryn Gerard

TEST FOR AUDITORY COMPREHENSION OF LANGUAGE

Test author   Elizabeth Carrow-Woolfolk

Purpose   This is a test for the auditory comprehension of meaning of word classes, meaning of grammatical morphemes and the meaning of elaborated sentence constructions. The test has been designed with the following applications in mind: the identification and selection of children with language problems; the planning of intervention programmes; as an indicator of readiness for early school academics; measuring improvement in language skills; use in research to evaluate the success of language programmes; and finally to assist in counselling parents about the nature and degree of the comprehension deficits. The aim in designing the test was to use pictures that depicted and contrasted the linguistic items being presented in a verbal stimulus. This test is the revised version and considerable research has gone into construction of both the original and into the revision.

Subject population   Children aged 3–10 years

Administration time   10–20 minutes; scoring time 5 minutes

Materials   The materials consist of a TACL-R test book, individual record forms and an examiner's manual. The TACL-R test book consists of 120 pages of pictures that the subject points to in response to a stimulus utterance.

Structure and administration   The test book is placed in front of the subject. Each page has three pictures on it and the subject is to select one in response to a stimulus utterance. The pictures have been selected to represent the item being tested and two contrasting grammatical constructions. The stimulus utterance is on the scoresheet as well as in front of the examiner on the test book. The examiner then ticks 1, 2, or 3 depending upon which picture the subject pointed to. The correct response is circled to assist in ease of scoring. There are 120 items, 40 each in three different subsections. The test book is indexed for each section to facilitate moving from one section to the other.

Scoring and interpretation   The items are either marked correct or incorrect and the correct items are then summed for each subgroup. Raw scores are transformed into percentile ranks which then can be transformed into z or t scores, deviation quotients or normal curve equivalents. Standard error measurements and age-equivalent scores can also be obtained. The individual record form has places on the front to note the child's personal details, raw score and other obtained scores. The centre of the form has the test-stimuli utterances and response coding. The back of the form has the standard score profile. The standard score profile is an easy-to-interpret chart which has the area of one standard deviation above and below the mean shaded in grey. The child's score can then be entered with easy visual cues as to where the score places in comparison to the mean and its standard deviations. The standard score profile allows each of the three subsections to be plotted individually as well as plotting a total score for the test.

Technical details

Standardization   The test was standardized on 1,003 children who presented with normal language development aged 3–9 years 11 months. The norming sample was selected by stratified random-sampling procedures. Each age band was stratified by family occupation, ethnic origin, age, sex, community size and geographical distribution.

Reliability   As there is little judgement to be made in marking a subject's response of pointing to a picture, inter-reliability was not considered an issue. Internal consistency was examined through the use of split-half correlations. The correlations are extremely high, with the lowest correlations occurring in the older age levels where performance was near ceiling level. Test–retest reliability was examined by retesting 100 subjects in the norming sample and 29 subjects with speech and language disorders 3–4 weeks after the first administration. The test–retest reliabilities range from 0.89 to 0.95 and indicate that the TACL-R scores are stable.

Validity   The relationship between item length and language comprehension was investigated with the conclusion that the item length had little effect on the subject's performance whereas comprehension of the language complexity of the item did have an effect. A relationship between the subject's age and score showed that performance is better on the items assessing simpler language structure than on items assessing more complex structures; the older the subject, the higher the score and the more complex language structures will be passed. As the earlier TACL had shown good validity with other language measures, the main concern was that the revised version would be consistent with the earlier version. The correlations offer strong support for the concurrent validity of the revised TACL.

Evaluation   The test is easy to administer and interpret. It covers a vast range of abilities (3–10 years) in three subsections of 40 items each. Therefore each age band and linguistic level is not tested fully; so it makes a comprehensive screening device rather than a full assessment procedure. It does, however, fulfil its aims and can be used for all the purposes for which it was designed.

Country of origin   USA

Publisher   DLM Teaching Resources, Allen, Texas. Distributed in the UK by NFER-NELSON.

Kathryn Gerard

TEST FOR RECEPTION OF GRAMMAR (TROG)

Test author   Dorothy Bishop

Purpose   This is an individually administered, multiple-choice test to assess the understanding of grammatical contrasts in English. It aims to provide not only a comparison of the child's comprehension with his or her peer group but also a qualitative analysis of errors to pinpoint specific areas of grammatical difficulty.

Subject population   Children aged 4–12 years. It can be used with adults, including those with dysphasia, for whom the norms for children in the 12-year-old age group are said to apply.

Administration time   10–20 minutes

Materials   All necessary materials are supplied with the test kit: a picture book of 80 test items, three double-sided vocabulary cards, test manual and record forms.

Structure and administration   The 80 test items are displayed in an A4-sized book. Each page is divided into four and there are four coloured line drawings, one in each quarter. The child is required to select the picture on the page that corresponds to the phrase or sentence spoken by the tester. The child may indicate this choice by pointing, including eye-pointing, or by stating the number (1–4) which corresponds to the picture chosen. The items are divided into 20 sections, or blocks, with four items demonstrating a particular grammatical contrast in each. In order to be credited with passing that section or block, the child must correctly select all four items in any one block. The test is then scored according to the number of blocks that are passed. The grammatical contrasts are arranged in order of increasing difficulty. Testing begins with a baseline of five consecutive blocks and is discontinued when five consecutive blocks are failed. Essentially this means that children under 7 years begin at block A, children 8–9 years start at block D and those over 10 years start at block H. However, this starting point can be adjusted according to the severity of the child's problem; older children can go back to an earlier section of the test if they make an error in the first five blocks administered so that a baseline may be established.

The tester should give the child a few seconds to scan each page and be sure that the child understands what to do. The co-operative child may wish to help by turning the pages after each item. The tester should speak each sentence clearly and naturally. Moderate stress can be placed on critical morphemes, like 'not' in block E, but this should not be artificial stress. The tester may repeat an item as many times as necessary if there is undue hesitation, if the child does not attend or if the child requests a repetition. A repetition may be recorded against the relevant item using the notation 'R'. If the child changes his or her response, then both the original and the final response should be recorded and the final response is circled to avoid confusion. It is this final response with which the child is credited. The test manual gives very clear instructions as to what to do in a number of possible situations that may arise during administration; the child is distracted, the child's response is difficult to interpret, etc., and these will help to clarify most possibilities. On the whole these are generous and allow for a full repetition of the test item where there is any doubt.

The vocabulary cards are used by the tester when uncertain whether the child knows the meaning of the particular words used in an item. In such a case the vocabulary card depicting that item would be shown and the child would be asked to indicate the picture concerned.

Scoring and interpretation   The test is scored according to a pass/fail scoring system. The tester marks on the record form which picture the child selected and this is compared with the correct responses for that block. Any error in any block means that the child has failed that block. The number of blocks passed is calculated at the end of the test and noted on the front of the response form. The total number of blocks passed can then be used to convert this result to an age-equivalent score or a centile score. In order to find the age-equivalent score, use the table in Appendix 2 of the manual. Find the total number of blocks passed in the left-hand column and read across the table to the right-hand column for the age equivalent in years. For the centile score, use the table in Appendix 1. The child's age should be calculated in years and months. This age should be found in the left-hand column of the table. Then moving along this row until the total blocks passed is reached, read off the centile score along the top of the table. This score gives a comparison with the child's peer group.

The TROG also gives information about the underlying nature of a child's comprehension problem which can further inform the performance of a child who is scoring below age level. First, if the child appears to have had problems with items containing similar vocabulary, then the vocabulary cards can be used to check that the child understands the meaning of specific items. Appendix 3 can be used to identify which test items contain particular items of vocabulary. For the blocks D–L it is also possible to examine the errors made to see if they are predominantly grammatical or lexical. This information is available in Appendix 4 of the manual. Further, if the British Picture Vocabulary Test (Dunn *et al.*, 1982) has also been given, then Appendix 5 can be used to discover whether there is any comparison between the child's comprehension problems on the two tests. The manual gives a full account of the possible ways in which TROG scores can suggest whether comprehension is delayed or deviant, related to limited span of processing or memory, etc., including a worked example in Appendix 6.

Technical details

Between 120 and 217 children in each age band were tested. Age bands covered one year, except for 4- and 5-year-olds where intervals of 3 months and 6 months respectively were used. As wide a range of population distribution as possible was included in this sample, both in terms of geographical and social class. Some of these effects are discussed in Appendix 8 of the manual.

Evaluation The test was first published in 1983 and has quickly become popular amongst paediatric speech and language therapists. It was originally designed as a research tool and both TROG and precursors to TROG have been used by Bishop and others in a number of research studies (e.g. Bishop 1982; Lees and Neville, 1990) to investigate comprehension problems in children with both developmental and acquired language disorders. The final clinical standardized version of TROG has several advantages including the fact that no expressive speech is required from the child to complete the test. This makes it particularly useful in several language disorders, acute acquired aphasia in childhood and even cerebral palsy (where eye-pointing is one method of item selection which can be used). The quantitative and qualitative methods available to analyse the results make a useful contribution to planning towards intervention. The qualitative aspect of the analysis could be further developed by the use of a scoring code which would simplify the notation of repeated and self-corrected items during the course of the test. Such a method is suggested by Lees and Urwin (1991) and used in a clinical research study of acquired childhood aphasia by Lees (1989).

The test is simple to use and the format quickly appeals to most children. Used in association with other tests it can be helpful in providing a profile of language ability in children with language disorders (Lees and Urwin, 1991).

Country of origin UK

Publisher Available from the author at MRC Applied Psychology Unit, 15 Chaucer Road, Cambridge, CB2 2EF

References

Bishop, D. V. M. (1982). 'Comprehension of spoken, written and signed sentences in childhood language disorders'. *Journal of Child Psychology and Psychiatry*, 23: 1, 1–20.

Bishop, D. (1983). *The Test for Reception of Grammar*. Available from the author at MRC Applied Psychology Unit, 15 Chaucer Road, Cambridge CB2 2EF.

Dunn, L. M., Pantile, D. and Whetton, C. (1982). *The British Picture Vocabulary Scale*. Windsor: NFER-NELSON.

Lees, J. A. (1989). 'A linguistic investigation of acquired childhood aphasia'. Unpublished M. Phil. thesis, City University, London.

Lees, J. A. and Neville, B. G. R. (1990). 'Acquired aphasia in childhood: case studies of five children'. *Aphasiology*, 4: 5, 463–78.

Lees, J. and Urwin, S. (1991). *Children with Language Disorders*. London: Whurr.

Janet Lees

THE TOKEN TEST FOR CHILDREN

Test author   Frank DiSimoni

Purpose   This form of the Token Test was designed to indicate receptive language function in children. The Token Test was first introduced by De Renzi and Vignolo (1962) to detect receptive language deficits in aphasic adults. Since its introduction the Token Test has been used in research and has undergone much scrutiny as well as subtle changes in format but the basic format has remained the same. Several objects (usually rectangles, squares or circles of various colours) are placed in front of the subject in a standardized manner. The examiner then presents a series of spoken commands that require the subject to manipulate the objects. The test consists of subtests that are composed of progressively longer and more complex commands. This form of the Token Test is described in the manual as being 'a rapid and effective measure for assessing subtle receptive language dysfunction in children when used by a conscientious examiner' (p. 13). It should be considered a rapid screening device that indicates a need for further testing of lexicon and syntax.

Subject population   Children aged 3–12½ years.

Administration time   Approximately 15–20 minutes. Scoring time: 2 minutes.

Materials   A comprehensive manual, scoresheets and 20 well-made wooden tokens are included. The tokens consist of 5 large and 5 small squares, 5 large and 5 small circles; in each set there is one of each colour: yellow, blue, green, red and white.

Structure and administration   This Token Test comprises five parts.

Parts I–IV have 10 commands and Part V has 21 commands. There are two arrangement methods for the tokens: Arrangement A uses the 10 large tokens and Arrangement B uses 20 tokens. The test alternates between the two arrangements with Part I using Arrangement A. The commands in Part I are all similar to 'Touch the red circle' with each colour and shape mentioned. The commands in Part II are all similar to 'Touch the small white square' with each size, colour and shape permutation mentioned. The commands in Part III are all similar to 'Touch the yellow circle and the red square'; and in Part IV they are all similar to 'Touch the small yellow circle and the large green square'. The final part uses prepositions, time words and a 'change of mind' strategy: 'put the red circle on the green square', 'before touching the yellow circle, pick up the red square' and 'pick up the red circle – No! – the white square'. The author stresses that the examiner should be thoroughly familiar with the token layout, test commands and scoring procedure before attempting to administer the test. A 'natural' spoken manner is required for some of the commands to be effective.

All parts should be presented in the specified sequence or the standardization results are invalid. If a child makes numerous errors in Part I, the test should be discontinued.

Scoring and interpretation Each item is scored as either correct or incorrect giving a total correct score of 61. In order for an item to be scored as correct it should be performed accurately in its entirety as no partial scoring is credited. If the child self-corrects before the next item is presented, then the item is scored as correct. Specific details for scoring criteria are given in the manual.

The scores are tallied and an overall raw score is obtained through summing the Part scores. To obtain standardized scores the examiner must consult the sets of tables. One of the tables is appropriate to the child's chronological age, the other is appropriate to the (US) grade level.

Technical details

Standardization This Token Test was standardized on 1,304 children who ranged in age from 3 to 12½ years. No children were included who had any known language or learning or reading problems. For the youngest and oldest age groups the numbers are small and the author warns that test results for these two subgroups should be interpreted with caution. Before including a child in the study they were tested on the terms circle, square, small, large and all five colour words. This greatly reduced the number of 3- and 4-year-old children who could be used in the study.

Reliability No reliability results are given. However, throughout the manual the author stresses the need for the examiner to be well acquainted with the presentation and scoring procedures, and the 85 examiners who carried out the standardization procedure had a pre-training session until they were judged to have mastered the administration procedure.

Validity Much research has been carried out to validate the Token Test, which was designed from a linguistic framework, with other tests that have differing initial construction frameworks. The Token Test has been shown to have a good correlation relationship with the Illinois Test of Psycholinguistic Abilities (Fusilier and Lass, 1973), with the Peabody Picture Vocabulary Test and Preschool Language Test (Lass and Golden, 1975), and with the Northwest Syntax Screening Test (Cartwright and Lass, 1974). The Token Test has also been shown to have a significant correlational relationship with the Brenner Developmental Gestalt Test of School Readiness and the Basic Grammatical Concepts Test (Robb and Lass, 1976).

Evaluation The Token Test is easy to administer and score with no training needed in either learning how to administer it or in interpreting the results. It can be a good quick screening device for the school-age child and could be carried out before calling in a language specialist. Although the research literature demonstrates a correlation between the results obtained on it and with other more specific language-ability assessments, if it is used as a screening device it will provide no information as to the nature of the problem and the type of help, or which further assessments, are needed.

Country of origin USA

Publisher DLM Teaching Resources, Allen, Texas. Distributed in the UK by NFER-NELSON.

References

Cartwright, L. and Lass, N. A. (1974). 'Comparative study of children's performance on the Token Test, Northwestern Syntax Screening Test, and Peabody Picture Vocabulary Test'. *Acta Symbolica*, 5, 19–29.

DeRenzi, E. and Vignolo, L. (1962). 'The Token Test: a sensitive test to detect receptive disturbances in aphasics'. *Brain*, 85, 665–78.

Fusilier, F. and Lass, N. (1973). 'A comparative study of children's performance on the Illinois Test of Psycholinguistic Abilities and the Token Test'. Unpublished manuscript, West Virginia University.

Lass, N. and Golden, S. (1975). 'A correlational study of children's performance on three tests for receptive language abilities'. *Journal of Auditory Research*, 15, 177–82.

Robb, E. and Lass, N. (1976). 'A correlational investigation of children's performance on the Token Test, the Brenner Developmental Gestalt Test of School Readiness and a basic grammatical concepts test'. *Journal of Auditory Research*, 16, 64–7.

Kathryn Gerard

NAME INDEX

260

SUBJECT INDEX